FOLKLORE CONCEPTS

FOLKLORE CONCEPTS

Histories and Critiques

Dan Ben-Amos

Edited by
Henry Glassie and Elliott Oring

INDIANA UNIVERSITY PRESS

This book is a publication of

Indiana University Press
Office of Scholarly Publishing
Herman B Wells Library 350
1320 East 10th Street
Bloomington, Indiana 47405 USA

iupress.indiana.edu

Manufactured in the United States of America

Cataloging information is available from the Library of Congress.

ISBN 978-0-253-04955-1 (hardback)
ISBN 978-0-253-04956-8 (paperback)
ISBN 978-0-253-05244-5 (ebook)

1 2 3 4 5   25 24 23 22 21 20

In memory of Roger David Abrahams (1933–2017),
a folklorist, a folk singer, and a friend.

CONTENTS

THE PROJECT

Henry Glassie

O N FRIDAY, JUNE 2, 2017, ROGER ABRAHAMS GAVE me a call. After Roger moved to California in 2013, we often enjoyed lengthy chats on the phone; our constant topics were the fortunes of the Philadelphia Phillies, the development of folklore scholarship, and the cultural richness of the black Atlantic. This time, Roger was excited by a recent article by our friend and colleague from the old days at Penn, Dan Ben-Amos. The paper inspired Roger to imagine editing a volume of Dan's theoretical writings. We had frequently talked about the need for such a volume of Roger's own writings, and had even sketched together the outline of an autobiographical introduction, but the task proved too much for him. Too big, too personal, it would launch him into a nightmarish whirl of endless revisions and explanations. Roger thought he could manage it for Dan, though, and he wondered if some press would be interested.

On the following Monday, I met with Gary Dunham, the director of the Indiana University Press. A man with a degree in anthropology, a firm friend of folklore, Gary said he would be interested in a volume of Dan's essays edited by Roger. He knew their work, admired them both. I called Roger with the news, and he was delighted. The next day, I was off to do fieldwork among the talented potters of North Carolina. When I returned, Roger was dead; he left on June 20, 2017. In passing, Roger had placed an obligation on me, an obligation both intellectual and emotional, to bring this last project to completion. To get it done, I brought into partnership my old friend Elliott Oring, who shares my commitment to folklore scholarship and my affection for Dan Ben-Amos.

Dan Ben-Amos gave our discipline its most generally accepted definition of folklore: artistic communication in small groups. That definition, offered without fanfare to undergraduates in introductory classes today, was startlingly fresh in the 1970s, and it served to propel the discipline forward when Dan Ben-Amos was among the leaders who were bringing into pragmatic adjustment the new directions set in the sixties.

In the sixties, the discipline came to professional stability, and in that decade, the long sweep of American folklore scholarship spun through a turning point in one miraculous year. All of this happened in 1964: Kenneth S. Goldstein (Kenny) published *A Guide for Field Workers in Folklore*, calling folklorists into awareness of the methods that would hasten a change from random collecting to rigorous ethnography. Edward D. Ives published *Larry Gorman: The Man Who Made the Songs*, featuring a singular individual, and he would follow that book with studies of Lawrence Doyle and Joe Scott. Roger D. Abrahams published *Deep Down in the Jungle: Negro Narrative Folklore from the Streets of Philadelphia*, deftly swinging from collected texts to cultural interpretation, as he would later do in his folkloristic masterpiece, *The Man-of-Words in the West Indies: Performance and the Emergence of Creole Culture*. Alan Dundes published *The Morphology of North American Indian Folktales*, demonstrating the importance of formal analysis and opening the door to structuralism and the logic of the unconscious. Alan Merriam published *The Anthropology of Music*, precipitating a paradigmatic shift in the adjacent and allied discipline of ethnomusicology that paralleled the change in folklore. And in 1964, Dell Hymes published two of the major essays that were leading him to the grand concept of committed and conditioned creation—generally called performance theory by folklorists—which Dell would later bring to full presence in *Foundations in Sociolinguistics: An Ethnographic Approach*.

The folkloristic interests in orderly methods, creative individuals, cultural interpretation, formal analysis, the patterned unconscious, and musical diversity were all comfortably accommodated in performance theory. It does no injustice to the bright, particular genius of Dell Hymes to say that he was articulating the common murmur, bringing into coherent clarity ideas scattered among his contemporaries. In fact, it helps to explain the acceptance and eventual prevalence of performance theory—though it is often enough debased and misunderstood in practice—among folklorists. Nor does it diminish Dell's originality to note that performance theory did not arrive as a flash in the dark but at the end of a long train of development, and Dell always scrupulously acknowledged his influences, notably Edward Sapir and Kenneth Burke.

Back before the disruptions of death and distance, we—Dell, Dan, Kenny, Roger, and I—were friends in Philadelphia, members of a small group united by communications that were not less artistic than those we studied. On the phone from California, Roger praised Dell but argued that performance theory was the logical consequence of many long years of fieldwork during which folklorists came to be more interested in the people they met than in the old theories that ostensibly took them into the field. It had to do with reading texts in context and understanding people amid their circumstances, and in retrospect, reading history backward. Roger and I agreed that signs of an emergent performance theory could be found in books published before 1960 by American folklorists who had done serious fieldwork: Vance Randolph, Zora Neale Hurston, George Korson, Leonard Roberts, and Richard Dorson.

Roger and I went into the field early, hunting for the singers of old songs. Separately, we befriended Paul Clayton Worthington and followed him as an apprentice does a master. Paul, a singer of folk songs who recorded many LPs and composed hit songs recorded by others, was also a dedicated scholar of the ballad. He lived in a beautiful log cabin on the eastern slope of the Blue Ridge, and he diligently recorded the full repertory of Mrs. McAllister, a neighbor of his in the mountains. In the sixties, Roger recorded the full repertory of Almeda Riddle, and I recorded the full repertory of Ola Belle Reed. All three were bold southern women and grand performers of song.

Here is the point. The norm when we began was to use the headnotes in ballad collections and the indexes compiled by Tristram Coffin and Malcolm Laws to place a song in relation to other versions in order to gain a historical and geographical understanding of the song. Following Paul, Roger and I placed a song in relation to other songs in the repertory in order to understand the singer. Those approaches were both old and new, the old one governed by historic-geographic considerations, the new one ethnographic and headed toward performance theory. But folklorists, of all people, should not be ruled by fashion, by the urge to the merely new. Both approaches, the old and the new, are rational and productive. As performance theory became dominant, historic-geographic methods still proved useful and enlightening in studies of material culture and in the search for the African sources of American traditions. Still, I am glad to say, performance theory prevailed and continued to direct folkloristic practice long past a time when it could reasonably be called new.

Now return to the time when performance theory was new. Fieldwork had prepared us to center ethnographic inquiry on individuals, to record their creations with precision, to stay long enough to be able to say something intelligent about them. The existentialists we had read encouraged us to encounter individuals as the authors of their own tragedies. No longer passive bearers of traditions, people appeared before us as actively volitional—as human beings, that is, who exploited traditions and adjusted to conditions in the predicament of the performative moment.

At this early point, Dan Ben-Amos provided us a definition of folklore fully congruent with performance theory. During the energetic debates his definition sparked, the absence of tradition was generally remarked. Tradition is clearly implicit; without tradition, there would be no art, no communication, no small groups. But Dan wisely left the word out because tradition can be misunderstood as a force that usurps human power and does things on its own. Traditions don't do things, nor do other abstractions, such as economics and politics. People do things, and Dan's definition staunchly focuses on people communicating artistically among others.

His definition is a signal instance of his thought, which is displayed throughout the essays gathered in this volume. Dan Ben-Amos looks critically at his discipline's past, understanding its history to move logically forward, hoping to bring others with him into an improved future for folklore scholarship.

Bibliography

Abrahams, Roger D. 1964. *Deep Down in the Jungle: Negro Narrative Folklore from the Streets of Philadelphia*. Hatboro: Folklore Associates.

———. 1970. *A Singer and Her Songs: Almeda Riddle's Book of Ballads*. Baton Rouge: Louisiana State University Press.

———. 1983. *The Man-of-Words in the West Indies: Performance and the Emergence of Creole Culture*. Baltimore: Johns Hopkins University Press.

Bauman, Richard. 1986. *Story, Performance, and Event: Contextual Studies of Oral Narrative*. London: Cambridge University Press.

Bauman, Richard, and Américo Paredes, eds. 1972. *Toward New Perspectives in Folklore*. Austin: University of Texas Press.

Coffin, Tristram P. 1963. *The British Traditional Ballad in North America*. Philadelphia: American Folklore Society.

Crowley, Daniel J. 1966. *I Could Talk Old-Story Good: Creativity in Bahamian Folklore*. Berkeley: University of California Press.

Dégh, Linda. 1995. *Narratives in Society: A Performer-Centered Study of Narration*. Folklore Fellows' Communications (FFC) 255. Helsinki: Suomalainen Tiedeakatemia.

Dorson, Richard M. 1952. *Bloodstoppers and Bearwalkers: Folk Traditions of the Upper Peninsula*. Cambridge: Harvard University Press.

Dundes, Alan. 1964. *The Morphology of North American Indian Folktales*. FFC 195. Helsinki: Suomalainen Tiedeakatemia.

Glassie, Henry. 1968. *Pattern in the Material Folk Culture of the Eastern United States*. Philadelphia: University of Pennsylvania Press.

———. 1989. *The Spirit of Folk Art*. New York: Harry N. Abrams.

———. 2016. *The Stars of Ballymenone*. Bloomington: Indiana University Press.

Glassie, Henry, Clifford R. Murphy, and Douglas Dowling Peach. 2015. *Ola Belle Reed and Southern Mountain Music on the Mason-Dixon Line*. Atlanta: Dust-to-Digital.

Glassie, Henry, and Pravina Shukla. 2018. *Sacred Art: Catholic Saints and Candomblé Gods in Modern Brazil*. Bloomington: Indiana University Press.

Goldstein, Kenneth S. 1964. *A Guide for Field Workers in Folklore*. Hatboro: Folklore Associates.

Haring, Lee. 1992. *Verbal Arts in Madagascar: Performance in Historical Perspective*. Philadelphia: University of Pennsylvania Press.

Hurston, Zora Neale. 1935. *Mules and Men*. Philadelphia: J. B. Lippincott.

———. 2018. *Barracoon: The Story of the Last "Black Cargo."* New York: Amistad.

Hymes, Dell. 1974. *Foundations in Sociolinguistics: An Ethnographic Approach*. Philadelphia: University of Pennsylvania Press.

———. 1981. *"In Vain I Tried to Tell You": Essays in Native American Ethnopoetics*. Philadelphia: University of Pennsylvania Press.

Ives, Edward D. 1964. *Larry Gorman: The Man Who Made the Songs*. Bloomington: Indiana University Press.

———. 1971. *Lawrence Doyle: The Farmer-Poet of Prince Edward Island: A Study in Local Songmaking*. Orono: University of Maine Press.

———. 1978. *Joe Scott: The Woodsman-Songmaker*. Urbana: University of Illinois Press.

———. 1980. *The Tape-Recorded Interview: A Manual for Field Workers in Folklore and Oral History*. Knoxville: University of Tennessee Press.

Jones, Michael Owen. 1975. *The Hand Made Object and Its Maker*. Berkeley: University of California Press.

Korson, George. 1938. *Minstrels of the Mine Patch: Songs and Stories of the Anthracite Industry*. Philadelphia: University of Pennsylvania Press.

———. 1943. *Coal Dust on the Fiddle: Songs and Stories of the Bituminous Industry*. Philadelphia: University of Pennsylvania Press.

Laws, G. Malcolm, Jr. 1957. *American Balladry from British Broadsides: A Guide for Students and Collectors of Traditional Song*. Philadelphia: American Folklore Society.

———. 1964. *Native American Balladry: A Descriptive Study and a Bibliographical Syllabus*. Philadelphia: American Folklore Society.

Merriam, Alan P. 1964. *The Anthropology of Music*. Evanston, IL: Northwestern University Press.

Oring, Elliott. 1981. *Israeli Humor: The Content and Structure of the Chizbat of the Palmah*. Albany: State University of New York Press.

Randolph, Vance. 1931. *The Ozarks: An American Survival of Primitive Society*. New York: Vanguard Press.

Roberts, Leonard W. 1959. *Up Cutshin and Down Greasy: Folkways of a Kentucky Mountain Family*. Lexington: University of Kentucky Press.

Shukla, Pravina. 2008. *The Grace of Four Moons: Dress, Adornment, and the Art of the Body in Modern India*. Bloomington: Indiana University Press.

THE CONTOURS OF THE BOOK

Elliott Oring

A NY MATURE DISCIPLINE IS LIKELY TO HAVE A body of writings that reflect on its definitions, concepts, and practices. If we reckon the history of the field of folklore only from the moment the term *folklore* was first coined in 1846, there is almost a century and three-quarters of definitions, concepts, and practices to consider. Dan Ben-Amos's academic career has spanned a good third of that disciplinary history. Although he has published widely in the field of folklore—especially in the areas of African and Jewish folk narrative—a persistent theme in his work has been the interrogation, criticism, extension, and revision of basic folklore definitions, terms, and concepts. This volume attempts to corral some of his most trenchant works of review and critique.

Chapter 1, "The Idea of Folklore: An Essay," identifies some of the original assumptions about peasant beliefs and practices—traditionalism, irrationality, rurality—held by those who first coined and employed the term *folklore*. It goes on to explore the corollary, though contradictory, assumptions—universality and communality—that arose in their wake. Chapter 2, "The Encounter with Native Americans and the Emergence of Folklore," reviews the impact on the human sciences of the discovery of the New World by the Old. The encounter pushed Europeans to confront their own national pasts through the study of their antiquities, and ultimately the artifacts, beliefs, practices, and narratives that they collected would constitute the subject matter of a discipline that would come to be. Chapter 3, "Toward a Definition of Folklore in Context," was a revolutionary proposal to move the concept of folklore away from tradition and toward the study of socially situated artistic performances. Ben-Amos's definition completely changed the trajectory of folklore research for the next half century. Chapter 4, "Analytical Categories and Ethnic Genres," characterizes the different conceptualizations of folklore genres. Scholars have their own set of categories—legend, myth, folktale, ballad, riddle—that are employed for cross-cultural and transhistorical analysis. The people whom folklorists study, however, have their own terms—*libogwo, hujwa, talla, okpohbie*—that articulate their own conceptions of their artistic communications and the appropriate situations for their expression. Chapter 5, "The Seven Strands of *Tradition*: Varieties in Its Meaning in American Folklore Studies," reviews the ways that folklorists have employed the term *tradition* and identifies seven distinct usages: as *lore, process, canon, mass, culture, langue,* and *performance*. Ben-Amos does not find any particular usage more adequate or more proper than any other but considers the variation reflective of the interests of folklorists of different theoretical persuasions in different historical periods. Chapter 6, "A History of Folklore Studies—Why Do We Need It?," claims that folklorists have lost sight of the questions that originally informed the field and argues that they need to stop to reexamine their disciplinary history in order to gauge the intellectual growth of the field and recalibrate its trajectory. Chapter 7, "The Concept of Motif in Folklore," addresses the history of this basic term in the folklorist's vocabulary and contrasts it with analogous terms in literary, artistic, and historical criticism. It also offers a sustained critique of folklorists' use of the concept over the past century. Chapter 8, "*Context* in Context," responds to the apprehension that the move away from text to an emphasis on context reduced folkloristics to particularistic ethnography. The essay argues that folkloristics shifted from explanation to interpretation, and context serves as the interpretant of folklore texts. The meaning of texts cannot be grasped without recourse to context. Chapter 9, "Two Benin Storytellers," is the only essay in the volume that focuses on actual folklore performances. Two professional narrators—one traditional, one innovative—are compared to reveal the personal, economic, and social dimensions of their art. The comparison points to differences in their relation to tradition and enlarges the sense of who constitutes a performer's relevant audience. Chapter 10, "Induced Natural Context in Context," focuses on Kenneth S. Goldstein's notion of induced natural context—the manipulation of fieldwork situations both to document folklore in action *and* to conduct experiments on folklore processes. Chapter 11, "The Name Is the Thing," is a response to suggestions made during the sesquicentennial anniversary year of the American Folklore Society that the term *folklore* be abandoned in favor of some other term. (The title of the essay alludes to D. K. Wilgus's essay "The Text Is the Thing," published in *Journal of American Folklore* in 1973.) Ben-Amos acknowledges the low esteem in which the field has been held by other disciplines but argues that a change of name is not a solution to the problem. The salvation of the discipline depends on folklorists always keeping in mind the intellectual traditions on which their field is based and to which they must continually strive to contribute. Chapter 12, "A Definition of Folklore: A Personal Narrative," is a retrospective that explores those influences that led Ben-Amos to redefine folklore in his 1971 essay "A Definition of Folklore in Context" (chap. 3).

Folklore, tradition, motif, performer, audience, genre, context, experiment, art: these are some of the terms and concepts to which Ben-Amos has brought his historical and critical perspective over the course of his career. In reading these essays, students will be introduced, and scholars reintroduced, to the intellectual history of the field. They will glimpse folklore's deep connections to broader intellectual currents and concerns. Most importantly, folklorists will have a solid base from which to engage the following questions: What are we doing? How are we doing it? And why?

A Note on the Sources

"The Idea of Folklore: An Essay" was first published in 1983, in *Studies in Aggadah and Jewish Folklore*, edited by Issachar Ben-Ami and Joseph Dan, Folklore Research Center Studies VII, 11–17, Jerusalem: Magnes; "The Encounter with Native Americans and the Emergence of Folklore" in 1984, in *Folk Culture Vol. V: Folk Culture and the Great Tradition*, edited by Shri Kulamani Mahapatra, 274–86, Cuttack, Orisaga, India: Institute of Oriental and Orissan Studies; "Toward a Definition of Folklore in Context" in 1971, in *Journal of American Folklore* 21 (331): 3–15; "Analytical and Ethnic Genres" in 1969, in *Genre* 2 (3): 275–301; "The Seven Strands of *Tradition*: Varieties in Its Meaning in American Folklore Studies" in 1984, in *Journal of Folklore Research* 21 (2/3): 97–131; "A History of Folklore Studies—Why Do We Need It?" in 1973, in *Journal of the Folklore Institute* 10 (1/2): 113–24; "The Concept of Motif in Folklore" in 1980, in *Folklore Studies in the Twentieth Century: Proceedings of the Centenary Conference of the Folklore Society*, edited by Venetia J. Newall, 17–36, Woodbridge: D. S. Brewer; "The Seven Strands of *Tradition*: Varieties in Its Meaning in American Folklore Studies" in 1980, in *Western Folklore* 52 (2/4): 209–26; "Two Benin Storytellers" in 1972, in *African Folklore*, edited by Richard M. Dorson, 103–14, Garden City, NY: Doubleday; "*Induced Natural Context* in Context" in 1998, in *Fields of Folklore: Essays in Honor of Kenneth S. Goldstein*, edited by Roger D. Abrahams, 11–20, Bloomington, IN: Trickster; "The Name Is the Thing" in 1998, in *Journal of American Folklore* 111 (441): 257–80; and "A Definition of Folklore: A Personal Narrative" in 2014, in *Estudis de Literatura Popular: Studies in Oral Folk Literature* 3:9–28.

PREFACE

Dan Ben-Amos

M Y FRIENDS HENRY GLASSIE AND ELLIOTT ORING HAVE kindly selected a few of my articles for publication in this book. My gratitude to them is boundless. Some of these articles were written in the late sixties and the early seventies. Others complement and comment on them. As single essays, I wrote them for specific occasions or by invitation. They do not compose a systematic exposition of folklore theory nor even a programmatic method. However, I recognize them, once assembled, as buoys marking developments in my own study of folklore as a subject and as a discipline. They float on a stream of thought that is making its way through obstacles and contradictions, exploring the nature of folklore and its study.

The earliest written essay in this collection, "Toward a Definition of Folklore in Context," was not only an introductory chapter to a yet-unwritten book, as I tell its story in the last essay in this collection, but also my personal way to chart a direction for my subsequent research. Once it was published, thoughtful folklorists reacted to it with comments that ranged from criticism to approval and humor. Mostly, they focused on the key terms of the essay and the definitions, such as *artistic, communication, performance, small groups,* and *context,* and my deliberate deletion of *tradition* as a defining term of folklore. I have learned from them all. Following the debates that ensued, in private conversations and in print, it has not occurred to me to modify my definition—I am too stubborn to do that—but I realize that it is necessary to broaden the perspective of folklore and consider it as a concept with three modalities: an act, a cultural symbol, and a research subject.

In society, folklore is a system of communicative acts that has cognitive, expressive, and social characterizing features, its own rhetorical or performative principles, and its learned rules, to which its speakers and participants adhere. Each ethnic folklore genre has its thematic, symbolic, and rhetorical range and its appropriate time and place for delivery. Some require particular verbal and musical proficiency, while others are accessible for performance to a broader range of individuals and groups, with possible conventions or even restrictions of age, gender, and social affiliation. The listeners are also an integral element of folklore genres and their delivery, since some are age and gender appropriate while others are all-inclusive. Narrators and singers may adjust their performances to accommodate their listeners. In society, folklore is a system of communicative acts. All of its elements, including its cognitive, expressive, and social characterizing features, are interdependent, and variations in one characterizing feature activate modifications in others.

It is not a closed system. Rather, it is interconnected with other social and cultural systems, such as those of religion, art, law, values, governance, kinship, and, in literate societies, literature, art, popular culture, film, and social media. These relations are mutual. As much as folklore themes and forms permeate literature, for example, so do themes, figures, and specific subjects and texts of literature and popular culture filter into oral tradition.

Historically, the transition to literacy was revolutionary, but not comprehensive. Initially, literacy was the prerogative of a small percentage of the population. Still, even when it became an integral part of the educational system, orality and literacy coexisted; in some cultures, they were recognized as two contrasting modes of communication and knowledge preservation. Eventually, literacy fractured society, and in many cultures, the literates assigned a negative value to orality and to those among them and those of other societies who did not make the transition to literacy. But this attitude was subject to personal ambivalence, alternating between nostalgia and progress, and to social-historical developments of ideas and thought. The European Enlightenment represented the most radical rejection of oral culture, but in reaction, Romanticism brought about its revaluation, generated the concept of folklore, and transformed its many manifestations into identity symbols of nations and emblems of their spiritual cores.

Thoughtful and articulate individuals constructed an idealized folk. Its life, songs, and stories combined to embody a genuine communal spirit that, together with language, unified peoples into nations. The symbolization of folklore began with Romantic nationalism, but subsequently other ideological movements appropriated it to advance their own political causes and purposes, with positive but also destructive results.

The national Romantic valuation and symbolization of folklore manifested politically, popularly, and canonically. Society's governing bodies (both its central and decentralized authorities) sponsored and promoted institutions, research projects, and festivals, preserving and exhibiting traditions that supported their respective political ideals and self-images. Historically, popular movements rose up and faded away, reviving idealized rural cultures in songs and stories in theatrical presentations of folksiness in city venues and festivals—for example, in the American and English folk song revival movements of the mid-twentieth century. Such celebrations of folklore as a cultural symbol are neither spurious nor inauthentic. Rather, they are authentic theatrical presentations of folklore within their urban and literate contexts.

These sentiments were not limited to popular movements. Culturally esteemed authors, poets, composers, and visual artists integrated folk motifs and themes into their own artistic creative works that then became part of the cultural canons of their respective societies. The transition of folk themes and forms from orality to literacy is selective, functional, and purposeful, subject to the communicative conventions of public space and the ideal images of nationhood.

The symbolization of folklore in literate societies motivated its scholarly study. Research offered a reality check on Romantic ideals and images. Yet universities were, and still are, slow to admit full-fledged folklore departments into their rosters of disciplines. Major influential thinkers and scholars taught folklore courses in departments of more conventional and established disciplines. No wonder that early publications in folklore studies adorned themselves with the word "science" in their titles, seeking entrance into the academic halls into which their admittance was denied. Still relentless, in America folklorists subversively established their learned society, which, about fifty years later, was admitted into the national American Council of Learned Societies, before the establishment of a single folklore department in any American university. The conflict between folklore and the academy is a continuous issue, and even at the present time, there are folklore departments in less than 1 percent of American universities and colleges.

Henry Glassie and Elliott Oring have selected for this lean volume several of my essays that, implicitly or explicitly, are concerned with the boundaries between and the interdependence of the academic and the symbolic modalities of folklore. As scholarship, folklore is not completely free from its ethnic—even nationalistic—objectives. The same ethnographic-historical method with which folklore scholars study folklore as a communicative act is applicable, with the necessary modifications, to folklore scholarship itself and to the symbolization of folklore in modern cultures, thereby freeing folklore from the burden of Romanticism.

FOLKLORE CONCEPTS

1

THE IDEA OF FOLKLORE

An Essay

THE CONCEPT OF FOLKLORE EMERGED IN EUROPE IN the mid-nineteenth century. Originally, it connoted tradition, ancient customs, and surviving festivals, old ditties and dateless ballads, archaic myths, legends and fables, and timeless tales and proverbs. As these narratives rarely stood the tests of common sense and experience, folklore also implied irrationality: beliefs in ghosts and demons, fairies and goblins, sprites and spirits. It referred to credence given to omens, amulets, and talismans. From the perspectives of the urbane literati, who conceived the idea of folklore, these two attributes of traditionalism and irrationality could pertain only to peasant or primitive societies. Hence they attributed to folklore a third quality: rurality. The countryside and the open space of wilderness were the proper breeding grounds for folklore. Man's close contact with nature in villages and hunting bands was considered the ultimate source of his myth and poetry. As an outgrowth of human experience with nature, folklore itself was thought to be a natural expression of man before city, commerce, civilization, and culture contaminated the purity of his life.

This triad of attributes—traditionalism, irrationality, and rurality—was to dominate the concept of folklore for many years to come; often, it still does. It provided standards for inclusion or exclusion of stories, songs, and sayings in terms of the domain of folklore proper. Those that possessed at least one of these qualities were christened folktales, folk songs, riddles, and folk sayings; those that had none were reprovingly rejected.

In their turn, these three terms of meaning generated additional attributes, which together constituted the sense of the concept of folklore in common use, in print and in speech. The cloak of tradition concealed the identity of those who authored folktales, ballads, and proverbs. Compounding matters, the transmission from generation to generation obscured their origin. Thus, by default and not by merit, anonymity became an earmark of folklore. Indigenous prose or poetry became part of folklore only after the memory of its creator had been erased. Then the seal of anonymity sanctioned tradition as genuine. It legitimized songs and tales as integral parts of the cultural heritage of society.

Yet the anonymity of folk narratives, rhymes, and riddles hardly solved the enigma of origin. The responsibility for authorship had to be assigned to some creator, divine or human. So in the absence of any individual who could justifiably and willingly claim paternity of myths and legends, the entire community was held accountable for them. After all, the existing evidence appeared to support such an allegation. Narrators and singers often attribute their tales and songs not to a single individual but to the collective tradition of the community. Even in the exceptional cases in which they indeed claimed authorship, scholarship succeeded in unveiling analogues in their own and other traditions. Such parallels cast doubt on any contention for originality and sustained the assertion of the communality of folklore.

In fact, communality has become a central attribute, rivaled only by tradition in the formulation of the concept of folklore. There was no room in folklore for private tales and poems. Any expression had to pass through the sieve of communal approval before it could be considered folklore. But the identification of the processes that would justify the attribution of communality to any story or song proved to be rather complex, even logically thorny. Were folktales and folk songs only in the communal domain, free to all to speak and sing? Or should these property rights have been limited to the moment of origin, thus rendering folk expressions a communal creation and solving, along the way, the question of authorship? Furthermore, how does the community foster its bond between people and their folklore, and exactly which of its aspects relate to the society at large: the themes, the language, the forms, or the particular tales, songs, and proverbs? These and other issues were the whetstones that sharpened debates that were crucial to the idea of folklore. From various viewpoints, the attribute of communality implied communal creation, recreation, or simply expression.

Communal creation involved some anachronistic reasoning: the tales, songs, and sayings that the community shared together were also created together. Such an explanation might have solved the problem of authorship, but inferring origins from results might be valid only biologically and not logically. In the cultural and social spheres, the mode of existence could not necessarily attest to the genesis of forms. Historical processes such as diffusion of themes, dissemination of ideas, and imitation of manners do affect the state and nature of folklore. Consequently, collective knowledge of tales and songs could not be an unequivocal indicator of creation. The notion of communal recreation countered this dilemma. It prolonged the moment of origin over historical periods and conceived of the formation of songs, for example, not in a single exhilarating burst of poetic creativity but through repetitive recitations of singers on communal occasions. Each improvised and embellished the text yet conformed to the communal aesthetic and ethical standards. Such an interpretation of the communality of folklore also allowed the viewing of folk prose and poetry as expressions of social fears and wishes, ideals and values. Folklore reflected the collective experience of society and was the mirror of itself that the community constantly faced.

Paradoxically, intertwined with the attribute of communality is the idea that folklore is universal. While folk songs and tales might be forged within a particular community and express its unique experience, they also transcend the boundaries that language and space impose, and emerge in diverse groups and remote countries, still maintaining sameness to a large extent. The attribute of universality appeared to be both formal and thematic. All peoples distinguish poetry from prose, pithy sayings from epic poems; all construct narratives, fictional or historical, stringing events in sequences; and all can combine music and movement with words and sing and dance to their heart's content. These are inherent abilities of humanity.

In that sense, folklore withstood the test that language failed. While modern discoveries about animals clearly demonstrate that some master the rudiments of language communication (whales sing), so far, neither monkeys nor rats have been caught telling legends to their infants. But the universality of folklore was not confined to the formal basis alone. The themes, the metaphors, and the subjects of stories, songs, and sayings of peoples who lived in countries remote from each other, and who spoke completely unrelated languages, exhibited a high degree of similarity that history could not explain. Migrations and contacts in war and peace could not account for the common features that the tales and poems of native Australians, Africans, and Americans shared. All include stories of gods, of creation, and of destruction; all tell about marvelous events, beings, and places; and all dwell on the supernatural, the extraordinary, the absolute, and the incongruous. Their metaphors relate to nature, beliefs, and societies, and their songs celebrate victories and lament failures in the struggle for survival. Often, similarities among folklores are even more striking, as the same narrative episodes and verbal or visual images appear in the expressions of unrelated peoples.

The dual attributes of universality and communality were locked together and created an apparent paradox in the idea of folklore, merging the general and the particular into a single concept. Evidence supported both. The themes and forms of folklore appeared to be universal, yet no other expression was so imbued with regional, local, and cultural references, meanings, and symbols. There were two ways to resolve this contradiction. First, universality and communality could be viewed not as contradictory but as complementary attributes. The relations that govern folklore are universal; the references to culture and history are specific. The principles of distinctiveness in form and in theme—the unusual, the incongruous, and conversely, the absolutely harmonious—are universal, but the languages, the social and historical experiences, the religious systems, and the moral values that make up the substance of the folklore of respective societies are communal. Second, these two attributes could be historically related, one preceding the other. If folklore was communal at first, later, its properties achieved universality by historical processes, such as diffusion of themes and population contacts through migration, trade, or warfare. Such an assumption would imply a single source, or place and time of origin, from which folklore features were universally diffused. But if folklore were universal first, then its basic characteristic forms and themes should have been formulated prior to any historical and evolutionary developments. In that case, folklore embodies the original homogeneity of the culture of man before diversity struck, following the Tower of Babel. Consequently, folklore also possesses the attribute of primariness, an attribute that made the impact of folklore on modern thought and art so powerful.

The mythology of all nations not only tells about but is the dawn of humanity. It incarnates the commonality, in all communities and voices, of the primordial expression of man. In its fundamental forms, folklore emerged before human diversity developed, and thus it embodies the most rudimentary forms of verbal and visual symbols. The primariness of folklore had historical and evolutionary aspects. Historically, folklore allegedly dated back to time immemorial, and hence, at its original stage, preceded any known recorded history. When man hunted and gathered his food, or even when he began to farm the land and to herd his cattle, but had not as yet quite mastered writing, he was already narrating tales and singing songs. The folklore of the world, it was hence assumed, abounds with symbols, themes, and metaphors that pertain to the beginning of human civilization, and could shed light on the dark corners of history that no other document could illuminate. The forms of folklore were regarded as the cores at the heart of artistic forms. They were the primitive, crude expressions out of which the literary, visual, and musical cultural heritage of the peoples of the world has emerged. Folklore comprised the symbolic forms at the base of the complex expressions of literate societies.

Naturally, folklore in its primary stage could not be accessible to modern man and would have been completely lost had it not been for the attempt to recapture tales and songs as they existed in nonliterate societies—that is, as they were told and sung orally, without recourse to any written devices to aid in the memorization and transmission of texts. No one claims that the current prose and poetry of peasants and nonliterate culture reflect human expression in its archaic, primordial form. Repeated recitations, loss of memorization, creative improvisation, and more general historical processes of cultural contacts amid technical evolution contributed to alterations in both the particular themes and the general tenor of folklore. However, in spite of the recognition of such historical factors, a basic assumption in folklore is that those stories, songs, and sayings continued to exist in the same way their ancient predecessors did—that is, in oral performance—and that they were transmitted from generation to generation only orally, as they were before the advance of literacy. Hence the oral nature of folklore became one of its crucial attributes, the touchstone of authenticity and originality. As long as stories, songs, and proverbs conformed with the principle of oral circulation and transmission, they qualified as "pure" folklore, but when, alas, somewhere along the line they came in contact with written texts, they were branded contaminated. No longer could they represent the primary expression of man.

The attributes of traditionalism, irrationality, and rurality; anonymity, communality, and universality; primacy and oral circulation became consolidated in the idea of folklore. They cluster, implying one another, and suggesting the existence of intrinsic relations between them. The occurrence of one quality in a song or tale often implies most of the others. A peasant song, for example, was considered as having long-standing tradition in the community. The possibility that it might be a recent composition, or borrowed from some external source such as an urban center, would have denied the song its folkloric nature and contradicted the basic assumptions held about it. Being rural, other attributes similarly follow: The author is anonymous, and the song belongs to the cultural heritage of the entire community. Most likely, as poetry, it would express deep-seated emotions or uncontrolled desires, which in turn project universal primary human qualities, unaffected by civilization. Thus, combined in a hypothetical song, these attributes convey the meaning of the concept of folklore.

Consequently, these attributes, which are only descriptive and interpretive terms at best, acquired a normative status, setting the standards and boundaries for the substance of folklore proper. They become defining terms, bound by an a priori notion of what folklore should have been but only occasionally

was, transforming the desired into necessary conditions and injecting interpretations into alleged observations. They became terms of value with which
to state the worth of songs and sayings and to rate their import in the light of
ideals only implicitly understood.

In the process of research and interpretation, desired goals could often
turn into a priori assumptions and serve as the initial premises rather than
the final results. This, in fact, had often happened with qualities attributed
to stories, songs, and sayings, which became the basic premises on which
research was designed and theory constructed. Naturally, there have been
sufficient examples that supported these contentions. Stories have circulated
orally, existing in the traditions of rural communities for many years; their
authors, if there were any, were long forgotten, and their analogues recovered
in distant lands. But even if there were texts that measured up to all the criteria of folklore, these standards should not have been the defining terms for
the substance of folklore.

The penalty for transferring norms into premises and ideal goals into
a priori conditions is a limited range for research and theory. Past folklore
scholarship paid its dues twice over. The diversity and richness that folklore is
was confined by the constraints that the notions about it imposed. The study
of traditions in villages flourished, but the equivalent manifestations in cities
went unnoticed. Anonymous tales and songs were avidly recorded, stored,
and dissected, but equally entertaining songs and stories whose authors were
alive and known were ignored as irrelevant. Other attributes became frames
for interpretation. The relationship between expressions and the community
was, and is, a major paradigm for analysis. The implicit irrationality of ideas
found in tales and metaphors has been the only basis for their explanation
and has opened the gate to a host of psychological interpretations. Significant
as they are, these notions blocked the way for alternate modes of explanation,
directions of research, and construction of theories. They predefined and
identified the substance and the problems of study, silencing the expressions
and the people themselves. In recent years, the clouds of a priori premises
began to disperse. Still, with a sense of innovation and intellectual rebellion,
Hermann Bausinger (1961/1990) expounded on folk culture in a technical
world, and American folklorists gathered to discuss *The Urban Experience
and Folk Tradition* (Paredes and Stekert 1971). Even more recently, Alan
Dundes and Carl R. Pagter (1975) published a collection of written materials
as urban folklore, and with a similar sense of innovation, Richard M. Dorson
(1978) convened a conference on the subject of modern folklore. But these
are recent developments, when scholarly traditions yielded to the demands of

reality. Throughout the formative years of folklore study, and in many years that followed, the attributes of the idea of folklore dictated the conception of its substance and the limits of its research. They became unchallenged premises and assumptions that were taken for granted.

Regardless of the validity of these attributes, they contributed to the popularity of the idea of folklore. At the same time, however, these very qualities impeded the transformation of folklore from an idea into a field of scholarship. These attributes burdened folklore research with unproved assumptions, untested beliefs, and a projection of popular attitudes toward the substance that makes up the subjects of folklore inquiry. In order to progress with research in the field of folklore, it is necessary to unload the attributes of the past and to observe folklore freshly as it exists in social reality, as some have already done. Within this context, folklore is a culturally unique mode of communication, and its distinctiveness is formal, thematic, and performative. There is a correlation between these three levels of expression, by which the speakers of folklore set it apart from any other communication in society.

As a distinct mode of communication, folklore exists in any society; it is the sole property of neither peasants nor primitives. No doubt folklore could be traditional, but it is not so by definition; it could be anonymous, but it is not essentially so. Any of the qualities that were, and still are, attributed to folklore might be inherent in some forms, in some cultures, and anytime that they are, it is up to the folklorists to demonstrate it anew.

Bibliography

Bausinger, Hermann. 1961. *Volkskultur in der technischen Welt*. Stuttgart: W. Rohlhammer.
———. 1990. *Folk Culture in a World of Technology*. Translated by Elke Dettmer. Folklore Studies in Translation. Bloomington: Indiana University Press.
Dorson, Richard M., ed. 1978. *Folklore in the Modern World*. World Anthropology. The Hague: Mouton.
Dundes, Alan, and Carl R. Pagter. 1975. *Urban Folklore from the Paperwork Empire*. Publications of the American Folklore Society Memoir Series, vol. 62. Austin: American Folklore Society.
Paredes, Américo, and Ellen J. Stekert, eds. 1971. *The Urban Experience and the Folk Tradition*. American Folklore Society Bibliographical and Special Series, vol. 22. Austin: University of Texas Press.

2

THE ENCOUNTER WITH NATIVE AMERICANS
AND THE EMERGENCE OF FOLKLORE

A PERIOD OF THREE HUNDRED AND FIFTY YEARS separates the discovery of America by Christopher Columbus and the coinage of the term *folklore* in 1846 (Merton 1846; see Boggs 1945; Dundes 1965, 4–6; Dorson 1968, 75–90; Emrich 1946). Any cautious historian would shudder at the attempt to establish a causal relationship between the two. So many other significant historical events occurred, and so many other important philosophical ideas developed in the interim, that this particular geographical event, crucial as it was, could not account for the verbal invention.

Yet since on the one hand, the discovery of America started a sequence of changes in European life and thought, and on the other hand, the coinage of the term *folklore* culminated a long process of ideational modifications, it is not so far-fetched as it initially seems to draw a direct, even causal, relationship between them. The first impression of America—the theme of the present conference[1]—had a traumatic effect on Europe, triggering a set of reactions to which it possible to attribute, although not exclusively, the formation of the idea of folklore and some of its basic tenets.

Less astounding would be the suggestion that the Europeans encountering the Native Americans influenced the development of anthropology, a sister discipline of folklore.[2] After all, the study of "other cultures," to use John Beattie's (1964) characterization of the field, thrives on the discovery of unknown tribes. In contrast to anthropology, folklore studies involved research in which the student and their subjects shared in broad terms, language, culture, and ethnic identity. It is a discipline in which national ties bind the students and the singers, narrators, and speakers whom they record. Thus, if there is any real connection between contact with the Native Americans—and for that matter, any other non-European peoples—and the emergence of the idea of folklore, then the essential lesson of this experience is the historical interdependence between contact with others and conceptions of self, the ethnic self. The Socratic quest for self-knowledge by European nations was generated by encounters with the peoples of the new lands.

A number of students of folklore, myself included, no longer distinguish between anthropology and folklore along the dividing line of the exotic versus the indigenous. We attempt to conceive of folklore as a qualitative, culturally defined system of communication that is universal, and its existence and definition does not depend on ethnic boundaries (Paredes and Bauman 1972; Bauman and Sherzer 1975; Ben-Amos and Goldstein 1975; Voigt 1972). Yet during the formative years of folklore studies, scholars focused, in theory and in practice, on their own traditional cultures. They studied the peasant narratives, songs, and sayings in a language they knew. The Swiss folklorist Hoffmann-Krayer (1864–1936) regarded the folk as *vulgus in populo*, the base strata of the civilized society, thus succinctly expressing an idea that others shared, and many still do (Hoffmann-Krayer 1902, 6–7).

Because of the preoccupation with national popular traditions that characterizes folklore, its students have traced the roots of their discipline to the Romantic period. Alexander Krappe (1930), for example, states explicitly, "In the Occident, folklore is a daughter of the Romantic Movement" (xix). Alan Dundes (1965) endorses this interpretation, saying that "during the middle and later portions of the nineteenth century, the discipline of folklore as it has developed in the twentieth century began to appear. The increasing awareness of folklore was closely associated with nineteenth century intellectual currents of romanticism and nationalism" (4). Even in the Soviet Union, where we have learned to expect the subordination of historiography to ideology, the same interpretation prevails: "[Folklore's] rise as a theoretical discipline dates from the first decades of the nineteenth century. Up to that time there had been only sporadic amateur collections of oral poetic material, and literary reworking of it. The origin of folkloristics is closely connected with that broad trend in the field of philosophy, science, and history, at the beginning of the nineteenth century which received the name romanticism" (Sokolov 1966, 47–48).

These are positivistic historical observations that are supported by complexes of ideas, by common concerns for subject matter, and by a common vocabulary that folklore shares with Romanticism, particularly in Germany (Prawer 1970; Furst 1969). After all, in spite of William Thoms's denial of any Germanic influence, *folklore* is a cognate of *Volkskunde*, a term that appeared in German earlier (Emrich 1946, 371–72; Lutz 1973). Furthermore, it is related to compound terms, such as *Volkspoesie*, *Volksseele*, and *Volkslieder*, that designate basic concepts in Herder's writings (Simpson 1921).

Yet the examination of thoughts and theories, even research methods, reveals that folklore is not the "daughter of Romanticism" but at most, if we preserve the kinship metaphor, its sister. The ideas that shaped folklore were similar to those that influenced European thought and literature in the direction of the Romantic paradigm. Mikhail Bakhtin correctly observes that "the narrow concept of popular character and folklore was born in the pre-Romantic period and was basically completed by Von Herder and the Romantics" (Bakhtin 1968, 4). Bakhtin himself, who studies folk humor, looks to the Renaissance and the Middle Ages as a cultivation period for the ideas that later crystalized in the concept of folklore. In the sixteenth century, he finds an intellectual and literary interest in "a boundless world of humorous forms and manifestations [that] opposed the official and serious tone of medieval ecclesiastical and feudal culture. In spite of their variety, folk festivities of the carnival type, the comic rites and cults, the clowns and fools, giants, dwarfs, and jugglers, the vast and manifold literature of parody—all these forms have one style in common: they belong to one culture of folk carnival humor" (Bakhtin 1968, 4).

No doubt the search for the historical roots of folklore can be extended back even beyond the Renaissance and the Middle Ages to ancient Mesopotamia, ancient Egypt, and Classical Greece. The extant texts from these extinct societies reveal both the flourishing of oral traditions and the literary, religion, intellectual, and scholarly interest in them. There is a continuity in Western thought and literature that exhibits concern with and usage of popular traditions. But the idea of folklore that finally was crystalized, recognized, and named in the middle of the nineteenth century was not merely the culmination of an ideational evolution of currents and undercurrents of thoughts that were part of the Western world. Rather, being an invention in itself, folklore was born in a situation of change, in a critical transition of life and thought in European society.

As an idea, folklore represents an interest in popular national traditions for their communal attributes on the one hand, and for their universal qualities on the other hand. It generates a concern for peasant songs, ancient proverbs, and simple narratives, because of the assumption that they encapsulate a primary, elemental expression of human creativity. At the same time, they express the essential spirit of the community. They have become the focus of identity and symbols of communality for the group of speakers.

Under these ideational and theoretical circumstances, popular traditions themselves symbolize the ethnicity, humanity, simplicity, and antiquity of peoples. The historical acquisition of these meanings did not come about through a progressive accumulation of connotations, but in contrast, by a departure from previous perspectives. The transition from the conception of popular traditions as an accepted part of a society and its culture to an attitude that is based on distance and alienation, and that regards traditions as a subject of intellectual inquiry and ideological focus, developed through a major revolution in the relations between man and society.

There is no attempt here to single out early encounters with the Native Americans as the sole cause for that revolution; historical reductions rarely stand the test of scrutiny (Fischer 1970, 172–75). Other events of the Renaissance period, such as the Copernican revolution and the Reformation, were equally, perhaps even more, significant. Similarly, the political adjustments of the period and the voyages along the shores of sub-Saharan Africa and other unknown regions of the globe also contributed to the new perspectives in which Europeans viewed themselves, their society, and their culture.

Yet once these qualifications are stated, it is possible to examine the particular effects and potential significance of the discovery of an unknown human society on the unexplored shores of the new land in the West. How did this discovery influence the development of thought and methods of research that later culminated in the idea and the discipline of folklore? Although the initial reactions to encountering Native Americans were often framed in terms of Judeo-Christian and Classical notions of history and man, this experience also generated ideas and trends that led, directly and indirectly, to the study of European popular traditions and to the development of a set of theories about them. In particular, the focus of the present discussion is on the method of research, the ethnic identity of European peoples, and the conceptions of the universality and relativity of culture as they contributed to the emergence of folklore.

Methods of Research

The encounter with the Native Americans frustrated voyagers and scholars alike. The newly contacted societies could not have been conceived of in any of the conventional terms. As non-Noachian man, the Native American fit neither into the biblical nor the Classical frameworks according to which histories were constructed in the Middle Ages. As nonliterate societies in most cases, whose languages were not understood by Europeans in any case, they lacked historical records or traditions that could have enabled European scholars to establish them in a familiar temporal framework. History, after all, served as a major mode of explanation for the present. Since travelers lacked, at first, any grasp of the social and political history of these peoples, the only recourse they had in describing them was to turn to narrative accounts of native life, customs, rituals and ceremonies, religious beliefs, and social institutions, as well as material culture such as dwellings, utensils, decorations, and art forms. Description was a mode of comprehension, and a form of explanation with which it was possible to relate to societies the history of which was unknown.

Thus, the encountering of the Europeans with the Native American was a catalyst in shifting the study of society from the historical to the antiquarian mode. Arnaldo Momigliano (1966) distinguishes between the two types of scholarship: "(1) historians write in a chronological order; (2) historians produce those facts which serve to illustrate or explain certain situations; antiquaries collect all the items that are connected with certain subject, whether they help to solve a problem or not. The subject-matter contributes to the distinction between historians and antiquaries only in so far as certain subjects (such as political institutions, religion, private life) have traditionally been considered more suitable for systematic descriptions than for a chronological account" (3). Momigliano points out that the antiquarian research had its origins at least in the fifth century BC in Greece, and it continued up to the nineteenth century in Europe. The works of Marcus Terentius Varro (116–27 BC) represent its highest achievement in the ancient world. Varro "attempted a systematic survey of Roman life as seen from the point of view of its founders in the past. None of the Hellenistic scholars seems to have aimed at describing all the aspects of the life of a nation as systematically as Varro did" (Momigliano 1966, 5). His work served as a model for future generations; however, during the Middle Ages, the idea of *antiquitates* was lost, and it was revived only in the Renaissance. Stuart Piggott (1956) thus commented that "medieval antiquarianism is no more than sporadic and exceptional. With the sixteenth century we come into a new world of learning in which antiquarian studies as such take place from the start. They took this place, not as a disinterested intellectual activity, but as part of the contemporary search for precedent and authority in all branches of life and thought, and above all in the quest for respectable antecedents" (98).

One of the factors that contributed to this new surge of interest in antiquities was, I would like to suggest, early encounters with the Native Americans. Piggott's observations could be used in support of this interpretation of history. He states, "This revelation of primitive man in the Americas was then of the greatest importance in molding antiquarian thought in the sixteenth and seventeenth centuries" (1956, 102). However, Piggott limits this influence to visual concepts. He points out that the Native Americans provided models for description of primitive man wherever they were, and the ancient Britons were described like the men from the New World.

However, the discovery of America had a much more profound impact on sixteenth-century antiquarianism. Equipped mainly with chronological rather than textual documentary evidence, I would like to suggest that encountering the Native Americans contributed significantly to the discovery of the native Europeans. The antiquarians of the post-Columbus voyages were no longer content in unearthing Roman ruins on their lands but were interested in the ancient remains and the life of the peoples who were native to Britannia, for example. Thus, they took up the conceptual framework that was revived in describing the life of the Native Americans and applied it to the description of the customs and manners of the people who lived in the countryside. The antiquarians discovered in their life the rituals, ceremonies, and religious beliefs that previously were of interest only among natives of faraway lands.

Thus, in the sixteenth century, there was an interdependence and mutual influence between the reports of customs and manners of the natives of remote lands and those of European peasants. In a guidebook for "merchants, students, soldiers, mariners, etc." employed in services abroad, Albrecht Meier suggested in 1587 that they note down, among other things, "the manners, rites and ceremonies of Espowsals, marriages, feasts and banquets, and the variatie and manner of their exercises for pastime and recreation" (Hodgen 1964, 186). Johann Boemus's collection of manners and customs appeared even earlier, first in Latin in 1520 and then in English in 1555. In Boemus's collection, there is not yet any information about the Native Americans, but in *Cosmographia* (1544), Sebastian Muenster (1489–1552) turns also to describing the "newe founde lands and Islandes" (Hodgen 1964, 145).

The popularity of such books leaves little doubt that they were read by John Leland (1506–51), William Camden (1551–1623), and other antiquarians. The new trends in sixteenth-century antiquarianism that emphasized local relics and peasant customs demonstrate the similarity in interests to those developed as a result of contact with the inhabitants of newly discovered lands. Among these, descriptions of Native Americans appear in a relatively high proportion. John Rowe (1964) comments, "A surprisingly high proportion of the ethnographic data published in the sixteenth century relates to the New World. There is some for Ethiopia, the Near East, Japan and China, but less than the frequency of European contacts with these areas or the popularity of books about them would lead one to expect. Ethnographic information on the New World in sixteenth century books is somewhat more abundant" (2).

For better and for worse, this antiquarian research of the sixteenth century was directly related to the development of folklore. Richard M. Dorson has already singled out William Camden as a precursor of folklore research. In Dorson's (1968) attempt to define the antecedents of folklore, he correctly observes that "the key phrase" in Thoms's proposal is "popular antiquities" (2). During the seventeenth and eighteenth centuries, antiquarian research continued in England. However, an even stronger support for this effort developed in the seventeenth century in Sweden. In the context of rivalry with Denmark and concern for the national spirit of his country, King Gustavus Adolphus (1594–1632) personally signed, on the May 20, 1630, instruction consisting of fifteen sections in which he established the office of the Council on Antiquities and outlined the ground rules of its research. Because of the significance of this document, it is cited here in full.

> Instructions that His Majesty graciously wishes that those who are appointed to be the antiquarians and historians of the Kingdom should follow.
>
> 1. First His Majesty wishes that they search and collect all kinds of ancient relics and objects that glorify the father-land. Foremost of all [they should collect] old runic inscriptions, in books as well as on stones, both broken and complete. [They should] record their locations, and give a complete account of how many of them there are in each Parish, writing down the old tales that exist about each stone, etcetera.
> 2. Next, [they should] copy and collect not only all the calendars, almanacs, and runic staves, in whatever from or shape they appear, and discover the difference between them, but also [they should] find out how their owners themselves understand them, and name the people who are knowledgeable in these matters, noting down how many of them live in each Parish.
> 3. [They should] search for all kinds of ancient law-books like the old Wastgibtha law, the Wastmanna, Sudermanna, and Tijharad's or Smaland's laws, and others either in manuscript or in print, etcetera. Also [they should collect] all kinds of ordinances and treaties, statutes, rights and regulations, that might be of use to our Royal Court.
> 4. Likewise [they should collect] all kinds of chronicles and histories, immemorial tales and poems about dragons, dwarfs and giants, as well as tales about famous persons, old monasteries, castles, royal residences and towns, from which you can have some knowledge about the ancient times. [They should] not forget to find out the music of old warriors and runic songs.
> 5. [They should] examine and copy all kinds of old letters or excerpts of letters that can serve as a guide in the evaluation of coins, nobility, genealogies, or court of arms and other evidence that can serve the annals of history.

6. [They should] search and collect all kinds of old coins and currencies.
7. All this information could be obtained from old farmers, burghers and others, as well as from noblemen, clergymen, bailiffs and lawmen, and it should be looked up in churches and libraries in the towns as well as in the country.
8. Wherever they travel they should make thorough inquiries about the topographical features of the country and record the salt and fresh water lakes, the rivers, streams and water-falls, mountains, forests and plains either inhabited or uninhabited. [They should note] the distances between one place and another, [note down] the existing roads and their condition, whether suitable for travel by coach or cart. [They should record] the sources of the streams and their flow into lakes or seas. [They should comment] whether they are navigable or can be made suitable for navigation by [the construction] of locks, and what could be their use. Everything should be observed and prepared for the drawing of geographical maps of the entire kingdom of Sweden.
9. [They should] take every opportunity to list all kinds of land-measurements as mark, ore and ortigland . . . fields and meadows.
10. [They should] look for all kinds of boundary stones and boundary clearings.
11. [They should] search for deposits of ore . . .
12. [They should] inquire about household records and all kinds of economic matters . . . [detailed examples of agricultural work, hunting and fishing]
13. [They should] record the different cures and search for medical books, noting down the names of herbs and trees. [They should find out about] the signs for forecasting the weather, with which those who live near the sea are usually familiar, etcetera. [They should] describe the old costumes and weapons that are used in each province and [write] about the drinking vessels, *kosor*, horns and other such objects etcetera.
14. And since the names of tools are necessary for compiling a complete dictionary, they should record the different field tools, ship tools and [the names of] other such objects. Likewise [they should note down] the names of hundreds of parishes, villages, forests, streams, lakes, mountains, islands, inlets, shoals, inquiring also for the origin of these names.
15. Finally [they should] find out what kind of temperament the people of each province have. As one sees, hardly anything is forgotten by the writers of history. (Almgren 1931, 37, 41–42; see also Roberts 1953, 1:520)[3]

In this comprehensive research plan, prepared at the urging of his teacher, Johannes Bureur, Gustavus Adolphus laid the foundation for the systematic research of Nordic antiquities. The results of these investigations gave rise to the Romantic enthusiasm for European native culture that is at the core of Romantic and folkloric concerns of the eighteenth and nineteenth centuries.

The Ethnic Identity of European Peoples

The surge of interest in antiquities in England and Sweden in the sixteenth and seventeenth centuries had other causes in addition to early encounters with Native Americans. As in the later Romantic period, the collection of antiquities in the Renaissance served the rising national sentiments in these countries. While nationalism was certainly associated with the political stature of England and Sweden in Europe, the promotion of ethnic-national consciousness also was related to encounters with the "barbarians" in the new land.

Since Classical times, and throughout the Middle Ages, European peoples referred to some ethnic groups as "barbarians." The concept underwent historical changes and variations in meaning from one cultural context to another. While in Classical times Herodotus used it mainly in reference to Asian non-Hellenic peoples, in the Middle Ages, its meaning shifted from an ethnic to a religious pejorative term, referring mostly to the heathen peoples of Europe. Since Christianity spread from the Mediterranean basin northward, the peoples that remained on the fringes of the new religion bore the label of barbarism longer. In this case, the term combined the notions of uncivility and paganism (Jones 1971). At the same time, the term retained its use as a negative slur in interethnic relations, as in the case of the Italians, who regarded the French as barbarians (Hay 1960).

The ethnic groups that bore the stigma of barbarism longer—that is, well into the Renaissance—were the Irish and Nordic peoples. William Camden, for example, took for granted that Ireland was "for the most part, rude, half barbarous and ignorant of literature." Its inhabitants were "the barbarous islanders" (1806, 4:467). In his description of the "Manners and Customs of the Ancient Irish," Camden cites Strabo's characterization of the ancient Irish as barbarians (4:468). His other casual remarks demonstrate that according to his views, little has changed since then. Cannibalism and sexual immodesty were the main attributions that were cited as example for their lack of civility.

Similarly, Europeans did not describe the Nordic peoples in complimentary terms, even when they intended to bestow praise on them. For example, in the collection of *Histories tragiques* (1571) that François de Belleforest (1530–83) prepared using a previous Italian collection of Matteo Bandello's, he substituted several Italian tales for Scandinavian stories. The reason for this change was quite noble. He wrote at the end of one of these tales, "J'ay proposé ceste histoire, non tant pour singulariser la vertu des dames, que pour monstrer qu'entre les peuples plus barbares, il y a des cœurs genereux et des dames aussi illustres que celles desquelles Rome nous fait parade" (Seaton 1935, 299).[4] The notion that the Nordic people were barbarians was widely accepted, and Cawley, who examined references to voyages in Elizabethan drama, concluded that this literature reflects an image of the Nordic people as "barbarous, insulated from culture; even their brains were frozen" (1938, 238).

But the discovery of America introduced a new reference to the term *barbarism*: the Native Americans. From the earliest encounter, writers referred to Native Americans as barbarians, often with no need for justification. Pietro Martire d'Anghiera casually writes, "The barbarians admit that there were forty thousands of them engaged in the battle" (1912, 2:31; see also Elliott 1970, 46–53). Later on, in the sixteenth century, Jose de Acosta addressed himself more directly to questions of culture and religion, yet automatically assumed the barbarism of the native Americans: "These people, although they are in actual fact barbarians and differ in many respects from what is right and from natural law, should nevertheless be called to the salvation of the gospel in the same way in which the Greeks and Romans and the rest of the peoples of Asia and Europe were in earlier times called by the apostles" (Rowe 1964, 17). De Acosta attempts to distinguish several types among them and comments, "Although the provinces, nations and kinds of these people are very numerous, it seems to me that there are three classes, as it were, of barbarians, differing greatly from one another, to which these Indian nations can in general be reduced" (Rowe 1964, 16).

Ethnic distinctions, however, are not just questions of objective scholarly analysis, since they often become subjective issues of social identity. The stigma of barbarity was hardly complimentary for the Irish and the Nordic peoples to begin with, but the discovery of the "new barbarians" and the extension of the reflection of the term to include "primitive societies" became even more threatening. This extension of the term cast the Nordic people, who by the first half of the seventeenth century had become a major European power, in the same class together with ancient uncivilized men. A design in *Cosmographia* is quite revealing, as it shows that "barbarians, savages, and monsters are included by Muenster in the same category" (Hodgen 1964, 127).

No European society could tolerate such an association. The most effective method to break away from this implicit relationship with the new barbarians would be to demonstrate the existence of a cultural tradition and ancient past that contradicted the image of barbarity. While the Irish lacked the social and political organization to assert themselves culturally, the Swedish people could do just that. The instruction to collect antiquities that Gustavus Adolphus signed was issued in the context of a scholarly and national contest with Denmark. However, scholars in private reflected on the needs and purposes of collecting antiquities. Thus, in 1635, Rhezelius, a student of

Bureus, jotted down the following notes, perhaps expressing the views of his
teacher and other antiquarians:

> The council of the kingdom expects from an antiquarian the following:
>
> 1. All relics and customs that glorify the Fatherland from heathen times.
> 2. A new and complete chronicle about the deeds of Svea kings, about tales
>   of feuds with which the Danes should be refuted.
> 3. A dictionary of our language in which the meaning of all old words is
>   given as it is found in law-books and *Frodhor.*
> 4. All of our runic stones that we can claim are earlier [than those of the
>   Danes].
> 5. Rune calendar staves that do not exist in any other country.
> 6. Because of the Danes, who boast of their monuments.
> 7. Since our kings, whom we commemorate praisefully, have enlarged this
>   country by force and subdued other nations: since also the literary arts
>   have reached new heights that surpassed those of other nations, it is nec-
>   essary that we prove that our forefathers have not been barbarians, as
>   foreigners call us, but that we had a history.
>   For no nation has more ancient and more praiseworthy monuments than
>   we have. Such relics prove that we are the oldest people, and that our
>   language is the oldest. From us others originated, from us other lands
>   have been populated. Otherwise, we see that the Danes take much honor
>   that belong to us.
> 8. The following can be of use to the country.
>   (1) Where there is opportunity, fields and meadows should be sought
>   out. (2) Mines should be explored. (3) All kinds of metals. (4) Look for
>   all old coins. (5) Where it is possible to, build towns and villages. (6)
>   Roads should be increased. (7) Our laws should be improved by useful
>   commentaries.
> 9. It would be necessary to look for old books in which there is information
>   about the events of old days, as well as books about household and agri-
>   cultural works.
> 10. A certain drawing and descriptions of the provinces of the country.
> 11. [Information] about noble families, courts of arms and lineages.
>   (Rhezelii 1915–17, 53–54; Roberts 1953, 1:519–22)

Certainly, further research is required to determine the exact references
of the term *barbarians* in Sweden in the seventeenth century. It is necessary to
find out whether the meanings of this term acquired in southern and central
Europe extended to the languages spoken in the North. If this indeed had
been the case, early encounters with the Native Americans resulted in negative reactions, which at the same time stimulated European nations to turn
inward and draw on the cultural resources and the traditional heritage of their
societies, asserting their ethnic identity and defining themselves nationalis-
tically. In the search for clear defining marks of ethnic distinction, cultural
superiority, and above all, nonbarbaric designation, the Swedes transformed

their immemorial legends and poems to symbols of ethnicity and civility and to evidence of a glamorous past.

The Contribution of Cultural Relativity to Folklore

While the idea of folklore had its roots in ethnocentric notions, its development into a theory of human creativity required the recognition of the relativity of cultures. Gustavus Adolphus's *Instructions* reflects the narrow nationalistic view of expressive traditions, the role of which was to assign to the Swedish people a position of historical priority and creative superiority. All other nations were in the role of recipients, imitators, or followers. However, before myths, tales, songs, and proverbs could become building blocks in the social and historical theories of the eighteenth-century Romantics, it was necessary to recognize these forms as universal elements of humanity that are related to particular cultures.

Early encounters with the Native Americans and the intellectual reflections on the meaning of this social experience contributed to the recognition of the relativity of cultural values. Thus, the notion of "barbarism" was also used by a thinker to point out the relativity of cultures and the meaningless of ethnic boundaries in relation to the universal humanity of man. Montaigne phrased this idea succinctly: "Each man calls barbarism whatever is not his own practice" (Frame 1965, 152).

Montaigne's reflections on barbarity, and his contribution to the emergence of the concern with folklore, do not stop at his recognition of the inherent validity of any behavior and values relative to their culture of origin. He proceeded to examine the poetry of the Native Americans, an area of culture that could well have been the most slighted and least understood by the European. The texts of songs of war and love that he included in his famous essay "Of Cannibals" and his commentary on their esthetic value speak for themselves:

> These prisoners are so far from giving in in spite of all that is done to them that on the contrary, during the two or three months that they are kept, they wear a gay expression; they urge their captors to hurry and put them to the test; they defy them, insult them, reproach them with their cowardice and the number of battles they have lost to the prisoners' own people.
>
> I have a song composed by a prisoner which contains this challenge, that they should all come boldly and gather to dine off him, for they will be eating at the same time their own fathers and grandfathers, who have served to feed and nourish his body. "These muscles," he says "this flesh and these veins are your own, poor fools that you are. You do not recognize that the substance of your ancestors' limbs is still contained in them. Savor them well; you will find in them taste of your own flesh." An idea that certainly does not smack of barbarity. Those that paint these people dying, and who show the execution, portray the

prisoner spitting in the face of his slayers and scowling at them. Indeed, to the last gasp they never stop braving and defying their enemies by word and look. Truly here are real savages by our standards, for either they must be thoroughly so, or we must be; there is an amazing distance between their character and ours.

Besides the warlike song I have just quoted, I have another, a love song, which begins in this vein: "Adder, stay; stay, adder, that from the pattern of your coloring my sister may draw the fashion and the workmanship of a rich girdle that I may give to my love; so may your beauty and your pattern be forever preferred to all other serpents." This first couplet is the refrain of the song. Now, I am familiar enough with poetry to be a judge of this: not only is there nothing barbarous in this fancy, but it is altogether Anacreontic. Their language, moreover, is a soft language, with an agreeable sound, somewhat like Greek in its endings. (Frame 1965, 158)

In conclusion, early encounters with the Native Americans had a traumatic effect on European society. The idea of folklore was one of the consequences of this event, and it emerged through concerns with antiquities, with ethnic identity and consciousness of cultural relativity. Yet, in spite of its import, discovery of America by Europeans must be viewed in the context of other historical events and ideas. Neither of these three themes in European culture could be related exclusively to the discovery of America, nor were they solely effective in the formation of the idea of folklore. However, in conjunction with other related discoveries, social and political trends, and scholarly and philosophical concerns, the encounter with other cultures generated the awareness of native European cultures that was the essence of folklore.[5]

Notes

1. The conference First Images of America: The Impact of the New World on the Old was held February 7–9, 1975, at the University of California, Los Angeles, as part of the 21st Annual Meeting of the Renaissance Society of America.

2. The relation between geographical explorations and anthropology is not universally accepted among historians of this discipline. Some tend to trace the study of anthropology back to the Classical period (Kluckhohn 1950). Most recently, Dell Hymes (1972, 21) starts with the Greek Enlightenment of the fifth century BC, though he does not discount the effect of explorations. In contrast, Marvin Harris (1968) considers the beginnings of anthropology to be in the European Enlightenment, and T. K. Penniman (1965) begins the history of the field in the nineteenth century. Others emphasize the significance of the Renaissance in the emergence of anthropology. The effect of the discovery of America by Columbus on anthropology is discussed by Edward G. Browne (1907), and the general period of the Renaissance by John Howland Rowe (1964, 1965). Further discussions and bibliographical information on the subject are in Margaret T. Hodgen (1964), Wilhelm E. Muhlmann (1968, 34–38), Michele Duchet (1971, 25–47), and De Wall Malefrit (1974, 58–65).

3. I would like to thank Mrs. Gunnil S. J. Sjoberg for rendering this document into English and for long discussions in which she clarified for me the historical background of this royal

proclamation. The English translation includes a number of necessary modifications, and the responsibility for the present English text rests with me.

4. "I proposed this story, not so much to single out the virtue of the ladies, but to show that between the most barbarous peoples, there are generous hearts and ladies as illustrious as those of which Rome would make us parade."

5. I would like to thank Regna Darnell, Wayland D. Hand, Dell Hymes, Alan Kors, and Gunnil S. J. Sjoberg for very helpful comments and criticism on an early version of this essay.

Bibliography

Almgren, Oscar. 1931. "Om tillkomsten av 1630 ars antikvarie-institution." *Fornvännen* 26:35–42.

Anghiera, Pietro Martire d'. 1912. *De Orbo Novo: The Eight Decades of Peter Martyr d'Anghera.* Translated by Francis Augustus MacNutt. New York: G. P. Putnam's Sons.

Bakhtin, Mikhail. 1968. *Rabelais and His World.* Translated by Helene Iswolsky. Cambridge, MA: MIT Press.

Bauman, Richard, and Joel Sherzer, eds. 1975. *Explorations in the Ethnography of Speaking.* Cambridge: Cambridge University Press.

Beattie, John. 1964. *Other Cultures: Aims, Methods and Achievements in Social Anthropology.* New York: Free Press.

Ben-Amos, Dan, and Kenneth S. Goldstein, eds. 1975. *Folklore: Performance, Communication.* Approaches to Semiotics, vol. 40. The Hague: Mouton.

Boggs, Ralph Steele. 1945. "Reprint of the Letter by W. J. Thoms in *The Athenaeum* of August 22, 1846, first proposing the work of 'Folklore,' with Spanish Translation." *Folklore Americas* 5:17–20.

Browne, Edward G. 1907. "Columbus, Ramon Pane and the Beginnings of American Anthropology." *Proceedings of the American Antiquarian Society* 17:310–48.

Camden, William. 1806. *Britannia, or a Chorographical Description of the Flourishing Kingdoms of England, Scotland, and Ireland and the Islands Adjacent; From the Earliest Antiquity.* 2nd ed. 4 vols. London: John Stockdale.

Cawley, Robert Ralston. 1938. *The Voyagers and Elizabethan Drama.* Modern Language Association of America Monograph Series, no. 8. Boston: D. C. Heath.

Darnell, Regna, ed. 1974. *Readings in the History of Anthropology.* New York: Harper and Row.

Dorson, Richard M. 1968. *The British Folklorists: A History.* Chicago: University of Chicago Press.

Dundes, Alan, ed. 1965. *The Study of Folklore.* Englewood Cliffs, NJ: Prentice-Hall.

Duchet, Michele. 1971. *Anthropologie et histoire au siecle des lumieres.* Paris: Francois Maspero.

Elliott, J. H. 1970. *The Old World and the New, 1492–1650.* Cambridge: Cambridge University Press.

Emrich, Duncan. 1946. "'Folklore': William John Thoms." *California Folklore Quarterly* 5, no. 4:355–74.

Fischer, David H. 1970. *Historians' Fallacies: Toward a Logic of Historical Thought.* New York: Harper and Row.

Frame, Donald M., trans. 1965. *The Complete Essays of Montaigne.* Stanford: Stanford University Press.

Furst, Lillian R. 1969. "Romanticism in Historical Perspectives." In *Comparative Literature: Matter and Method,* edited by A. Owen Aldridge, 61–89. Urbana: University of Illinois Press.

Harris, Marvin. 1968. *The Rise of Anthropological Theory*. New York: Thomas Y. Crowell.

Hay, Denys. 1960. "Italy and Barbarian Europe." In *Italian Renaissance Studies: A Tribute to the Late Cecilia M. Ady*, edited by E. F. Jacod, 48–68. London: Faber and Faber.

Hodgen, Margaret T. 1964. *Early Anthropology in the Sixteenth and Seventeenth Centuries*. Philadelphia: University of Pennsylvania Press.

Hoffmann-Krayer, Eduard. 1902. *Die Volkskunde als Wissenschaft*. Zürich: F. Amberger.

Hymes, Dell, ed. 1972. *Reinventing Anthropology*. New York: Pantheon Books.

Jones, W. R. 1971. "The Image of the Barbarian in Medieval Europe." *Comparative Studies in Society and History* 13, no. 4:376–407.

Kluckhohn, Clyde. 1950. *Anthropology and the Classics*. Providence: Brown University Press.

Krappe, Alexander H. 1930. *The Science of Folk-Lore*. London: Methuen.

Lutz, Gerahrd. 1973. "Johann Ernst Fabri und die Anfuange der Volksforschung im Ausehenden 18. Jahrhundert." *Zeitschrift für Volkskunde* 69:19–42.

Malefrit, Annemarie De Wall. 1974. *Images of Man: A History of Anthropological Thought*, New York: Knopf.

Momigliano, Arnaldo. 1966. *Studies in Historiography*. New York; Harper and Row.

Muhlmann, Wilhelm E. 1968. *Geschichte der Anthropologie*. Frankfurt am Main: Athenaum.

Paredes, Américo, and Richard Bauman, eds. 1972. *Toward New Perspectives in Folklore*. American Folklore Society Bibliographical and Special Series 23. Austin: University of Texas Press.

Penniman, T. K. 1965. *A Hundred Years of Anthropology*. 3rd. ed. London: Gerald Duckworth.

Piggott, Stuart. 1956. "Antiquarian Thought in the Sixteenth and Seventeenth Centuries." In *English Historical Scholarship in the Sixteenth and Seventeenth Centuries*, edited by Levi Fox, 93–114. London: Oxford University Press.

Prawer, Siegbert, ed. 1970. *The Romantic Period in Germany*. New York: Schocken Books.

Rhezelii, Ion Haquini. 1915–17. *Monumenta Uplandica: Reseanteckningar Från Åren 1635, 1636, 1638*, edited by C. M. Stenbock and Oskar Lundberg. Uppsala: Akademiska Boktryckeriet.

Rowe, John Howland. 1964. "Ethnography and Ethnology in the Sixteenth Century." *Kroeber Anthropological Society Papers* 30:1–19.

———. 1965. "The Renaissance Foundations of Anthropology." *American Anthropologist* 67, no. 1:1–20. Reprinted in Darnell (1974, 61–77).

Roberts, Michael. 1953. *Gustavus Adolphus: A History of Sweden, 1611–1632*. 2 vols. London: Longmans, Green.

Seaton Ethel. 1935. *Literary Relations of England and Scandinavia in the Seventeenth Century*. Oxford: Clarendon.

Simpson, Georgiana R. 1921. *Herder's Conception of "Das Volk."* Chicago: University of Chicago Libraries.

Sokolov, Y. M. 1966. *Russian Folklore*. Translated by Catherine Ruth Smith. Introduction and bibliography by Felix J. Oinas. Hatboro, PA: Folklore Associates. Originally published in English in 1950 by the American Council of Learned Societies Devoted to Humanistic Studies, Russian Translation Project Series, 7. New York: Macmillan.

Vilmos, Voigt, 1972. "Some Problems of Narrative Structure Universals in Folklore." *Acta Ethnographica* 21:57–72.

3

TOWARD A DEFINITION OF
FOLKLORE IN CONTEXT

DEFINITIONS OF FOLKLORE ARE AS MANY AND VARIED as the versions of a well-known tale. Both semantic and theoretical differences have contributed to this proliferation. The German *Volkskunde*, the Swedish *folkminne*, and the Indian *lok sahitya* all imply slightly different meanings that the English term *folklore* cannot syncretize completely (Eriksson 1955; Hultkranz 1960, 243–49; Legross 1962; Lutz 1958). Similarly, anthropologists and students of literature have projected their own biases into their definitions of folklore. In fact, for each of them, folklore became the exotic topic, the green grass on the other side of the fence, to which they were attracted but which, alas, was not in their own domain. Thus, while anthropologists regarded folklore as literature, scholars of literature defined it as culture (cf. Bascom 1949; Espinosa 1949; Herskovits 1949; Leach 1949). Folklorists themselves resorted to enumerative (Bayard 1953, 9–10; Dundes 1965, 1–3; Merton 1846), intuitive (Botkin 1944, xxi; Utley 1968), and operational (Utley 1961) definitions; yet while all these certainly contributed to the clarification of the nature of folklore, at the same time, they circumvented the main issue—namely, the isolation of the unifying thread that joins jokes and myths, gestures and legends, costumes and music into a single category of knowledge.

The difficulties experienced in defining folklore are genuine and real. They result from the nature of folklore itself and are rooted in the historical development of the concept. Early definitions of folklore were clouded by romantic mist and haunted by the notion of "popular antiquities," which Thoms sought to replace.[1] Implicit in these definitions are criteria of the antiquity of the material, the anonymity or collectiveness of composition, and the simplicity of the folk, all of which are circumstantial and not essential to folklore. The age of a song, for example, establishes it chronologically; the identification of the composer describes it historically; and its association with a particular group defines it socially. Each of these factors has an explanatory and interpretive value, but none of them defines the song as folklore. Thus, the principles that united "customs, observance, superstitions, ballads, proverbs, etc." in Thoms's initial definition of folklore were not intrinsic to these items and could only serve as a shaky framework for the development of a scientific discipline concentrating on them.[2]

Subsequent attempts to construct a definition that would hold together all these apparently diversified phenomena encountered a difficulty inherent in the nature of folklore. On the one hand, folklore forms—such as mentifacts and artifacts—are superorganic in the sense that once they are created, their indigenous environment and cultural context are not required for their continuous existence (Bidney 1953, 125–31). Background information may be essential for the analytical interpretation of the materials, but none of it is crucial for the sheer existence of the folklore forms. Tales and songs can shift media, cross language boundaries, pass from one culture to another, and still retain sufficient traces of similarity to enable us to recognize a core of sameness in all their versions. Folk art objects can outlive their users and even exist when their culture as a whole has become extinct, so that they are literally survivals of ancient times. A folk musician nowadays can perform for millions of people on a television network, in a style and manner that approximate his own singing and playing in the midst of his own small group, thus extending his art far beyond his social circle. In sum, the materials of folklore are mobile, manipulative, and transcultural.

On the other hand, folklore is very much an organic phenomenon in the sense that it is an integral part of culture. Any divorce of tales, songs, or sculptures from their indigenous locale, time, and society inevitably introduces qualitative changes into them. The social context, the cultural attitude, the rhetorical situation, and the individual aptitude are variables that produce distinct differences in the structure, text, and texture of the ultimate verbal, musical, or plastic product. The audience itself, be it children or adults, men or women, a stable society or an accidental grouping, affects the kind of folklore genre and the manner of presentation (see Dégh 1957). Moreover, the categorization of prose narratives into different genres depends largely on the cultural attitude toward the tales and the indigenous taxonomy of oral tradition. Thus, in the process of diffusion from one culture to another, tales may also cross narrative categories, and the same story may be myth for one group and *Märchen* for another. In that case, the question of the actual generic classification of the tale is irrelevant, since it does not depend on any autonomous intrinsic features but rather on the cultural attitude toward it. Finally, unlike written literature, music, and fine art, folklore forms and texts are performed repeatedly by different peoples on various occasions. The performance situation, in the final analysis, is the crucial context for the available text. The particular talent of the professional or lay artist, his mood at the moment of recitation, and the response of his audience may all affect the text of his tale or song.

Thus, definitions of folklore have had to cope with this inherent duality of the subject and often did so by placing the materials of folklore in different, even conflicting perspectives. In spite of this diversification, it is possible to distinguish three basic conceptions of the subject underlying many definitions; accordingly, folklore is one of these three: a body of knowledge, a mode of thought, or a kind of art. These categories are not completely exclusive of each other. Very often, the difference between them is a matter of emphasis rather than of essence; for example, the focus on knowledge and thought implies an emphasis on the contents of the materials and their perception, whereas the concentration on art puts the accent on the forms and the media of transmission. Nevertheless, each of these three foci involves a different range of hypotheses, relates to a distinct set of theories about folklore, and consequently leads toward divergent research directions.

However, since knowledge, thought, and art are broad categories of culture, folklorists have had to concentrate mainly on distinguishing their subject matter from other phenomena of the same kind. For that purpose, they have qualified folklore materials in terms of their social context, time depth, and medium of transmission. Thus, folklore is not thought of as existing without or apart from a structured group. It is not a phenomenon *sui generis*. No matter how defined, its existence depends on its social context, which may be either a geographic, linguistic, ethnic, or occupational grouping. In addition, it has required distillation through the mills of time. Folklore may be "old wine in new bottles" and also "new wine in old bottles" (Botkin 1944, xxi–xxii), but rarely has it been conceived of as new wine in new bottles. Finally, it has to pass through time at least partially via the channels of oral transmission. Any other medium is liable to disqualify the material from being folklore.

Further, folklorists have constructed their definitions on the basis of sets of relations between the social context, the time depth, and the medium of transmission on the one hand and the conception of folklore as a body of knowledge, mode of thought, and kind of art on the other, as illustrated in the following table.

	Social Context	Time Depth	Medium of Transmission
Knowledge	Communal possession	Antiquity	Verbal or imitative
Thought	Collective representation	Survival	Verbal
Art	Communal creation or re-creation	Antiquity	Verbal or imitative

It is possible to distinguish three types of relations between the social context and folklore: possession, representation, and creation or re-creation. Basically, a literal interpretation of the term *folklore* sets up the first type of relationship. Accordingly, folklore is "the learning of the people" (Burne 1914, 1), "the wisdom of the people, the people's knowledge" (Sokolov 1966, 3), or more fully, "the lore, erudition, knowledge or teaching of a folk" (Boggs 1943, 1). This view of folklore as the lore shared by the whole group communally applies, in practice and theory, to different degrees of public possession. First, folklore can be the sum total of knowledge in a society. Since no single member of the community has a complete command of all its facets, folklore in this sense must be an abstract construct based on the collective information as it is stored with many individuals, "the whole body of people's traditionary beliefs and customs" (Frazer 1918, 1:vii).

Second, and in contrast, folklore has been considered only that knowledge shared by every member of the group. This definition excludes any esoteric information to which only selected experts in the community have access, since it restricts folklore to "popular knowledge" (Espinosa 1949) alone. In that case, folklore is the real "common property" (Bayard 1953, 8) of the community. Third, this real communal lore can be expressed by the group at large in "collective actions of the multitude," as Frazer defines it (1918, 1:vii), including public festivities, rituals, and ceremonies in which every member of the group partakes. Last, folklore can be restricted to customs and observances that each individual adheres to in the privacy of his home, though all the people in the society abide by them. Although this last interpretation is theoretically possible, no definition has limited the scope of folklore so narrowly. The construction of the second set of relations between folklore and its social context is based on British evolutionary theory and French sociological anthropology. Accordingly, folklore represents a particular mode of collective and spontaneous thought, as André Varagnac has formulated his definition: "Le folklore, ce sont des croyances collectives sans doctrine, des pratiques collectives sans théorie" (Varagnac 1938, 18).[3] In that case, the actual customs, rituals, and other observances are representations of the mode of thought that underlies them. The notion of collective thought in the context of definitions of folklore has several connotations. First, it refers to the average, unexceptional thought that lacks any marks of individuality, conventional modes of human thought. Second, it implies the particular thinking patterns of primitive man, as they were conceived by early folklorists and anthropologists. Edwin Sidney Hartland, for example, defined tradition, the subject matter of the science of fairy tales, as "the sum total of the psychological phenomena of uncivilized man" (1891, 34). In that sense, folklore is the expression of the psychology of early man as it concerns any field, either philosophy, religion, science, or history.

All these aspects of thought are represented collectively in the folklore of the people. The conception of a special mode of thinking pertaining to primitive people was developed by Lévy-Bruhl (1910) as "the collective representation." Folklore, as other social facts, is a manifestation of this particular mode of thought. It expresses the particular mystique that characterizes primitive mentality in its perception of natural and social reality. Although Lévy-Bruhl's theories are no longer accepted without reservations, they still serve as a basis for defining folklore, as exemplified in Joseph Rysan's (1952) definition: "Folklore can be defined as the collective objectifications of basic emotions, such as awe, fear, hatred, reverence, and desire, on the part of the social group" (10).

When the principle of collectivity or communality is applied to the definition of folklore as art, reference is made particularly to the creation of folk literature. Two concepts have been developed in that regard: communal creation and re-creation. The first—whose main exponent in America was Francis Gummere (1907)—implies that folk songs, especially ballads, are a product of communal creation. This notion, long discarded, is not as absurd as Louise Pound (1921) would have liked us to believe. Although its particular application to the origin of the ballad is rather doubtful, it is possible to conceive of such a process in relation to other kinds of folklore. Paul Bohannan (1961) reports a case of communal creation in the decoration of a walking stick and of other objects. Many members of the group, including the anthropologist himself, contributed to the formation of the wooden pieces. Some of my own informants, composers of songs from Benin City, in midwestern Nigeria, admitted readily, and without perceiving the theoretical difficulties such admissions impose on us, that they often composed a song alone, but that the group of singers to whom they belonged reworked it afterward until everybody was pleased. However, by now the notion of communal creation has been completely discarded from any definition of folklore and replaced, when applicable, by the concept of communal re-creation. Archer Taylor (1949), for example, incorporated the concept explicitly into his definition of folklore. Actually, this process is implied in the notion of oral transmission and the variability of the text. The concept of re-creation differs from that of creation only in regard to the duration of the creative moment. The main feature of folklore remains the same: verbal art is the sum total of creation of a whole community over time. Actually, when this hypothesis itself is challenged, the notion of passive creativity is introduced. Accordingly, the audience reaction is as much a part of the act of creation as the active imagination of the folk artist (von Sydow 1948, 11–43; Anderson 1923, 397–403).

By its very nature, the notion of communal re-creation involves a relationship between folklore and a second factor: time depth. The persistence of the materials in circulation in a culture, "bequeathed from generation to generation" (Boggs 1943, 1), has become the determining criterion for the identification of folklore items. For Thompson, "the idea of tradition is the touchstone for everything that is to be included in the term folklore" (1951, 11). According to this notion, however, there cannot be any innovation in tradition, and if there is, it still has to "live in people's mouth for at least several generations" (Dorson 1952, 7). This conception of folklore was contained in the original definition of Thoms's and maintained by folklorists up to the present time. Francis Utley, who made a content analysis of the definitions in the *Funk and Wagnalls Standard Dictionary of Folklore, Mythology, and Legend* (1961, 193), found the great preponderance of the term *tradition* to be unchallenged by any other concept. The idea of tradition refers to folklore both as knowledge (the "wisdom" of the past) and as art (old songs and tales). In relation to thoughts and beliefs, the relative time depth qualifies folklore even further. It designates the materials as survivals, as implied by the evolutionary theories of Edward Tylor (1958, 1, 70–159) and Andrew Lang (1884). In that case, *folklore* applies only to that item in culture that had vital currency in previous stages of human evolution and either survived the changes of time and became "a lively fossil" (Potter 1949) or remained alive among those segments of society least exposed to the light of civilization.

Of the three factors, it is the medium of transmission that has been the most persistent in folklore definitions. Almost from the beginning, the most accepted characteristic of folklore—whether conceived of as knowledge, thought, or art—has been its transmission by oral means. In order for an item to qualify as folklore, the prime prerequisite is that it have been in oral circulation and passed from one person to another without the aid of any written texts. When a visual, musical, or kinetic form is considered, the transmission can be through imitation (Boggs 1943, 1). The basic assumption is that this particular form of transmission introduces some distinct qualities into the materials that would be lost otherwise. In this sense, folklore as a discipline preceded Marshall McLuhan in declaring "the medium is the message" (1964, 23–39).

The criterion of oral tradition has become the last citadel of folklore scholars in defending the uniqueness of their materials. When the theories about communal creation collapsed and the doctrine of survivals fell through, scholars were able to hold firm to the idea that folklore is "verbal art," "unrecorded menti-facts," and "literature orally transmitted" (Bascom 1955; Kangas-Maranda 1963, 85; Utley 1961.) This conception of folklore was hailed both by anthropologists who worked in nonliterate societies and by scholars of literature, who found it an operational distinction separating folklore from literature. Although folklorists concede that the purity of this transmission has often been contaminated by literary texts, the final standard for the identification of materials as folklore is the actual circulation, even once, through verbal media.

In spite of its popularity, the criterion of medium of transmission has not defined what folklore really is; it has merely provided a qualifying statement about the form of circulation. Moreover, such definitions impose a preconceived framework on folklore. Rather than define it, they establish certain ideals as to what folklore should be. These attempts to reconcile romantic with empirical approaches have held back scientific research in the field and are partially responsible for the fact that, while other disciplines that emerged during the nineteenth century have made headway, folklore is still suffering growing pains.

It is still necessary to ask, "What is it that circulates verbally and is transmitted through time within a distinct social entity?" This rhetorical question in itself reflects the wrong direction that various attempts to define folklore have taken. They have searched for a way to describe folklore as a static, tangible object. The enumerative definitions consisted of lists of objects, while the substantive definitions regarded folklore as art, literature, knowledge, or belief. In actuality, it is none of these and all of them together. Folklore does contain knowledge; it is an expression of thought, formulated artistically, but at the same time, it is also a unique phenomenon that is irreducible to any of these categories.

In order to discern the uniqueness of folklore, it is first necessary to change the existing perspective we have of the subject. So far, most definitions have conceived of folklore as a collection of things. These could be either narratives, melodies, beliefs, or material objects. All of them are completed products or formulated ideas; it is possible to collect them. In fact, the last characteristic has been at the base of the major portion of folklore research since its inception. The collection of things requires a methodological abstraction of objects from their actual context. No doubt this can be done; often, it is essential for research purposes. Nevertheless, this abstraction is only methodological and should not be confused with, or substituted for, the true nature of the entities. Moreover, any definition of folklore on the basis of these abstracted things is bound to mistake the part for the whole. To define folklore, it is necessary to examine the phenomena as they exist. In its cultural context, folklore is not an aggregate of things, but a process—a communicative process, to be exact.

It should be pointed out that this conception of folklore differs substantially from previous views of folklore as a process. Focusing on the dynamics of transmission, modification, and textual variation (for example, Abrahams 1963, 102; Goldstein 1967; and Utley 1958, 139), such views perpetuated the dichotomy between processes and things. They stressed the transmission of objects in time and society, and allowed for a methodological and theoretical separation between the narrators and their tales. These views of folklore are logically justified, since after all, there is a distinction between the man and his songs, the child and his games. But the ever-increasing emphasis on the situational background of tales, songs, and proverbs that developed from Malinowski's functionalism into Hymes's (1962) "ethnography of speaking" enables us not only to study but to define folklore in its context. And in this framework, which is the real habitat of all folklore forms, there is no dichotomy between processes and products. The telling is the tale; therefore, the narrator, his story, and his audience are all related to each other as components of a single continuum, which is the communicative event.

Folklore is the action that happens at that time. It is an artistic action. It involves creativity and esthetic response, both of which converge in the art forms themselves. Folklore in that sense is a social interaction via the art media and differs from other modes of speaking and gesturing. This distinction is based on sets of cultural conventions, recognized and adhered to by all the members of the group, that separate folklore from nonart communication. In other words, the definition of folklore is not merely an analytical construct, depending on arbitrary exclusion and inclusion of items; on the contrary, it has a cultural and social base. Folklore is not "pretty much what one wants to make out of it" (Foster 1949); it is a definite realistic, artistic, and communicative process. The locus of the conventions marking the boundaries between folklore and nonfolklore is in the text, texture, and context of the forms, to apply Dundes's (1964) three levels for the analysis of folklore in somewhat modified form.

The textual marks that set folklore apart as a particular kind of communication are the opening and closing formulas of tales and songs and the structure of actions that happen in between. The opening and closing formulas designate the events enclosed between them as a distinct category of narration, not to be confused with reality. As the Ashanti storyteller states most explicitly, "We don't really mean to say so, we don't really mean to say so," referring to the imaginary nature of the story (Rattray 1930, x). Tales, however, do not necessarily relate to denotative speech as fiction does to truth. A folkloristic historical narrative, such as a legend (Bascom 1965), is nevertheless formally distinct from a chronology of events. This contention, admittedly, requires further research. However, the phrase "it is like in a folktale"—which people employ whenever reality duplicates the sequence of actions in an artistic narration—attests to the awareness of a particular folktale structure. Also, other genres, such as proverbs and riddles, have distinct syntactic and semantic structures that separate them from the regular daily speech into which they are interspersed. Furthermore, these artistic forms are culturally recognized categories of communication. They have special names or identifying features distinguishing them from each other and from other modes of social interaction, pointing to the cultural awareness of their unique character.

Each of these forms may also have distinct textural qualities that separate them from other kinds of communication. These can be rhythmical speech, musical sounds, melodic accompaniment, or patterned design. In a sense, this is a reverse argument for the arts. Accordingly, a message is not considered artistic because it possesses these qualities, but it is these textural features that serve as markers to distinguish it as artistic. Since folklore forms are often interspersed in the midst of other modes of social interaction, they require such textural marks to single them out and prevent mistaking them for what they are not. Thus the telling of a story may necessitate a distinct speech pattern, such as recitative, and the saying of a proverb may involve a shift in intonation (Herzog and Blooah 1936, 8).

Finally, there are contextual conventions that set folklore apart. These are specifications as to time, place, and company in which folklore actions happen. "To everything there is a season and a time to every purpose" (Eccles. 3:1). Narratives can be told during the daytime in the marketplace, at the country store, and on the street corner, or at night in the village square, the parlor, and the coffeehouse. Songs and music have other occasions when they are performed. Although such specifications may have other functions, such as confining folklore to leisure and ceremonial activities, they also separate art from nonart in cultures that otherwise lack a complex division of time, space, and labor. In a sense, they provide a spatial, temporal, and social definition for folklore in culture.

These communicative marks of folklore do not necessarily exist on all three levels—text, texture, and context. The identification of social interaction as folklore by the people who tell the stories, sing the songs, play the music, and paint the pictures may be in terms of only one or all of these three. In any case, for them, folklore is a well-defined cultural category.

Although folklore is a distinct category in terms of social interaction patterns and communication media, it is not necessarily recognized by the culture as a separate concept. In fact, within the cognitive system, its forms may be classified into such apparently unrelated categories as history, tradition, dance, music, games, and tales. The reason for this categorization is inherent in the nature of the folkloristic communication itself. Folklore, like any other art, is a symbolic kind of action. Its forms have symbolic significance reaching far beyond the explicit content of the particular text, melody, or artifact. The very syntactic and semantic structure of the text, the special recitative rhythm of presentation, and the time and locality in which the action happens may have symbolic implications for which the text itself cannot account. Consequently, it is quite plausible that in their classification of these materials, people will use as a criterion not the symbolic mode of the form but its reference. Legend, for example, often signifies a chronological truth; myth symbolizes a religious truth; and parable implies a moral truth. A definition, according to these references, would regard them as history, religion, and ethics, respectively. However, if their actual cultural mode of communication is the key for definition, then all these forms are but different phases in the same process of folklore.

The allowance for a possible disparity between ethnic taxonomy and behavior implies that, in a certain instance, the definition of folklore in its context depends on actual modes of communication and not necessarily on the particular cultural concept of them. There may be an overlap between the analytical view, which depends on observation, and the internal interpretation, which results from participation; however, for the purpose of a cross-cultural application of this definition, the analytical approach to the material must have methodological priority.

Similarly, the acceptance of the possible disparity between the analytical and the cultural views in regard to processes of social interaction permits the extension of the scope of folklore beyond the limits imposed on it by the concept of verbal art. As an artistic process, folklore may be found in any communicative medium: musical, visual, kinetic, or dramatic. Theoretically, it is not necessary for the people themselves to make the conceptual connection between their melodies, masks, and tales. From the cultural point of view, these may well be separate phenomena unrelated to each other and not even existing in the same situation. Sufficient is the cultural recognition of their qualitative uniqueness in relation to other modes of communication in the respective media of sound, motion, and vision. The factor of rhythm changes human noise to music, movement and gesture to dance, and object to sculpture. Thus, they are artistic communication by their very essence. Furthermore, they are recognized as such by the people, since there are definite contexts of time and place in culture in which these actions are permissible. In the case of music and dance, there is no need to differentiate them from nonart communication. Their artistic qualities are intrinsic and essential to their very existence. There is, however, some necessity to distinguish these media as folklore. The distinguishing factor would be the particular social context of folklore.

As a communicative process, folklore has a social limitation as well—namely, the small group. This is the particular context of folklore. The concept of the small group, so popular among sociologists in the early fifties (Golembiewski 1962), somehow bypassed the ranks of folklorists, who preferred the more romantic, even corny, term *folk*. Since, in America at least, the connotations of marginality and low socioeconomic status that once were associated with the term *folk* have long been abandoned (Boggs 1943; Clarke 1963, 1; Dundes 1966, 229–33), the concept of *folk* has become almost synonymous with the group concept. A group is "a number of persons who communicate with one another, often over a span of time, and who are few enough so that each person is able to communicate with all the others, not at second-hand through other people, but face-to-face" (Homans 1950, 1). A group could be a family, a street-corner gang, a roomful of factory workers, a village, or even a tribe. These are social units of different orders and qualities, yet all of them exhibit, to a larger or smaller extent, the characteristics of a group. For the folkloric act to happen, two social conditions are necessary: Both the performers and the audience have to be in the same situation and be part of the same reference group. This implies that folklore communication takes place in a situation in which people confront each other face to face and relate to each other directly.

It is necessary to remember at this point that even when a certain literary theme or musical style is known regionally, nationally, or internationally, its actual existence depends on such small-group situations. In these cases, the storytellers know their audience and relate specifically to them, and the listeners know the performer and react to his particular way of presentation. Of course, this familiarity is often relative to the size of the general reference group. A storyteller who has a regional reputation may entertain people whom he does not know as intimately as he knows the people in his own village. Yet, even in such cases, both the performers and the audience belong to the same reference group; they speak the same language; share similar values, beliefs, and background knowledge; and have the same system of codes and signs for social interaction. In other words, for a folklore communication to exist as such, the participants in the small-group situation have to belong to the same reference group, one composed of people of the same age or of the same professional, local, religious, or ethnic affiliation. In theory and in practice, tales can be narrated and music can be played to foreigners. Sometimes this accounts for diffusion. But folklore is true to its own nature when it takes place within the group itself. In sum, folklore is artistic communication in small groups.

Two key folklore terms are absent from this definition—namely, tradition and oral transmission. This omission is not accidental. The cultural use of tradition as a sanction is not necessarily dependent on historical fact. Very often, it is merely a rhetorical device or a socially instrumental convention. The combination of a narrative content concerned with olden times with the cultural conviction in the historicity of tales necessitates a presentation of the stories as if they were handed down from antiquity. Further, in past-oriented cultures, the sanction of tradition may be instrumental to the introduction of new ideas, and tales may serve as the vehicle for that purpose. Thus, the traditional character of folklore is an accidental quality, associated with it in some cases, rather than an objectively intrinsic feature of it. In fact, some groups specifically divorce the notion of antiquity from certain folklore forms and present them as novelty instead. Thus, for example, the lore of children derives its efficacy from its supposed newness. Often, children consider their rhymes as fresh creations of their own invention (Opie 1959, 12). Similarly, riddles have to be unfamiliar to the audience. A known riddle is a contradiction in terms and cannot fulfill its rhetorical function any more. In fact, riddles may disappear from circulation exactly because they are traditional and recognized as such by the members of the group (Goldstein 1963).

In both cases, the traditional character of folklore is an analytical construct. It is a scholarly and not a cultural fact. The antiquity of the material has been established after laborious research, and the tellers themselves are completely ignorant of it. Therefore, tradition should not be a criterion for the definition of folklore in its context.

There are methodological reasons as well for releasing folklore from the burden of tradition. The focus on those items alone that have stood the test of time cannot provide us with a systematic understanding of the principles of diachronic transmission, selection, and memorization of folklore. Since the criterion of tradition determines a priori the selection of items, any research into these problems lacks the "control data" to check its conclusions. After all, the study of transmission requires the inquiry into the principles both of forgetting and of remembering. Thus, even the study of tradition itself should demand that we broaden the scope of folklore and not limit it to time-proven tales and songs alone. The artistic forms that are part of the communicative processes of small groups are significant, without regard to the time they have been in circulation. The statement that "all folklore is traditional, but not all traditions are folklore" (cf. Bascom 1953, 285) might well be revised to "some traditions are folklore, but not all folklore is traditional."

Furthermore, if folklore as a discipline focuses on oral transmission and tradition only, it "contradicts its own *raison d'être*" (Hymes 1962b, 678). If the initial assumption of folklore research is based on the disappearance of its subject matter, there is no way to prevent the science from following the same road. If the attempt to save tradition from oblivion remains the only function of the folklorist, he returns to the role of the antiquarian from which he tried so hard to escape. In that case, it is in the interest of folklore scholarship that we change the definition of the subject to allow broader and more dynamic research in the field.

The same applies to the notion of oral transmission; an insistence on the "purity" of all folklore texts can be destructive in terms of folklore scholarship. Because of the advent of modern means of communication, folklorists who insist on this criterion actually saw off the branch they are sitting on. They inevitably concentrate on isolated forms and ignore the real social and literary interchange between cultures and artistic media and channels of communication. In reality, oral texts cross into the domain of written literature and the plastic and musical arts; conversely, the oral circulation of songs and tales has been affected by print. This has long been recognized, and yet it has been a source of constant frustration for folklorists who searched for materials uncontaminated by print or broadcast. The notion of folklore as a process may provide a way out of this dilemma. Accordingly, it is not the life history of the text that determines its folkloristic quality but its present mode of existence. On the one hand, a popular melody, a current joke, or a political anecdote that has been incorporated into the artistic process in small-group situations is folklore, no matter how long it has existed in that context. On the other hand, a song, a tale, or a riddle that is performed on television or appears in print ceases to be folklore because there is a change in its communicative context.

This definition may break away from some scholarly traditions, but at the same time, it may point to possible new directions. A major factor that prevented folklore studies from becoming a full-fledged discipline in the academic community has been the tendency toward thing-collecting projects. The tripod scheme of folklore research as collecting, classifying, and analyzing emphasizes this very point. This procedure developed as a nineteenth-century positivistic reaction to some of the more speculative ideas about folklore that prevailed at that time. Since then, however, the battle for empiricism has been won twice over. Folklore scholarship—which developed since the rejection of unilinear cultural evolutionism and the solar and psychoanalytical universal symbolism—has had its own built-in limitations and misconceptions. These resulted in part from the focus on facts. Because of the literary and philological starting point of folklore studies, the empirical fact was an object, a text of a tale, song, or proverb, or even an isolated word. This approach limited the research possibilities in folklore and narrowed the range of generalizations that could be induced from the available data. It might have been suitable for Krappe's notion of folklore as an historical science that purported to reconstruct the spiritual history of man, but it completely incapacitated the development of any other thesis about the nature of folklore in society. Consequently, when social sciences such as anthropology, sociology, and psychology came of age, they incorporated folklore into their studies only as a reflection and projection of other phenomena. Folklore was a mirror of culture but not a dynamic factor in it; a projection of basic personality, but not personality in action. Once viewed as a process, however, folklore does not have to be a marginal projection or reflection; it can be considered a sphere of interaction in its own right.[4]

Notes

1. Ambrose Merton [William J. Thoms], "Folklore," *Athenaeum*, no. 982 (August 22, 1846), 862–63. Reprinted in Alan Dundes, *The Study of Folklore* (Englewood Cliffs, NJ: Prentice-Hall, 1965), 4–6; and William J. Thoms, "'Folk-Lore,' from 'The Athenæum,' August 22, 1846," *Journal of Folklore Research* 33, no. 3 (1996): 187–89.

2. Ibid.

3. "Folklore is collective beliefs without doctrine, collective practices without theory."

4. A shorter version of this essay, titled "Folklore: The Definition Game Once Again," was read at the American Folklore Society Annual Meeting in Toronto, November 1967.

Bibliography

Abrahams, Roger D. 1963. "Folklore in Culture: Notes toward an Analytical Method." *Texas Studies in Literature and Language* 5:98–110.

Anderson, Walter. 1923. *Kaiser und Abt, die Geschichte eines Schwanks.* Folklore Fellows' Communications (FFC), no. 42. Helsinki: Suomalainen Tiedeakatemia.

Bascom, William R. 1949. "Folklore." In *The Funk and Wagnalls Standard Dictionary of Folklore, Mythology, and Legend*, edited by Maria Leach and Jerome Fried, 1:398. New York: Funk and Wagnalls.

———. 1953. "Folklore and Anthropology." *Journal of American Folklore* 66, no. 262:283–90.

———. 1955. "Verbal Art." *Journal of American Folklore* 68, no. 269:245–52.

———. 1965. "The Forms of Folklore: Prose Narratives." *Journal of American Folklore* 78, no. 307:3–20.

Bayard, Samuel P. 1953. "The Materials of Folklore." *Journal of American Folklore* 66, no. 262:1–17.

Bidney, David. 1953. *Theoretical Anthropology*. New York: Columbia University Press.

Boggs, Ralph Steele. 1943. "Folklore: Materials, Science, Art." *Folklore Americas* 3, no. 1:1–8.

Bohannan, Paul. 1961. "Artist and Critic in an African Society." In *The Artist in Tribal Society: Proceedings of a Symposium Held at the Royal Anthropological Institute*, edited by Marian W. Smith, 85–94. New York: Free Press of Glencoe.

Botkin, Benjamin A. 1944. *A Treasury of American Folklore*. New York: Crown.

Burne, Charlotte Sophia. 1914. *The Handbook of Folklore*. Rev. ed. London: Sidgwick and Jackson.

Clarke, Kenneth W., and Mary W. 1963. *Introducing Folklore*. New York: Holt, Rinehart and Winston.

Dégh, Linda. 1957. "Some Questions of the Social Function of Story-telling." *Acta Ethnographica* 6:91–147.

Dorson, Richard M. 1952. *Bloodstoppers and Bearwalkers: Folk Traditions of the Upper Peninsula*. Cambridge: Harvard University Press.

Dundes, Alan. 1964. "Text, Texture and Context." *Southern Folklore Quarterly* 28:251–65.

———. 1965. "What Is Folklore?" In *The Study of Folklore*, edited by Alan Dundes, 1–3. Englewood Cliffs, NJ: Prentice-Hall.

———. 1966. "The American Concept of Folklore." *Journal of the Folklore Institute* 3, no. 3:226–49.

Eriksson, Manne. 1955. "Problems of Ethnological and Folkloristic Terminology with Regard to Scandinavian Material and Languages." In *Papers of the International Congress of European and Western Ethnology Stockholm, 1951*, edited by Sigurd Erixon, 37–40. Stockholm: International Council for Philosophy and Humanistic Studies.

Espinosa, Aurelio. 1949. "Folklore." In *The Funk and Wagnalls Standard Dictionary of Folklore, Mythology, and Legend*, edited by Maria Leach and Jerome Fried, 1:399. New York: Funk and Wagnalls.

Foster, George M. 1949. "Folklore." In *The Funk and Wagnalls Standard Dictionary of Folklore, Mythology, and Legend*, edited by Maria Leach and Jerome Fried, 1:399. New York: Funk and Wagnalls.

Frazer, James G. 1918. *Folklore in the Old Testament: Studies in Comparative Religion Legend and Law*. 3 vols. London: Macmillan.

Goldstein, Kenneth S. 1963. "Riddling Traditions in Northeastern Scotland." *Journal of American Folklore* 76, no. 302:330–36.

———. 1967. "Experimental Folklore: Laboratory vs. Field." In *Folklore International: Essays in Traditional Literature, Belief, and Custom in Honor of Wayland Debs Hand*, edited by D. K. Wilgus and Carol Sommer, 71–82. Hatboro, PA: Folklore Associates.

Golembiewski, Robert T. 1962. *The Small Group: An Analysis of Research Concepts and Operations*. Chicago: Chicago University Press.

Gummere, Francis B. 1907. *The Popular Ballad*. Boston: Houghton, Mifflin. Reprint, New York: Dover Publications, 1959.

Hartland, Edwin Sidney. 1891. *The Science of Fairy Tales: An Inquiry into Fairy Mythology.* Contemporary Science Series. London: Walter Scott.

Herzog, George, and Charles G. Blooah. 1936. *Jabo Proverbs from Liberia: Maxims in the Life of a Native Tribe.* London: Oxford University Press.

Homans, George C. 1950. *The Human Group.* New York: Harcourt, Brace.

Herskovits, Melville J. 1949. "Folklore." In *The Funk and Wagnalls Standard Dictionary of Folklore, Mythology, and Legend*, edited by Maria Leach and Jerome Fried, 1:400. New York: Funk and Wagnalls.

Hultkranz, Ake. 1960. *General Ethnological Concepts.* International Dictionary of Regional European Ethnology and Folklore, vol. 1. Copenhagen: Rosenkilde and Bagger.

Hymes, Dell. 1962a. "The Ethnography of Speaking." In *Anthropology and Human Behavior*, edited by Thomas Gladwin and William C. Sturtevant, 15–53. Washington, DC: Anthropological Society of Washington.

———. 1962b. "Review of *Indian Tales of North America: An Anthology for the Adult Reader*, by Tristram P. Coffin." *American Anthropologist*, n.s., 64, no. 3, pt. 1:676–79.

Kangas-Maranda, Elli Kaija. 1963. "The Concept of Folklore." *Midwest Folklore* 13, no. 2:69–88.

Lang, Andrew. 1884. "Introduction." In *Grimm's Household Tales*, translated by Margaret Hunt, 1:xi-lxxv. London: George Bell and Sons.

Leach, MacEdward. 1949. "Folklore." In *The Funk and Wagnalls Standard Dictionary of Folklore, Mythology, and Legend*, edited by Maria Leach and Jerome Fried, 1:401. New York: Funk and Wagnalls.

Legros, Elisee. 1962. *Sur les noms et les tendances du folklore.* Collection d'études, no. 1. Liège: Éditions du Musée Wallon.

Lévy-Bruhl, Lucien. 1910. *Les fonctions mentales dans les sociétés inférieures.* Paris: F. Alcan.

Lutz, Gerhard. 1958. *Volkskunde: Ein Handbuch zur Geschichte ihrer Probleme.* Berlin: Erich Schmidt.

McLuhan, Marshall. 1964. *Understanding Media: The Extensions of Man.* Paperback ed. New York: New American Library.

Merton, Ambrose [William J. Thoms]. 1846. "Folk-Lore." *The Athenæum*, no. 982:862–63. Reprinted in Dundes (1965, 4–6); and Thoms (1996).

Opie, Peter, and Iona Opie. 1959. *The Lore and Language of Schoolchildren.* Oxford: Clarendon.

Pande, Trilochan. 1963. "The Concept of Folklore in India and Pakistan." *Schweizerisches Archiv fiir Volkskunde* 59:25–30.

Potter, Charles Francis. 1949. "Folklore." In *Funk and Wagnalls Standard Dictionary of Folklore, Mythology, and Legend*, edited by Maria Leach and Jerome Fried, 1:401. New York: Funk and Wagnalls.

Pound, Louise. 1921. *Poetic Origins and the Ballad.* New York: Macmillan.

Rattray, R. S. 1930. *Akan-Ashanti Folk-Tales.* Oxford: Clarendon.

Rysan, Joseph. 1952. "Is Our Civilization Able to Create a New Folklore?" *South Atlantic Bulletin* 17, no. 3:10.

Sokolov, Y. M. 1966. *Russian Folklore.* Translated by Catherine Ruth Smith. Introduction and bibliography by Felix J. Oinas. Hatboro, PA: Folklore Associates. Originally published in English by American Council of Learned Societies Devoted to Humanistic Studies, Russian Translation Project Series, 7. New York: Macmillan.

Sydow, C. W. von. 1948. "On the Spread of Tradition." In *Selected Papers on Folklore*, 11–43. Edited by Laurits Bødker. Copenhagen: Rosenkillde and Bagger. Reprint, New York: Arno Press, 1977.

Taylor, Archer. 1949. "Folklore." In *The Funk and Wagnalls Standard Dictionary of Folklore, Mythology, and Legend*, edited by Maria Leach and Jerome Fried, 1:402. New York: Funk and Wagnalls.

Thompson, Stith. 1951. "Folklore at Midcentury." *Midwest Folklore* 1, no. 1:5–12.

Thoms, William J. 1996. "'Folk-Lore' from 'The Athenæum,' August 22, 1846." *Journal of Folklore Research* 33, no. 3:187–89.

Tylor, Edward Burnett. 1958. *The Origins of Culture*. 2 vols. New York: Harper and Brothers. Originally published as chapters 1–10 of *Primitive Culture*. London: John Murray, 1871.

Utley, Francis Lee. 1958. "The Study of Folk Literature: Its Scope and Use." *Journal of American Folklore* 71, no. 280: 139–48.

———. 1961. "Folk Literature: An Operational Definition." *Journal of American Folklore* 74, no. 293:193–206. Reprinted in Dundes (1965, 7–24).

———. 1968. "A Definition of Folklore." In *Our Living Traditions: An Introduction to American Folklore*, edited by Tristram P. Coffin, 3–14. New York: Basic Books.

Varagnac, André. 1938. *Définition du folklore suivi de notes sur folklore et psychotechnique et sur l'agriculture temporaire, la prèhistoire et le folklore*. Paris: Société d'Édition.

4

ANALYTICAL CATEGORIES
AND ETHNIC GENRES

"Was ist eine Sage?" This question ("What is a legend?"), raised by Carl-Herman Tillhagen (1964) a few years ago, is equally applicable to other folklore genres. The search for the thematic and structural attributes that distinguish one form from another has continuously occupied folklorists who aspire to establish research in this field on a systematic basis. Thus, Alan Dundes states that "the problem . . . of defining folklore boils down to the task of defining exhaustively all the forms of folklore. Once this has been accomplished, it will be possible to give an enumerative definition of folklore. However, thus far in the illustrious history of the discipline, not so much as one genre has been completely defined" (1964b, 252).

The blame, however, does not rest so much with the folklorists as with the very incongruity between ethnic genres of oral literature and the analytical categories constructed for their classification. Whereas ethnic genres are cultural modes of communication, analytical categories are models for the organization of texts. Both constitute separate systems that should relate to each other as substantive matter to abstract models. Yet this relationship has not materialized. The basic problem inherent in any analytical scheme for folklore classification is that it must synchronize different folklore communication systems, each with its own internal logical consistency, each based on distinct sociohistorical experiences and cognitive categories. This is methodologically, if not logically, impossible. Yet, as folklorists, we did not heed this incongruity and, in our zeal for scientific methodology, we abandoned the cultural reality and strove to formulate theoretical analytical systems. We attempted to construct logical concepts that would have potential cross-cultural applications and to design tools that would serve as the basis for scholarly discourse, providing it with defined terms of reference and analysis. In the process, however, we transformed traditional genres from cultural categories of communication into scientific concepts. We approached them as if they were not dependent on cultural expression and perception but autonomous entities that consisted of exclusive inherent qualities of their own; as if they were not relative divisions in a totality of an oral tradition but absolute forms. In other words, we attempted to change folk-taxonomic systems that are cultural bound and vary according to the speakers' cognitive systems into culture-free, analytical, unified, and objective models of folk literature. The failure, now admitted, almost could have been anticipated.

I.

Scholarly attempts to establish folklore studies on scientific grounds have followed four distinct paths: thematic, holistic, archetypal, and functional, all of which were followed in the hope of discovering the formula for methodological definitions of genres at the end of each road. Each of these conducts of inquiry aimed at the construction of a valid, objective order of categories of folk literature. Yet, naturally, the tools, terms, and concepts that emerged were generated by definite theories and geared toward distinct sets of problems.

The Thematic Approach

Comparative folklore research concerns itself with the diffusion of themes in different traditions. Consequently, in this framework, genre is a thematic category. The touchstone for such a generic classification of texts is the answer to the question, "What is it about?" Legends are about saints, heroes, miracles, and other kinds of supernatural phenomena. *Märchen* are about "humble heroes [who] kill adversaries, succeed to kingdoms and marry princesses" (Thompson 1946, 8). Fables are about plants and animals, and proverbs encapsulate traditional wisdom. Underlying such an approach to folk literature is the premise that thematic similarity implies universal generic identity. The formal nature of an expression is inherent in its content. Tales about the same themes automatically constitute a single genre. This assumption of direct correlation between subject matter and folkloristic typology does have some significant methodological value. It provides clear clues for the classification of tradition and hence for the comparative examination of texts from different cultures. Yet, at the same time, this premise begets evolutionary and diffusionist notions about folklore genres that cannot be maintained by the examination of historical and cultural facts. Some examples illustrate this point. The *Märchen* is a European form that flourished in literary circles from the seventeenth through the nineteenth centuries. Simultaneously and during earlier and later periods, it enjoyed oral circulation among nonliterate rural and urban people of this and other continents. Thematically, this genre has its antecedents in oriental and Classical literatures; yet to refer to similar subjects in biblical and Greek traditions as examples of the genre *Märchen* is sheer anachronism. Hermann Gunkel's *Das Märchen in Alten Testament* (1921) is a milestone in biblical research. In this book, Gunkel emphasized the role of oral tradition in the formulation of the scriptures and proposed to conceive of many biblical tales not as history, as religion dictates, but as poetic narrations that share themes in common with European and Asian nations. Gunkel, like the Grimm brothers before him (Grimm 1891, vii), defined *Märchen* as poetic narrations, in contrast with legends, which are historical narrations. As far as this definition is concerned, many of his new interpretations of biblical stories as poetry no doubt are valid. But the use of the generic term *Märchen* implies a particular literary form that is absent from the Bible.

The thematic approach for generic definition is even more apparent in Herbert Jennings Rose's discussion of the "*Märchen* in Greece and Italy" (1959, 286–304). He simply used a list of folktale themes compiled by Joseph Jacobs in Burne's *Handbook of Folklore* (1914, 344–55; cf. Baring Gould 1866, 299–311) and similar subjects singled out from classical literature as examples of ancient Greek and Italian *Märchen*. However, among his examples are such stories as "Cupid and Psyche" and "Beauty and Beast," themes that, although indeed part of the European *Märchen* tradition, in Greece belonged to a completely different genre—the comic romance (Perry 1967, 236–82).

Thus, the a priori assumption of direct correlation between themes and genres has resulted in an anachronistic conception of literary kinds. In other cases, the same premise has suggested genealogical relationships between various forms. For example, historians of literature have outlined the direction of literary development from fable to proverb or vice versa (Taylor 1931, 27–32), from epic (Ker 1897, 123–32) and romance (Courthope 1895, 1, 445–68) to ballad. Among the ancestors of the later genre, ballad, are listed lyrical poetry (Pound 1921, 28, 45–46) and metrical religious legends (Mackey 1968). These relationships are based on the assumptions that no theme can be the subject of two genres simultaneously and that where such thematic similarity does exist, it reflects a direct historical relationship. Neither of these assumptions is necessarily true. The story of "The King and the Abbott" is a widely found prose narrative (Anderson 1923). Antti Aarne and Stith Thompson (1961, 320–21) classify it with romantic tales; in Jewish tradition, it is a joke (Schwarzbaum 1968, 115–16; Noy 1963, 94–97), and in English folklore, a ballad (Child 1882, 1:403–14, no. 45).

No generic relationship necessarily exists between these forms. Similarly, the theme of the ballad "The Maiden Freed from the Gallows" (Child 1884, 2:346–55, no. 95) appears in the West Indies in a *cante fable* (Parsons 1918, 152–54; Beckwith 1924). Although this form provides more background details, which are missing from the abrupt balladic description, it does not imply that one genre evolves out of the other, even though here there are closer formal affinities. Moreover, even within the tradition of a single culture, the same theme can appear both in prose and in poetry, as, for example, the motif of the "singing bone" that reveals the murderer (Aarne and Thompson 1961, 269, type 780).

Realization of the lack of correspondence between themes and genres led students of folklore to embrace a kind of Crocean aesthetics and to forego any systematic order of forms in oral tradition. Thompson considered "useless" the "effort devoted to the establishment of exact terms for the various kinds of folktale" (1946, 7) and even went as far as to make a virtue out of this vagueness, as "it frequently avoids the necessity of making decisions and often of entering into long debates as to the exact narrative *genre* to which a particular story may belong" (1949, 408). Ruth Benedict said flatly, "No folktale is generic" (1935, 1:xiii). This categorical statement reflects Benedict's field research among the Zuni, whose "tales," she found, "fall into no clearly distinguishable categories" (1:xxx). Consequently, she adapted Croce's aesthetics to the study of verbal art among nonliterate people and stated, "It is always the tale of one particular people, with one particular livelihood and social organization" (1:xiii).

No doubt, thematic classification of folk literature has had pragmatic value in the promotion of comparative studies; yet its basic principle of direct correlation between themes and genres does not stand the test of empirical examination, as we have just seen. The premise that thematic similarity implies generic identity may be valid in regard to the oral literature of a single culture within a definite period, but it is simply incongruent with the facts of folk literatures of different peoples or of the same society during different historical periods.

However, themes are not necessary standards of order. Any number or combination of attributes can serve as the basis for generic distinctions. Moreover, thematic classification itself involves subjective selection and discrimination, which inevitably biases the system. The choice of some themes as essential and the dismissal of others as irrelevant involves either personal, cultural, or theoretical subjective judgments that defy analytical objectivity. Furthermore, because thematic classification of folklore genres involves selective procedures, it can be only an incomplete representation of the literary forms themselves. For example, legends about saints and heroes are often classified as separate genres because they differ in regard to the nature of the protagonist. However, this approach ignores a whole range of narrative and content relationships, such as prosody, structure, and performance, which may or may not contribute to the differentiation between these two genres.

The Holistic Approach

According to the holistic conception of folklore genres, tales and songs, riddles and proverbs are not aggregates of episodes or accidental combinations of metaphors. Rather, they are formal and thematic entities that have an organic unity of their own. This unity is the intrinsic ontological reality of any folklore form. It is not dependent on any theoretical orientation or conditioned perception, and it does not change with any analytical shift in point of view. Genres, hence, are subject to structural description in the sense that it is theoretically possible to illustrate how the different elements in these forms relate to each other and constitute distinct unified fields of actions. Since the distinctive unity of each folklore genre is the basic premise of the holistic approach, its principal mode of inquiry is that of discovery rather than of systematization, which is characteristic of the comparative school. Students of folklore who pursue research in this direction purport to discover the existing structure of a verbal message of which the speaker or singer and his addressees are not necessarily aware. Although they may respond intuitively to any violation of the structural principles of such a message, they cannot pinpoint the exact source of their frustration. Only the person who has discovered the formal structure of the genre is able to do so.

Of course, it is possible to describe the particular structural properties of folklore genres as they exist on any linguistic level: phonetic, syntactic, and semantic. It is possible to analyze them in terms of sequences of episodes and actions or to construct abstract models of the relations inherent in the genres.[1] Essentially, the holistic approach affirms the ontology of folklore forms and changes the concept of genre from a nominalistic to a realistic entity. A genre is no longer just a label for a relatively similar corpus of themes but is a real form, which exists regardless of any interpretation or classification. The holistic conception of folklore genres provides, in other words, for the fulfillment of Carl Wilhelm von Sydow's demand to build up a "natural system" of traditional forms (1948, 127–45). Indeed, Vladimir Propp, one of the pioneers in the application of the holistic approach to folklore genres, emulated the classification methods in natural sciences and regarded his own description as a morphology of the folktales. In analogy with the term *morphology* in botany, he considered it "a description of the tale according to its component parts and the relationship of these components to each other and to the whole" (1968, 19).

Inadvertently, the application of the scientific principles of botany to folklore can exceed its heuristic value and lead to conclusions logically and empirically possible in the natural sciences but incompatible with the very nature of oral literature. For example, if structural similarity between forms is regarded as having the same consequences as in botany, the inevitable conclusion would be that there is a genealogical relation between two genres. Propp himself probably would not have objected to that conclusion. After all, one of the main purposes of his research was the formulation of a method that would replace Alexander Veselovskij's thematic discussions of the history of folklore genres with more objective and accurate methods. He himself conceived of the variant versions of a tale as relating to the basic structural model as "*species* to *genus*" (Propp 1968, 25). Other scholars, in partial criticism of Propp, extended these relations in terms of two distinct genres. Archer Taylor (1964) demonstrated that the biographical pattern of the mythic hero, as outlined by J. G. von Hahn, Otto Rank, Lord Raglan, and Joseph Campbell, actually corresponds to the wanderings of the *Märchen* protagonist. Thus, in structural terms, myth and folktale are identical, or at least related to each other genealogically. Claude Lévi-Strauss, who regards the relationship between myth and tales in modalic, not genealogical, terms, phrased it more succinctly: "Les contes sont les mythes en miniature" (1960, 136).[2] When it takes this direction, structural analysis no longer serves its original purpose of delineation of folklore forms. Instead, it implies a conception of genres based on approximation rather than differentiation. The genealogy of forms rather than their distinctive attributes may become the central question.

Structural analysis of folklore raised still another problem. The shift from a nominalistic to a realistic conception of folklore genres implied in morphological analysis involves the question of the universality of these forms. Are they only structures of local tradition, or are they inherent qualities of human creative imagination? Are they part of an ethnic system of folkloric communication, or are they intrinsic to any artistic expression, and do they transcend cultural boundaries? Propp himself limited his investigation to Russian folktales, but, since he analyzed only "ordinary tales" (AT 300–749) that are spread widely throughout Europe, it is possible to assume that this structure is common to the European tradition at large. However, Dundes's (1964a) successful application of the same method and basically the same structural pattern to the oral tradition of the North American Indians implies the possible universality of this folktale structure. The similarity in narrative forms between cultures as remote as the Slavic and the North American Indian could have taken place either through historical diffusion, population migration, or independent creation. Any of these possibilities points, at the very minimum, to the universal appeal of these forms.

The Archetypal Approach

For folklore genres to be universal categories, there must be a convergence of the structural patterns, thematic content, and social usage of each of these genres. If the legend, for example, is to be considered a cross-cultural category, stories about saintly people must follow the same distinct pattern in all traditions. If such universality does exist, it means that folklore genres are ontologically independent of culture and are not subject to variability of social differences. Hence it is necessary to account for their thematic similarity and formal stability by transcendental, transcultural, universal archetypes. André Jolles's (1930) thesis of *einfache Formen* provides, indeed, such a theory of folklore genres.[3] Accordingly, these genres are primary verbal formulations (*Sprächgebarden*) of basic mental concerns (*Geistesbeschäftigung*). He postulates that the human mind is preoccupied with the holy, the family, the essence of the universe, the soluble problem, the accumulated experience. It is occupied with the choice between moral principles, the verbal reproductions of facts, the suspension of immoral reality, and the inadequacies of reality. These are basic mental concerns, and, theoretically, they exist independent of any verbal expression. The *einfache Formen* constitute the elementary, primary linguistic formulations of these attitudes. Thus, the legend, the *Sage*, the myth, the riddle, the proverb, the *Kasus*, the memorabilia, the *Märchen*, and the joke are the respective verbal representations of the above mental attitudes. The folklore genres are not *about* these subjects, but they themselves, in their totality, are the verbal realization of them. Each form constitutes a holistic entity, a field of network interactions that in its entirety is a representation or a verbal formulation of these mental attitudes. These primary forms serve, in turn, as the genealogical model for the secondary forms, the artistic genres, which appear in written literature. In other words, in a Platonic fashion, the genres of oral tradition are an imitation of mental concerns, and the literary forms constitute a secondary development of them.

Kurt Ranke (1967) proposed to view the creative process of the primary forms from a different perspective and to conceive of them as verbal representations not of intellectual concerns but of human emotions. Thus, for Ranke, they are not imitations of mental attitudes but manifestations of a creative spiritual force, a psychological *enérgeia* that rises to the level of consciousness. For the mental concerns of Jolles, Ranke substitutes a postulation of basic needs of the human soul, which are the "ontological archetypes of various genres" (1967, 27). Thus, folktales, legend, myth, and jest are the respective functions of needs for a sublimated world of mythical perfection, psychological resignation in the face of human destruction, the religious meditative relations between the present world and the next world, and the psychological ability of man to laugh at human things and actions.

Both Jolles and Ranke shift the categorization of oral tradition from the verbal to the intellectual and psychological level, depending on their respective views. Both of them, however, derive their notions about the nature of the ontological archetypes that generate these genres from the very texts of *Märchen*, legends, jokes, and proverbs themselves. In that way, their suggestions involve circularity of reasoning. First, they reduce the existing genres to either intellectual or psychological levels, assuming the existence of distinct categories; then, they proceed to suggest direct causal generative relationships between the hypothetical system and the folklore forms. Theoretically, the postulation of an existing intellectual or psychological system on the basis of its overt evidence, the verbal expression, is indeed possible, but the argument that these hypothetical categories are the models or the source of the texts from which they were derived to begin with involves logical circularity. Jolles and Ranke lack a third dimension in which the two sets of categories they correlate exist independent of each other. It is necessary to demonstrate that the mental concerns that Jolles postulates and the basic psychological needs that Ranke surmises do indeed exist independent of folklore genres.

The Functional Approach

The functional approach to the categorization of oral literature actually has focused on the relationships between forms of verbal art and existing cultural, psychological, and social needs. Yet the anthropologists who pursued this mode of inquiry were not concerned with the ontology but the phenomenology of folklore kinds. Their distinction of genre is based not on any intrinsic qualities of oral literary forms, but on the perception and identification of their attributes by the people themselves. The functional approach is concerned not with what genres are, but with what the members of the society say they are. Thus the taxonomy of verbal art has become a categorization of cultural experiences, which are represented in the overt cultural attitudes toward themes and forms. In most cases, these attitudes are represented in the set of relations of belief and nonbelief, which has since become the basis for the categorization of formal expressions and for the analytical interpretation of their function in culture. As cultural experiences, such categorizations of oral traditions are unique. No two systems duplicate each other exactly. Hence the construction of a cross-cultural analytical model on the basis of a particular cultural system is a contradiction in terms and amounts to mistaking a deductive model for the real ethnic taxonomies. William Bascom (1965), who proposed a tripartite system of classification for prose narratives, was quite aware of this inherent discrepancy. Hence, he regarded the defined terms *myth*, *legend*, and *folktale* only as "analytical concepts which can be meaningfully applied cross culturally even when other systems of 'native categories' are locally recognized" (1965, 5). As far as agreement between folklorists is concerned, such an application of clearly defined terms of reference can indeed be meaningful. However, this type of model inevitably falls short of deciphering the ethnic system of folklore categorization whenever it compares an actual cultural experience with an analytical model, a unique phenomenon with a general scheme. When the actual native genres do not agree with the ideal construction, adjustments are necessary. Thus, for example, when some West African societies have a binary rather than tripartite classification of prose narratives, Bascom suggests that "myth and legend apparently *blend* into a single category, 'myth legend'" (10; my emphasis). In making this adjustment, Bascom oversteps the limits he himself set for the system he proposed, treating it as if it has a historical-cultural reality and is subject to change. In spite of his constant resort to native terminology, the inherent premise of such a model does not allow for the consideration of the native classification of prose narratives as a complete, complex symbolic system.

II.

The frustration felt by comparative folklorists who are struggling to synchronize diversified and incompatible taxonomic systems may result in statements of desperation, such as the declaration by John Greenway that "most preliterate people are quite indiscriminate about their classification," or that the "primitive mind . . . is [characterized by] unwillingness to abstract" (1964, 35). Such pronouncements reflect more the methodological problems of folklore studies than the native powers of perception, distinction, and abstraction. In effect, misconceptions like these arise because of the failure to recognize the

differences in function and purpose between analytical and ethnic taxonomies of genres. The former is concerned with the ontology of literary forms.
Its ultimate objective is the definition of what a folklore genre is, the description of its literary "mode of existence" (Wellek and Warren 1956, 129–45) in
either thematic, morphological, archetypal, or functional terms. Analytical
categories of genres have been developed in the context of scholarship and
serve its varied research purposes. Native taxonomy, on the other hand, has
no external objective. It is a qualitative, subjective system of order. The logical principles that underlie this categorization of oral tradition are those that
are meaningful to the members of the group and can guide them in their
personal relationships and ritualistic actions. They are reflections of the rules
for what can be said, in what situation, in what form, by whom, and to whom.
When a person in our society retracts his words by saying, "I was only joking," he actually redirects his words via another genre. Whatever he said vio-
lated the rules of regular conversation but is allowed in the joke genre. Hence
the incongruity between the analytical and the ethnic systems does not imply
that one is more logical, more abstract, or more sophisticated than the other.
Any evaluation of that sort is simply irrelevant to ethnic taxonomy. As the
grammar of each language is unique and has its own logical consistency, so
the native categorization of oral literature is particular and does not need to
conform to any analytical delineation of folklore genres.

The ethnic system of genres constitutes a grammar of folklore, a cultural
affirmation of the communication rules that govern the expression of complex messages within the cultural context. It is a self-contained system by
which society defines its experiences, creative imagination, and social commentary. It consists of distinct forms, each of which has its particular symbolic connotations and scope of applicable social contexts.

Each genre is characterized by a set of relations between its formal features, thematic domains, and potential social usages. For example, alliera-
tion is a formal phonetic feature of redundancy that often appears in proverbs,
riddles, rhymes, and songs (see Sackett 1964) but is rare in narratives. When
occasionally it does appear in tales and legends, it occupies a conspicuous
position. On the other hand, prose and poetic narratives can accommodate
redundancy on a thematic and structural level. The *Märchen* plot as a story
that develops from "villainy or a lack, through intermediary functions to
marriage" (Propp 1968, 92) can appear, with some modification, in epics, but
in most European traditions, it is rarely a subject for proverbs, as fables and
legends often are. The communication of folklore in society operates on the
basis of such a system of distinctions and correlations. The native speaker is

sensitive to the grammatical rules of his own folklore, though not necessarily conscious of them. These the analyst can discover.[4]

From another perspective, it is possible to regard the ethnic system of genres as a cultural metafolklore. Alan Dundes, who first introduced the term, regarded it mainly as oral literary criticism or, in his words, "a folkloristic commentary about folklore genres" (1966, 509). As examples he cited proverbs about proverbs, jokes about jokes, and the interpretations of expressions by the speakers themselves. However, the term *metafolklore* yields itself semantically to a further extension. Metafolklore can be understood to mean the conception a culture has of its own folkloric communication as it is represented in the distinction of forms, the attribution of names to them, and the sense of the social appropriateness of their application in various cultural situations.

The ethnic system of genres is a cognitive correlative of metafolklore, a culturally explicit statement of the conception of the speakers have of their expressive forms, formulated in both verbal and behavioral terms. The names of genres are indicative of the attributes people perceive in their verbal art forms. The interpretation of names of genres should not be literal. Such an explanation might point to the etymology of a word but not necessarily to its current meaning. *Märchen* is not simply a short tale, but a complex European narrative form that has a definite thematic domain and stock of characters. The Bini term *umaȓamwẹn* means literally "a council of animals" (Melzian 1937, 12, 206). Yet in my own work, I found only one informant who applied it strictly to animal tales and regarded its contents as purely fictional. Other people understood *umaȓamwẹn* to mean a tale without songs (Ben-Amos 1978).[5]

The behavior of folklore performance also has a defining capacity in terms of genres. The time in which a story is told, for example, places it in a particular position in the temporal sequence of the social, economic, and political activities of a group. The Marshallese fairy tale *inoñ* "must be told only at night" (Davenport 1953, 224). Nothing in the term itself provides any clue to this behavioral pattern, yet the rule is strictly observed, and thus it becomes a component part of the Marshallese concept *inoñ*. Similarly, Melville and Frances Herskovits tell us that the Dahomean, "in his classification of narrative . . . identifies two broad categories, the *hwenoho*, literally 'time-old-story,' which he translates variously as history, as traditional history, or as ancient lore; and *heho*, the tale. It is a distinction that the youngest story-teller recognizes. It has bearing on culturally defined attitudes toward traditional lore and improvisation, on the one hand, and on priori ties in narration, as governed by seniority rights, professional specialization and sexual differentiation of roles, on the other" (Herskovits 1958, 14–15).

In the final analysis, each society defines its genres by any number or combination of terms. Yet the distinctive attributes that speakers of folklore recognize in their communication can be analytically confined to three levels: prosodic, thematic, and behavioral. The conception of the prosodic nature of an expression is a function of the perception of the relationship between verbal sounds and time; the formulation of the thematic attributes is dependent on the relationships between actions, actors, or metaphors; and the recognition of the behavioral characteristics derives from the potential social composition of the communicative event. An ethnic definition of a genre may incorporate distinctions made on any or all three levels. A song can differ from a tale in the prosodic contour of the message, the subject matter, and the occasions the society provides for its performance.

Probably the most commonly recognized attribute of speech is its prosodic quality. Franz Boas pointed out that "the two fundamental forms, song and tale, are found among all the people of the world," and hence he suggested that "they must be considered the primary forms of literary activity" (1925, 329). For Boas, the notion of primacy, in this context, refers to the position these two forms have in the development of literary creativity. Rhythmic forms constitute the lowest common denominator of world literatures and hence must be basic to any verbal expression. However, it is possible to conceive of the primacy of prose and poetry not in evolutionary but in perceptual terms, in relationship to the immediacy or latency of recognition. The existence or absence of metric substructure in a message is the quality first recognized in any communicative event and hence serves as the primary and most inclusive attribute for the categorization of oral tradition. Consequently, prose and poetry constitute a binary set in which the metric substructure is the crucial attribute that differentiates between these two major divisions. It serves as the definitive feature that polarizes any verbal communication and does not provide any possible intermediary positions. A message is either rhythmic or not. However, within the category of poetry, speakers may be able to perceive several patterns of verbal metrical redundancy that they would recognize as qualitatively different genres. For example, B. W. Andrzejewski and I. M. Lewis note that "the Somali classify their poems into various distinct types, each of which has its own specific name. It seems that their classification is mainly based on two prosodic factors: the type of tune to which the poem is chanted or sung, and the rhythmic pattern of the words" (1964, 46).

The very existence or absence of a metric substructure in the verbal message can signify the conception the society has of a particular theme or can provide clues to the narrator's intent. The speaking of prose, for example, associates a message with everyday speech. In spite of the extraordinary events related in a legend, its narration in prose signifies reality and plausibility. However, when the approximation to daily discourse has only an artistic value and the narrator does not seek the credence of his audience, he is likely to preface his tales with cautionary clues such as opening or closing formulae, special vocabulary and phrases inserted into the body of the story, which enable the listeners to grasp the real nature of the message and to not confuse fiction with reality. Thus, among the Marshallese, "the fairy tale always begins with the word *kininwante*, which without specific meaning signifies 'this is a fairy tale; it may or may not have happened long ago; it is not to be taken seriously; it is not always supposed to be logical'" (Davenport 1953, 224). Similarly the Ashanti people open their fictional tales with the formula "we don't really mean to say so; we don't really mean to say so" (Rattary 1930, 8). In current American usage, the phrase "have you heard about . . ." often demarcates the joke from the regular prose speech into which it is inserted.

Similarly, the speaking of poetry signifies the conception the speakers have of their subject matter or of the occasion. The usage of metric prosody can have a wide range of significance, varying from religious sanctions to magical power to mere play, each depending on the circumstances of delivery. Common to all poetic expression, however, is the deliberate deviation from everyday speech, and with it the departure from the profane, the realistic, or the true. This, of course, does not imply that any information communicated in a poetic form is ontologically false or intended to be imaginary. Most ballads and epics do contain a nucleus of historical truth. Jan Vansina, for example, went so far as to construct a method for the induction of the possible historical truth in African poetic recitations (Vansina 1965, 148–51). The ballad "Tom Dooley," made popular in the United States by the Kingston Trio in 1958 (Blake, Rubeck, and Shaw 1986), was based on a local historical incident (Belden and Hudson 1952, 703–14; West 1970). However, the delivery of this story in a metric form indicates an intent to affect the audience emotionally and not merely to transmit factual information to them. As a matter of fact, in prose fiction, there is a contradiction between the signification of prose speech and the cultural attitude to the subject matter; hence such narration often requires special disclaimers of any truth value. In contrast, because poetic forms signify a departure from reality, any intent on the part of the speaker to establish his story as true needs validating statements, such as the opening formulae in broadside ballads that establish the story as a testimony.

In spite of the fact that prose and poetry are mutually exclusive forms of verbal art, the prosodic structure of a single expression, or even of a whole genre, does not have to be metrically uniform. It may include segments of varied prosodic nature. In fact, in Africa, where singing is often an integral part of the storytelling event, some peoples regard the existence or absence of songs interspersed in the prose text as a primary distinctive attribute for the categorization of narratives. Thus Clement Doke informs us that "Lamba folk-lore is classified by the natives in two ways, according to the mode of recitations. First and foremost comes the prose story, called *Icisimikisyo*. The other, which, for want of a better term, is translated as 'Choric Story,' is variously called by the natives . . . *Ulusimi*, *Icisimi*, *Akasimi* and *Akalawi*. This is a prose story interspersed with songs" (Doke 1927, xiv).

The Gbaya and the Bini peoples also divide their prose narratives in such a way. Among the Gbaya, "the main distinguishing feature between the *tô* and the *lizang* is the song [*gima*]" (Noss 1967, 38). The Bini, who distinguish between songs, *ihuan*, and tales, categorize the latter in terms of the metric composition of the entire narrative: Tales with songs are *okha*, and tales without them are *umaṟamwẹn*. This kind of classification is by no means universal in cultures where these two modes of storytelling exist. Other societies may ignore the form of recitation as a distinctive attribute between genres and focus on other characteristics of their narratives.

The basis for the categorization of verbal art into prose and poetry is the concrete, physiological reality of speech. It is an objective, observable, and verifiable process, the attributes of which are not dependent solely on the subjective perception of the speakers. Metric speech constitutes an ontological system objectively distinct from prose. Although various peoples may draw the demarcation line between the two categories at different points, and boundaries between the two divisions may fluctuate even within a single group, there will always be a substantive distinction between them. In contrast, the ethnic taxonomy of verbal art in terms of its secondary attributes, the thematic and behavioral features, is a phenomenological system. It is a function of the social experience of folkloric communication. Because the speaking of folklore involves a process of exchanging messages that have to be mutually comprehensive to be effective, it must adhere to consistent rules of communication. An ethnic genre must have defining features that signify its potential connotations and clearly distinguish it from other forms of verbal art. This fact of cultural consistency and coherence may permit future discussions of folkloric systems, similar to such studies in other social sciences.

For the time being, any suggestions in this direction must be hypothetical in nature. All the facts required for the deciphering of any given system of verbal art are simply not available, since folklorists previously have sought solutions to other types of problems.

Because the folkloric system in any given culture functions in society in both thematic and behavioral terms, it seems reasonable to assume, at this preliminary stage of our inquiry, that each genre consists of distinctive attributes on both these levels. Furthermore, because an ethnic genre is a part of a whole folkloric system, it must relate to other forms in the same network of communication. Hence these distinctive attributes are, at the same time, also in contrastive relations to the defining features of other genres. Of course, such relations are possible only between attributes that share a dimension of relevance. Thus, it is possible to contrast two types of protagonists, two kinds of social situations, and two different narrative endings.

On the basis of the foregoing assumptions, it is possible to consider an ethnic genre as a verbal art form consisting of a cluster of thematic and behavioral attributes and to formulate the relationships between the various elements of the folkloric system in the form of a paradigm.[6] For illustrative purposes, it seems best to quote, at some length, a discussion of folklore genres in which there is an attempt to define the nature of each form in a deductive method, in the light of established notions about the nature of *myth, legend,* and *tale,* and then to examine the same genres inductively, in the light of the previous argument. William Bascom's description of two prose genres of the Yoruba people of Nigeria will serve that purpose.

> The Yoruba recognize two classes of stories: the folktale *(alǫ)* . . . and the myths, traditions, or "histories" *(itan).* The folktales are ordinarily told for amusement about the fire on moonlight evenings during the season of harmattan. The myths on the other hand are regarded as historically true, and are quoted by old men to settle a difficult point in a serious discussion of ritual or political matters. Both types, however, are recited under the same conditions by the diviners as part of the Ifa verses.
>
> By and large the myths or histories are distinguished by having deities or legendary figures as characters rather than animals, and by explaining or justifying present-day ritual behavior. But as Boas pointed out, because of the ease of substitution of characters and explanatory elements, these distinctions do not make it possible to classify any plot as either myth or a tale in the generic sense. In some verses the deities Ifa and Eshu appear in the role of trickster instead of Tortoise; but there are many others . . . where the characters are animals, and some in which Tortoise himself is the trickster. And in the Ifa verses, the purpose

of both myths and tales is to justify the prediction that is made and to explain to the client why a particular sacrifice is necessary. It is obvious that these stories are not recited by the diviners simply for the amusement of their clients, and that their function is not limited to providing entertainment or aesthetic satisfaction.

They are not non-utilitarian, but have practical application of a type that can be compared to the use of elaborate costumes, carved masks, or highly decorated paraphernalia in religious ceremonies. It is generally accepted that graphic and plastic art in primitive cultures is seldom pure art; in this instance we have a case of applied art in the field of literature. The verbal incantations, the myths, and the songs used as a part of magical and religious ritual can also be cited as examples of "applied" literary art.

While the full significance of this point may not have been previously recognized, it is implicit in the attempts that have been made to distinguish myths from folktales on the basis of whether or not they are employed as a part of ritual. However since both myths and folktales, according to the Yoruba categories, are associated with the ritual of divination, a distinction between them on this basis is no more satisfactory than one based on the type of characters which appear in the plot. The real basis of the Yoruba categories seems to be whether the accounts are to be regarded as fact or fiction. (Bascom 1943, 129–30)

Thus Bascom carefully describes the characteristics of each of these genres, weighs the evidence one way or another before he categorizes them, and finally, in conclusion, he reduces the differences between *itan* and *alọ* to the contrast between belief and nonbelief. Yet this very evaluation of narratives as truth or fiction is actually not a primary but a secondary formulation of attitudes toward the thematic and behavioral attributes the speakers perceive in the narratives themselves. There is a whole gamut of distinctions between these two genres, and, although the reduction of their differences to just a single set of contrastive attributes may be analytically convenient, it is ethnographically simplistic.

Yet Bascom's description can serve as a basis for a preliminary formulation of the relations between *itan* and *alọ* as two communicative entities within the Yoruba folkloric system. Accordingly, *itan* is a verbal art form consistently related to ritual or politics, its narrators are either diviners or old men, it revolves around either deities or human heroes, and it is considered as either religious or historical truth. On the other hand, *alọ* is told for amusement, by any person in the society, its protagonists are often animals, and it is regarded by the Yoruba as fiction. The attributes of *itan* and *alọ* relate to each other within the framework of several dimensions. Thus, in terms of the social situations in which people narrate the two genres, *itan* relates to *alọ* as ritual or politics to amusement. The singularity of *itan* in Yoruba folklore is analogous to the distinctions diviners and older men have in this society. Thematically, it is possible to consider, for the time being, only the nature of the protagonist, and, in this context, the contrast between the two genres is equivalent to that between deities and heroes on the one hand and animals on the other. In their totality, the Yoruba consider *itan* as a true account of historical or religious events, whereas *alǫ* is a narration of fictional matters. On the basis of the features that coexist within a single genre and the contrastive attributes on each dimension, it is possible to formulate a paradigm of relations between *itan* and *alǫ* as the Yoruba themselves conceive of them. Thus in the Yoruba grammar of folklore:

> *itan* : *alǫ* : ritual/politics : amusement :: old men/diviners : any sex/any age :: deities/human heroes : animals :: religious or historical truth : fiction

These relationships are shown in another form in the accompanying table.

Of course, the more extensive the analytical study of the texts is, and the more detailed the observations of its performance and the inquiry into the attitudes are, the more closely these paradigmatic relations between the distinctive attributes of *alǫ* and *itan* will reflect the ethnic conception of these two genres. Such details should include the distinct thematic domains of each genre, their particular formal qualities, and connotative references. The paradigm should point to the entire range of social components that constitute the situations in which they are applicable and any other kinds of relations that can be induced from the formal expressions in the ethnic genre system.

Bascom's description of the Yoruba genres *alǫ* and *itan* and the frustrations he encountered in the definitions of the exact distinctions between them illustrate an additional relationship of attributes, that of equivalence. Some generic features are not distinctive, but under certain circumstances they are, borrowing a term from linguistics, in free variation with each other. That is to say, the substitution of one attribute for another does not produce any significant changes in the symbolic value of the verbal form and has equivalent effect. Attributes in free variation with each other are culturally determined. Thus, for example, it is no accident that the deity Eshu is substituted for Tortoise in these narratives, for in the Yoruba belief system Eshu is the trickster among the deities (Idowe 1963, 80–85), as Tortoise is among the animals; hence under certain circumstances they are found in free variation with each other without producing any qualitative changes in the genres themselves.

Similarly, the Ha diviner has a particular conception of Yoruba tradition that deviates from the generally accepted one. Although diviners do quote from and refer to *alǫ* as well as *itan* in their divinations, they conceive all narrative traditions as a single category, of which the appropriate usage is in the ritualistic situation. As far as they are concerned, all tradition has the same

Table 4.1. Yoruba Paradigm for *itan* and alọ

Dimension	itan	alọ
Situation	ritual/politics	amusement
Narrator's status	old men/diviners	any age/any sex
Protagonist	deities/human heroes	animals
Attitude	truth: religious or historical	fiction

symbolic value and hence the same name, and they "describe all Ifa narratives as *itan*" (Bascom 1969, 130), ignoring the generally accepted dichotomy between the two prose genres. Consistent with their conception of these narratives, and in spite of the fact that "the diviners are recognized as knowing more folktales than other individuals . . . they may not use this knowledge for secular purposes." Moreover, "in Ifa it is a professional tabu for diviners to tell folktales *(pa alọ)* for amusement, or even to join in singing the songs in the tales when they are being told by someone else" (Bascom 1969, 131). Thus, what appeared to be an irreconcilable feature of Yoruba genres from an analytical standpoint in an earlier description later turns out to be consistent with the rules of grammar of folklore as the Yoruba diviner conceives of them.

The set of contrastive attributes represents the structure of relations between the distinct genres in the system of folklore communication. They are contrastive only in their cultural context. There is no inherent opposition between amusement and ritual or politics, as there is no ontological reason for the association of ritual and politics or of religion and history as equivalent attributes. Similarly, the clusters of attributes within a single genre have logical consistency within the cultural context. Animals, for example, might be associated with totemism in other societies and would have closer affinity with ritual and social structure than with amusement and fiction, as is the case in Yoruba trickster tales. Yet for the Yoruba man who lives in a society in which divine kingship is the dominant religio-political order, these contrasts and associations are sound and valid. They are congruent with the social and religious systematization of his culture. In that sense, the analysis of ethnic genres has a diagnostic value as well. Since the cultural conception of the folkloric communicative system is part of the general cultural cognitive reality, it should be methodologically possible to infer from the categorization of folklore some general principles underlying the taxonomy of the cosmic natural and social universe.

The summation of thematic and behavioral attributes of a genre and its position in the folkloric system are best indicated by the terms people use for their expressive forms. The names of genres often reflect their symbolic value in the network of formal communication and their position in the cultural cognitive categories. Each name signifies the semantic component of the genre in all its manifestations, the basic common denominator that unifies all its attributes in the culture. Thus even expressions that are formally similar have different symbolic meanings in separate ethnic systems of genres. Proverbs, for example, often deviate from the regular syntactic structure of a language and thus relate to everyday speech in similar manner in different societies. Yet in each culture they have their particular symbolic connotations and communicative value. The Hausa people of Northern Nigeria regard a proverb, *karin magana*, in terms of its application in verbal context (Bargery 1934, 569), whereas the Jabo of Liberia regard it as "old matter," *da' di kpa* (Herzog and Blooah 1936, 1). The proverbs are "first principles" for the Marshallese (Davenport 1953, 231), and in biblical Hebrew, *mashal* (Johnson 1955) means an exemplary dictum as well as a fable.

Not all cultures have an explicit linguistic taxonomy of verbal art beyond the primary prosodic distinction between prose and poetry. This is so despite the fact that the people are likely to perceive the thematic and behavioral distinctive attributes of the various genres. In such cases, the name of the general category points to the primary attribute that unifies all these different forms in the cultural cognition. The Limba people of Sierra Leone, for example, have a single term for their prose expression—*mbɔrɔ*. According to Ruth Finnegan, who recorded their tales, "the Limba themselves do not make any further clear division. In most dialects the same term is used to cover a wide range of formulations, from 'folktales' in the accepted sense of the word to shorter forms such as riddles and proverbs, as well as what we would normally call historical accounts. None of these classes are strictly differentiated by the Limba" (1967, 28).

From Finnegan's further discussion, it is not quite clear whether the Limba really do not distinguish between the various prose forms or whether the term *mbɔrɔ* is simply a polysemic word with different meanings in different linguistic and social contexts. However, the Limba people seem to differentiate behaviorally, if not overtly verbally, between the various forms of *mbɔrɔ*. The speakers use the shorter forms, which Finnegan compares with proverbs or analogies, in the context of persuasion, argument, oratory, and joking. On the other hand, storytellers narrate the longer *mbɔrɔ* forms in the relaxed atmosphere before retirement in the evening (1967, 42–48). Thus the social behavior of the Limba does indicate that the term *mbɔrɔ*, which seems to be all-inclusive, has different meanings and refers to distinct forms on separate occasions.

In any case, although the concept of *mbɔrɔ* seems to parallel a somewhat extended notion of the English term *prose narrative*, its connotations are completely different. In their categorization, the Limba people are concerned neither with the prose nor with the narrative qualities of its forms. According to Finnegan,

> The concept of *mbɔrɔ* is an integrated one . . . [and has] two main strands. . . . These are first the connexion with age and tradition, and secondly, the idea of analogical expression. . . . In the first place the word *mbɔrɔ* seems to be connected with the root *bɔrɔ*, old. *Mabɔrɔma* are the "old times" or "ancient ways," *bebɔrɔrɔ* the "old people," usually referring to the dead ancestors, and *bɔrɔ* commonly occurs in various grammatical forms as the ordinary adjective meaning "old." . . . Moreover, whatever the linguistic facts about the derivation of the word *mbɔrɔ* the concept does seem to be closely associated in Limba eyes with the idea of age and tradition. . . . The Limba very often are very conscious of the wisdom and presence of "the old people." (1967, 46–47)

In an earlier discussion, Finnegan mentioned that "artistic expression and inspiration, whether of singers, storytellers, dancers or drummers, is thought to come from essentially the same source—the dead, 'the old people'" (1967, 25). "The second main connotation of *mbɔrɔ*, apparent in at least the majority of the many usages of the term, is that of a comment or reflection in analogical terms. This is naturally specially clear when is used to mean metaphor, parable and analogy; but even when *mbɔrɔ* means the more straight-forward stories, it seems to suggest this aspect" (47).

The inquiry into the names for genres must extend beyond the limits of etymological interpretation. Historically and geographically, the same names may mean different things in the same language in separate periods and in distinct regional dialects. Conversely, two different words may acquire the same meanings in different periods. Moreover, with usage, the names may develop a complex semantic structure, for which etymology alone would not account. Hence the study of the ethnic system of genres must combine the cognitive, expressive, and behavioral levels of genres in each culture.

Although the significance of ethnic classifications of folklore has long been recognized, in most cases, its actual study was frustrated by the discrepancy between the analytical and the ethnic systems. The preceding discussion is merely an exploratory outline that attempts to point to areas of promise rather than to present conclusive theory and method. However, if folklore communication, allusive and complex as it is, is based on culturally defined rules, then discovery of them is essential. The system of genres is the primary ethnic formulation of such a grammar of folklore.[7]

Notes

1. A brief discussion of the syntagmatic, sequential, and paradigmatic types of structural analysis and their application to folklore is in Dundes (1968, xi–xvii). That article includes a short, valuable bibliography about the various approaches to structural analysis in folklore and related texts. Other relevant essays are Barthes et al. (1966); Donato (1967); Hymes (1968); and Retel-Laurentin (1968).

2. "Folktales are myths in miniature."

3. Discussions of his theory are in Bausinger (1968, 51–64); (Berendsohn (1930–33); Mohr (1958); and Petsch (1932).

4. The idea that the social usage of folklore in culture follows some principles and regulations is by no means new and was expressed, implicitly and explicitly, in Arewa and Dundes (1964); Bogatyrëv and Jakobson (1929); and Hymes (1962, 1964).

5. The examples from Benin interspersed in the present essay are based on my fieldwork in the Benin region of midwestern Nigeria in 1966.

6. The notions of distinctive features and contrastive attributes as used here constitute extensions and modifications of similar concepts developed by Roman Jakobson and his collaborators in regard to language and by Claude Levi-Strauss in regard to social structure and myth (Jakobson, Fant, and Halle 1952; Jakobson and Halle 1956; Lévi-Strauss 1963, 1966).

7. In writing this essay, I profited from discussions with Kenneth Goldstein and Joel Sherzer.

Bibliography

Aarne, Antti, and Stith Thompson. 1961. *The Types of the Folktale*. 2nd rev. ed. Folklore Fellows Communications, no. 184. Helsinki: Suomalainen Tiedeakatemia.

Andrzejewski, B. W., and I. M. Lewis. 1964. *Somali Poetry: An Introduction*. Oxford Library of African Literature. Oxford: Clarendon.

Arewa, E. Ojo, and Alan Dundes. 1964. "Proverbs and the Ethnography of Speaking Folklore." In "The Ethnography of Communication," edited by John J. Gumperz and Dell Hymes. Special issue, *American Anthropologist* 66, no. 6, pt. 2:70–85.

Anderson, Walter. 1923. *Kaiser und Abt: Die Geschichte eines Schwanks*. Folklore Fellows Communications, no. 42. Helsinki: Suomalainen Tiedeakatemia.

Bargery, G. P. 1934. *A Hausa-English Dictionary and English-Hausa Vocabulary*. London: Oxford University Press.

Baring-Gould, S. 1866. "Household Tales." In *Notes on the Folk Lore of Northern Counties of England and the Borders*, edited by William Henderson, 299–311. London: Longmans, Green.

Barthes, Roland, ed. 1966. "Recherches sémiologiques: L'analyse structurale du récit." *Communications*, no. 8:1–172.

Bascom, William R. 1943. "The Relationship of Yoruba Folklore to Divining." *Journal of American Folklore* 56, no. 220:127–31.

———. 1965. "The Forms of Folklore: Prose Narratives." *Journal of American Folklore* 78, no. 307:3–20.

———. 1969. *Ifa Divination: Communication between Gods and Men in West Africa*. Bloomington: Indiana University Press.

Bausinger, Hermann. 1968. *Formen der "Volkspoesie."* Grundllagen der Germanistik. Berlin: Erich Schmidt.

Beckwith, Martha Warren. 1924. "The English Ballad in Jamaica: A Note on the Origin of the Ballad Form." *PMLA* 39:475–76.

Belden, Henry M., and Arthur Palmer Hudson, eds. 1952. *The Frank C. Brown Collection of North Carolina Folklore.* 2 vols. Durham, NC: Duke University Press.

Ben-Amos, Dan. 1978. "The Modern Local Historian in Africa." In *Folklore in the Modern World,* edited by Richard M. Dorson, 327–43. World Anthropology. The Hague: Mouton.

Benedict, Ruth. 1935. *Zuni Mythology.* Columbia University Contribution to Anthropology, no. 21. 2 vols. New York: Columbia University Press.

Berendsohn, Walter A. 1930–33. "Einfache Formen." In *Handworterbuch des deutschen Märchen,* edited by Johannes Bolte and Lutz Mackensen, 1484–98. Berlin: Evangelische Verlagsanstalt.

Blake, Benjamin, Jack Rubeck, and Allan Shaw. 1986. *The Kingston Trio on Record.* Naperville, IL: Kingston Korner.

Boas, Franz. 1925. "Stylistic Aspects of Primitive Literature." *Journal of American Folklore* 38, no. 149:329–39. Reprinted in Boas (1940, 491–502).

———. 1940. *Race, Language and Culture.* New York: Macmillan Co.

Bogatyrëv, Peter, and Roman Jakobson. 1929. "Die Folklore als eine besondere Form des Schaffens." In *Donum natalicum Schrijnen, verzameling van opstellen opgedragen aan . . . Jos. Schrijnen bij gelegenheid van zijn zestigsten verjaardag, 3 Mei 1929.* Utrecht: Dekkera and Van der Vegt, 900–13. Revised version, *Roman Jakobson: Selected Writings.* The Hague: Mouton, 1966; see vol. 4, pp. 1–15. Published in English as "Folklore as a Special Form of Creativity," in *The Prague School: Selected Writings, 1919–1946,* edited by Peter Steiner, 32–46. Austin: University of Texas Press, 1982.

Child, Francis James. 1882–98. *The English and Scottish Popular Ballads.* 5 vols. Boston: Houghton, Mifflin. Reprint, New York: Dover, 1965.

Courthope, William John. 1895. *A History of English Poetry.* New York: Macmillan.

Davenport, William H. 1953. "Marshallese Folklore Types." *Journal of American Folklore* 66, no. 261:219–37.

Doke, Clement. 1927. *Lamba Folk-Lore.* American Folklore Society Memoir Series, no. 20. New York: American Folklore Society.

Donato, Eugenio. 1967. "Of Structuralism and Literature." *Modern Language Notes* 82, no. 5:549–74.

Dundes, Alan. 1964a. *The Morphology of North American Indian Folktales.* Folklore Fellows Communications, no. 195, vol. 81. Helsinki: Suomalainen Tiedeakatemia.

———. 1964b. "Texture, Text, and Context." *Southern Folklore Quarterly* 28:251–65.

———. 1966. "Metafolklore and Oral Literary Criticism." *The Monist* 50, no. 4:505–16.

———. 1968. "Introduction to the Second Edition." In Vladímir Propp, *Morphology of the Folktale,* xi–xvii. Austin: University of Texas Press.

Finnegan, Ruth. 1967. *Limba Stories and Story-Telling.* Oxford Library of African Literature. Oxford: Clarendon.

Greenway, John. 1964. *Literature among the Primitives.* Hatboro, PA: Folklore Associates.

Grimm, Jacob and Wilhelm. 1891. *Deutsche Sagen.* 3rd ed. Edited by Herman Grimm. Berlin: Nicolaische Verlags-Buchhandlung. Originally published in Berlin: In der Nicolaischen Buchhandlung, 1816–18.

Gunkel, Hermann. 1921. *Das Märchen in Alten Testament.* Religionsgeschichtliche Volksbücher, 2nd series, Die Religion des Alten Testament, nos. 23–26. Tübingen: Mohr.

Herskovits, Melville J., and Frances S. 1958. *Dahomean Narrative: A Cross-Cultural Analysis.* Evanston, IL: Northwestern University Press.

Hymes, Dell. 1962. "The Ethnography of Speaking." In *Anthropology and Human Behavior,* edited by Thomas Gladwin and William C. Sturtevant, 15–53. Washington, DC: Anthropological Society of Washington.

———. 1964. "Introduction: Toward Ethnographies of Communication." In "The Ethnography of Communication," edited by John J. Gumperz and Dell Hymes. Special issue, *American Anthropologist* 66, no. 6, pt. 2:1–34.

———. 1968. "The 'Wife' Who 'Goes Out' Like a Man: Reinterpretation of a Clackamas Chinook Myth." *Social Science Information* 7:173–99.

Idowu, E. Bọlaji. 1963. *Olódùmarè: God in Yoruba Belief.* New York: Frederick A. Praeger.

Jacobs, Joseph. 1914. "Some Types of Indo-European Folktales." In *The Handbook of Folklore,* edited by Charlotte Sophia Burne, 344–55. Rev. ed. London: Sidgwick.

Jakobson, Roman, Gunnar M. Fant, and Morris Halle, 1952. *Preliminaries to Speech Analysis: The Distinctive Features and Their Correlates.* Cambridge, MA: MIT Press.

———. 1956. *Fundamentals of Language.* The Hague: Mouton.

Johnson, A. R. 1955. "משל" *Vetus Testamentum.* Supplement, 3:162–69.

Jolles, André. 1930. *Einfache Formen: Legende, Sage, Mythe, Rätsel, Spruch, Kasus, Memorabile, Märchen, Witz.* Halle (Saale), Germany: M. Niemeyer. Published in English as *Simple Forms.* Translated by Peter J. Schwartz. London: Verso, 2017.

Ker, William Paton. 1897. *Epic and Romance: Essays on Medieval Literature.* New York: Macmillan.

Lévi-Strauss, Claude. 1960. "L'analyse morphologique des contes populaires russes." *International Journal of Slavic Linguistics and Poetics* 3:122–49.

———. 1963. *Structural Anthropology.* Translated by Claire Jacobson and Brooke Grundfest Schoepf. New York: Basic Books.

———. 1966. *The Savage Mind.* Chicago: University of Chicago Press.

Mackey, Julie R. 1968. "Medieval Metrical Saints' Lives and the Origin of the Ballad." Doctoral diss., University of Pennsylvania.

Melzian, Hans. 1937. *A Concise Dictionary of the Bini Language of Southern Nigeria.* London: Kegan Paul, Trench, Triibner and Co.

Mohr, Wolfgang. 1958. "Einfache Formen." In *Reallexikon der deutschen Literaturgeschichte,* edited by Paul Merker and Wolfgang Stammler, 1:321–28. 2nd edition revised by Werner Kohlschmidt and Wolfgang Mohr. Berlin: Walter de Gruyter.

Noss, Philip. 1967. "Gbaya Traditional Literature." *Abbia* 17–18:35–67.

Noy, Dov, ed. 1963. *Folktales of Israel.* With the assistance of Dan Ben-Amos. Folktales of the World. Chicago: Chicago University Press.

Parsons, Elsie Clews. 1918. *Folk-Tales of Andros Island, Bahamas.* American Folklore Society Memoir Series, no. 13. New York: American Folklore Society.

Perry, Ben Edwin. 1967. *The Ancient Romances: A Literary-Historical Account of Their Origins.* Berkeley: University of California Press.

Petsch, Robert. 1932. "Die Lehre von den 'Einfache Formen'." *Deutsche Vierteljahrsschrift fiir Literaturwissenschaft und Geistesgeschichte* 10:335–69.

Pound, Louise. 1921. *Poetic Origin and the Ballad.* New York: Macmillan.

Propp, Vladímir. 1968. *Morphology of the Folktale.* 2nd ed. Translated by Laurence Scott. Revised by Louis A. Wagner. Introductions by Svatava Pirkova-Jakobson and Alan Dundes. Austin: University of Texas Press. Originally published in 1928; first English edition in 1958.

Ranke, Kurt. 1967. "Einfache Formen." Translated by William Templer and Eberhard Alsen. *Journal of the Folklore Institute* 4:17–31. First published in German in *Internationaler Kongress der Volkserzahlungsforscher in Kiel und KopenhagenInternationaler Kongress der Volkserzahlungsforscher in Kiel und Kopenhagen (1959)—Vortrage und Referate*, edited by Kurt Ranke, 1–11. Berlin: De Gruyter.

Rattray, R. S. 1930. *Akan-Ashanti Folk-Tales*. Oxford: Clarendon.

Retel-Laurentin, Anne. 1968. "Structure et symbolisme: Essai methodologique pour l'etude des contes africains." *Cahiers d'etudes africaines* 8, no. 30:206–44.

Rose, Herbert Jennings. 1959. *A Handbook of Greek Mythology Including Its Extension to Rome*. New York: Dutton. Originally published in London: Methuen, 1928.

Sackett, S. J. 1964. "Poetry and Folklore: Some Points of Affinity." *Journal of American Folklore* 77, no. 304:143–53.

Schwarzbaum, Haim. 1968. *Studies in Jewish and World Folklore*. Berlin: Walter de Gruyter.

Sydow, C. W. von. 1948. *Selected Papers on Folklore*, edited by Laurits Bødker, 11–43. Copenhagen: Rosenkillde and Bagger. Reprint, New York: Arno Press, 1977.

Taylor, Archer. 1931. *The Proverb*. Cambridge, MA: Harvard University Press.

———. 1964. "The Biographical Pattern in Traditional Narrative." *Journal of the Folklore Institute* 1:114–29.

Thompson, Stith. 1946. *The Folktale*. New York: Holt, Rinehart and Winston.

———. 1949. "Folktale." In *Funk and Wagnalls Standard Dictionary of Folklore, Mythology and Legend*, edited by Maria Leach and Jerome Fried, 1:408. New York: Funk and Wagnalls.

Tillhagen, Carl-Herman. 1964. "Was ist eine Sage? Eine Definition und ein Vorschlag fiir ein europiiisches Sagensystem." *Acta Ethnographica* 13:9–17.

Vansina, Jan. 1965. *Oral Tradition: A Study in Historical Methodology*. Translated by M. Wright. Chicago: Aldine.

Wellek, René, and Austin Warren. 1956. *Theory of Literature*. 2nd rev. ed. New York: Harcourt, Brace and Co.

West, John F. 1970. *The Ballad of Tom Dula*. Durham, NC: Moore.

5

THE SEVEN STRANDS OF *TRADITION*

Varieties in Its Meaning in American Folklore Studies

Introduction

In folklore studies in America, *tradition* has been a term to think with, not to think about. Few define it, but many define with it folklore itself, employing nominal forms, adjectives, and adverbs. *Popular tradition, folk tradition, oral tradition*, even simply *traditions* in the plural, have been the descriptive terms for folklore; its genres are *traditional* and they are transmitted *traditionally*.[1] Tradition, particularly oral, has been the sine qua non of folklore, with no apparent need to belabor its own meaning (Utley 1961; Honko 1983b, 223).[2] In a survey conducted by the American Folklore Society's Committee on Research in Folklore in 1945 and 1946, "one thing was clear even when not explicitly stated: that even in the most inclusive sense (equating folklore with folklife) *folklore* carried a traditional or vestigial quality" (Gayton 1947, 351). For Stith Thompson, "tradition . . . [is] the touchstone for everything that is to be included in the term folklore" (1951a, 11), and similarly, Jan Brunvand states unequivocally that "the key to studies of American folk artifacts remains the same as for all folklore—it is *tradition*" (1968, 274; 1978, 308), the meaning of which he takes for granted.

For that matter, *tradition* does not defy definition, but simply does not need one. Its meaning appears lucid beyond clarification, perspicuous beyond explanation. The connotations of its Latin root *tradere*, to give, to deliver, to hand down, still resonate in the abstract noun *tradition*, making superfluous any further explication. Often emotive (Royce 1982, 28, 147),[3] yet unambiguous, *tradition* has persisted with but vague definitions not only in folklore but in humanistic and social scientific discourse in general. When Edward Shils explores the phenomenon of tradition, he finds numerous books about particular cultural, religious, artistic, even scholarly traditions, but "no book about tradition which tries to see the common ground and elements of tradition and which analyzes what difference tradition makes in human life" (1981, vii). Standard major reference works have shunned the subject. *Encyclopedia Britannica, Encyclopedia Americana, The International Encyclopedia of the Social Sciences, The Encyclopedia of Philosophy*, and the *Dictionary of the History of Ideas* neither enter nor index *tradition* as a distinct concept. Even folklore's own *Funk and Wagnalls Standard Dictionary of Folklore, Mythology and Legend* does not devote a separate entry to *tradition*. Only two relevant reference works demonstrate awareness of tradition as a distinct scholarly concept: the *International Dictionary of Regional European Ethnology and Folklore, Vol. I: General Ethnological Concepts*, and the *Encyclopaedia of Religion and Ethics*; the latter examines tradition only in its Christian context.

Absence, however, is not an omission. Definitions flourish when the semantics are vague, and the neglect from which the term *tradition* has suffered reflects, paradoxically, a healthy position in scholarly and literary discourse. In folklore studies, tradition has served as a motive for and a subject of research. It has been a fundamental theoretical concept indispensable in the analysis of texts, cultures, and societies. The impulse to salvage the diversified forms of tradition has motivated folklore research from its inception. Whether the sentiment be nationalistic, romantic, literary, or historical, the imprint of antiquity on customs, songs, and tales has been a sufficient reason for their scrutiny by folklorists. Often, these vestiges have been major analytical concerns: the recovery of past meanings, uses, and references has been a primary research goal. Consequently, any explanation of their survival has placed tradition at the center of many a theory in folklore. Furthermore, folklore, unlike sociology (Eisenstadt 1969, 1973a, 1973b), has never contemplated replacing tradition with modernity. The passing away of tradition from society, to paraphrase Daniel Lerner's (1958) title, is inconceivable in folklore terms, and therefore the persistence of tradition in modern life has never been an enigma.

Yet, as deep rooted as tradition is in our discipline, its clarity has been only apparent. Multiple, sometimes conflicting, meanings infest the term, and not only in folklore. Commenting on the critical writings of T. S. Eliot, Stanley Edgar Hyman points out that the word *tradition* is the key term in Eliot's critical writing and that what he means by it is "shifting and complex." Sometimes Eliot's *traditional* means no more than *good*, while at other times it is "simply a metaphorical way of telling a writer not to be 'too new.' Actually Eliot's 'tradition' is a utilitarian concept, and he constantly emphasizes the *using* of the tradition" (Hyman 1955, 54–55).

In folklore, *tradition* has been even far more shifting and complex. Charles Seeger (1950) has already pointed out the extent of its intricacy in modern scholarship. He observes that in American folklore writings, it is possible to distinguish three separate meanings in the use of *tradition*. It is "1) an inherited *accumulation* of material; 2) the *process* of inheritance, cultivation, and transmission thereof; 3) the *technical* means employed" (emphasis in the original). For Seeger, this multiplicity of meaning is not "an unusual semantic complication and does not confuse us unduly as long as we remain in the field of folk music" (826). But in the discussions held at the 22nd Congress of Nordic Ethnology and Folkloristics in Liperi, Finland, in 1982, the participants sought to establish the adequate analytical uses of the term *tradition*, bringing rigor and setting standards for folklore scholarly discourse. Descriptively, they have found that *tradition* has been used to mean, as Bengt Holbek (1983) summarizes so well, the process of handing down, the material that has been handed down, and the quality—positive or negative, depending on the speaker's perspectives—that people attribute to the subjects that connote either the process or the material. Prescriptively, however, these informal, self-reflective discussions lacked the desired precision. If "the whole point of discussing the concept of tradition is to make clear how it can be used" (Holbek 1983, 240), the conference participants appear to have been enlightened by the exchange of ideas, but frustrated by the lack of conclusions. A synthesis that would take into consideration emic views and analytical demands, stability and change, learned discourse and popular use, past and past projected into the future, simply could not be achieved in the use of a single term that already has a history of its own.

Rare as they are, there are indications that *tradition* has frustrated folklorists ever since their earliest efforts to define the term for scholarly use. In 1885, Edwin Sidney Hartland, a member of the "Great Team" (Dorson 1951; 1968a, 239–48) of British folklorists, demonstrated in his use of the term its potential for inherent contradictions. He argued that "Tradition is always being created anew, and that traditions of modern origin wherever found are as much within our province as ancient ones" (Hartland 1885, 120). The phrase "new tradition" may appear as a contradiction in terms, but in fact, it is an acceptable linguistic paradox that, astonishingly, always occurs in folklore scholarship with an aura of a daring theoretical innovation. Ninety years after Hartland's suggestion, and with direct reference to it, Richard M. Dorson proposed that in light of developments in the modern world, "'tradition' . . . needs reassessment, for traditions are continually being updated" (1978, 23).

When Hartland made his suggestion, in the formative stage of folklore studies, he was still groping for an adequate definition not only of *tradition*, but also of folklore itself. In 1891, he stated that "By tradition [he meant] the entire circle of thought and practice, custom as well as belief, ceremonies, tales, music, songs, dances, and other amusements, the philosophy and the superstitions and the institutions, delivered by word of mouth and by example from generation to generation through unremembered ages: in a word, the sum total of the psychological phenomena of uncivilized man. Every people has its own body of Tradition, its own Folk-Lore, which comprises a slowly diminishing part, or the whole, of its mental furniture, according as the art of writing is, or is not, known" (34).

Under the influence of the nineteenth-century ideas of progress (Bury 1932; Pollard 1968; Doren 1967; Wager 1972) and cultural evolution (Burrow 1966; Cocchiara 1981, 375–446; Dorson 1968, 187–201), Hartland transforms the past that *tradition* connotes from a temporal to a social dimension and predicates it on social and cultural backwardness. *Tradition* becomes the attribute not just of time but, more pronouncedly, of societies of earlier cultural stages. Consequently, *tradition* and *civilization* become an oppositional pair along the axis of literacy. *Tradition* has been the descriptive term for the culture of nonliterate societies, and civilization has become the designation for literate societies. Such a linkage of time past with social, cultural, and economic underdevelopment has prevailed in the conception of tradition throughout the years in folklore as well as in other disciplines.[4]

Toward the turn of the century, Hartland further refines his notion of tradition and examines it in the context of the emerging respective sciences of folklore and anthropology. For him, "Tradition as an object of science means the whole body of the lore of the uneducated" (Hartland 1899/1904, 10–11; Dorson 1968b, 1:233). These "uneducated" are to be found primarily among the "savages," such as "the Australian blackfellows and the Red Indians of North America" (Hartland 1899/1904, 10–11; Dorson 1968b, 1,233). For comparative purposes, Hartland is ready to turn "from savage nations to the peasantry of civilized Europe" (Hartland 1899/1904, 10–11; Dorson 1968b, 1:233), where he finds "the very same conditions of thought . . . wherever they are untouched by modern education and the industrial and commercial revolution of the last hundred years" (Hartland 1899/1904, 10–11; Dorson 1968b, 1:234). He interprets this phenomenon in terms of the premises of cultural evolution: "The human mind, alike in Europe and in America, in Africa and in the South Seas, works in the same way, according to the same laws. And the aim of the science of Tradition is to discover those laws, by the examination of their products, the customs and beliefs, the stories and superstitions handed down from generation to generation" (Hartland 1899/1904, 10–11; Dorson 1968b, 1:234). In Hartland's case, folklore is distinct from, yet part of, anthropology:

> The portion of Anthropology with which folklore deals is the mental and spiritual side of humanity. It is now well established that the most civilized races have all fought their way slowly upwards from a condition of savagery. Now, savages can neither read nor write; yet they manage to collect and store up a considerable amount of knowledge of a certain kind, and to hand on from one generation to another a definite social organization and certain invariable rules of procedure in all events of life. The knowledge, organization, and rules thus gathered and formulated are preserved in the memory, and communicated by word of mouth and by actions of various kinds. To this mode of preservation and communication, as well as to the things thus preserved and communicated, the name of Tradition is given; and Folklore is the science of Tradition. (Hartland 1899/1904, 6–7; Dorson 1968b, 1:231)

Hartland's use of *tradition* exposes the differences between folklore and nineteenth-century social sciences, as well as between the British and the continental folklore traditions. To a large extent, sociology, anthropology, and political sciences have retained the nineteenth-century meaning of *tradition* that Hartland reflects in his writings. Traditional are those societies that operate along the principles of tradition as Hartland spells them out. In that sense, tradition is a form of social and cultural order that exists alongside other forms of order (Acton 1952–53). The relationship between these organizations of society, and particularly between tradition and modernity, motivated research in those disciplines. Initially, social scientists positioned tradition and modernity as contrasts, but later, acknowledging reality, they shifted to a conception of a gradual continuum in which the two are conceived as mutually complementary social and cultural phenomena (see Cantlie 1979; Coleman 1968; Eisenstadt 1973a; Rudolph 1967; Rudolph, S. H., 1979; and Singer 1972).

Folklorists, on the other hand, had come to this realization much earlier. In fact, the initial premise in folklore, to paraphrase Stanley Diamond, does not assume tradition as dead; rather, the death of tradition is a dilemma (1980, 11). Folklorists study tradition, record narratives and songs, classify and analyze them, and in addition, endeavor to revive and maintain the traditions of their own peoples. After all, this was the romantic goal of Herder, who wished to restore greatness to the Germanic peoples by bringing his nation closer to its roots in nature so that it would experience a rising swing in its cyclical history (Barnard 1965; Ergang 1966). Consequently, continental folklorists differ with Hartland in the emphasis on their use of *tradition*. For them, the term refers primarily to the lore of their own peasantry. Such a difference underscores the need to examine not only the meaning of *tradition*, but also, to use Lauri Honko's (1983a) apt title, the "Research Traditions in Tradition Research."

Since it is a key term in folklore studies, the uses of *tradition* unfold the history of folklore theory and uncover variations in interpretation, shades of meaning, and subtleties in significance. The shifts in uses and meanings of *tradition* differ from country to country, language to language, and generation to generation. They expose the internal dynamics of folklore scholarship in specific countries and outline their scholarly traditions as they have consolidated in the pursuit of specific issues, definitions of research goals, and the acceptability of research solutions (see Boberg 1953; Diamond 1980; Dorson 1961, 1968; Hautala 1969; Herzfeld 1982; Rearick 1974; and Stromback 1971).

Unlike the discussions of our Nordic colleagues, the present examination of *tradition* has only descriptive and not prescriptive purposes. Here, there is no intention to outline the proper use of the term, nor to suggest that there is one. On the contrary, this is an inductive examination of the ways *tradition* has been used in folklore writings in the United States. It is a self-reflective scrutiny that addresses to ourselves the same questions we constantly wish to address to narrators, singers, and speakers of proverbs. It is a study of the emic view of *tradition*, albeit the reference group is neither a nation nor a tribe but the students of folklore in the United States. If, as Wittgenstein asserts, "the meaning of words lies in their use" (Wittgenstein 1953, 80; Halbett 1967), such a study should reveal the meaning, or meanings, of *tradition* in American folklore scholarship and explore the cumulative connotations of the term in scholarly folklore discourse.

Ideally, the exploration should have been done by scanning the uses of the term in a variety of rhetorical and theoretical contexts, aiming at establishing a correlation between meanings, historical periods, and research trends and subjects. Unfortunately, the present analysis cannot claim that much. Instead, this survey is often intuitive, impressionistic, and inevitably selective. That this is so is regrettable, but the alternative would have required resources that are unavailable. Therefore, the following findings are more preliminary than conclusive. Fully aware of these methodological shortcomings, in the vein of a traditional formula in folklore, I have discerned seven semantic strands that *tradition* has in our midst. Obviously, they overlap and intertwine; they extend over several historical periods in scholarship and carelessly cross from one research trend to another. Consistency even eludes a single writer who might use *tradition* in two or more of its meanings without having even the slightest awareness of the shifts he made. There is nothing unusual about that, and folklorists will undoubtedly continue to employ the entire semantic gamut of *tradition*. The way they have done so in the past is part of the history of ideas about folklore.

Tradition as Lore

Let us start at the beginning with the folklore manifesto of William Newell inaugurating the *Journal of American Folklore* (1888b, 3–7). The term *tradition* occurs rather sparingly in this essay; instead, the term *lore* appears in a key position in the four-tiered goal that Newell sets forth for the newly formed society:

> 1. For the collection of the fast-vanishing remains of Folk-Lore in America, namely:
>   (a) Relics of Old English Folk-Lore (ballads, tales, superstitions, dialect, etc.).
>   (b) Lore of the Negroes in the Southern States of the Union.
>   (c) Lore of the Indian Tribes of North America (myths, tales, etc.).
>   (d) Lore of French Canada, Mexico, etc. (Newell 1888b, 3)

But when Newell does use the term *tradition*, he does so as if it were an obvious synonym of *lore*. For example, expounding on the first research target, he writes, "As to Old English lore, the early settlers, in the colonies peopled from Great Britain, not only brought with them the *oral traditions* of the mother country, but clung to those *traditions* with the usual tenacity of emigrants transported to a new land" (1888b, 3; my emphasis). Later, as he further elaborates on the working of the society, he states, "The collection of the third kind of American folklore—the *traditions* of the Indian tribes—will be generally regarded as the most promising and important part of the work to be accomplished" (5). For him, *tradition* means a "system of myth, rituals, feasts, sacred customs, games, songs, tales [which] exist in such profusion that volumes would be required to contain the lore of each separate tribe" (5). Newell's use of the term is consistent with that of Hartland, both writing in the same decade, the same language, only an ocean apart. Newell predicates *tradition* on a social entity, particularly but not exclusively of oral cultures, and uses it synonymously with *lore*.

Seven years later, when he discusses the relationship between the study of folklore and folklore societies, he specifies that "the name folk-lore was originally invented to denote the *traditional* inheritance of educated Europe" (Newell 1895, 231; my emphasis). Later, he states his theory of tradition, referring directly to his *Games and Songs of American Children* (1883): "In certain

cases it was evident that for many thousand years oral tradition had maintained even the formulas of popular games. The collection made in a country
relatively new proved of value in determining the general theory of tradition;
it seemed that these rhymes were not confined to English-speaking peoples,
but with slight change were also European; it was thus clear that the persis-
tency of oral tradition, under favorable circumstances, is not incompatible
with a continued diffusion from country to country, and translation from
language to language" (Newell 1895, 232–33).

This theory of tradition basically concerns issues of diffusion, transmission, and translation, and hence while Newell employs the term as *lore*, he
also considers and uses *tradition* as process.

Although in Newell's writings, *lore* and *tradition* appear to be inter-
changed freely, there is a proclivity to associate *tradition* with the term *races*,
which at that time referred to so-called *primitive races*, and more specifically
to the American Indians. He made a special plea for the "Necessity of Collecting the Traditions of Native Races" (1888a) and discusses "the record of the
oral tradition of primitive races" (1895, 233), suggesting that "the admixture of
the traditions of these races with those of the conquering whites, the remains
of their ceremonies, subject to gradual alteration, present composite survivals, from which extensive record and careful comparison may hereafter be
able to infer the true character of aboriginal pre-Columbian lore" (1895, 235).

But Newell does not associate tradition with non-European peoples exclusively. Later in the essay, he poses a series of questions about both indigenous
and immigrant groups: "What is their distinctive racial character; what are
their peculiar ideas and traditions? The German, Irishman, and French Canadian, the Bohemian and Russia, the Armenian and Japanese, bring to our
doors the spectacle of the whole civilized and semi-civilized world" (1895, 238).

The interchangeability of *lore* and *tradition* results in the attribution of
the apparent qualities of *lore* to *tradition*. Ever since William Thoms's coinage
of *folk-lore*, the term *lore* refers to a slowly but surely disappearing knowledge.
In this context, tradition also acquires the quality of being on the verge of total
demise. Like lore, tradition is past knowledge that has accidentally survived,
and without adequate attention will suffer a natural death. It is only with such
a perception of tradition that the phrase *living tradition* makes tropic sense.
In Newell's writings, the phrase occurs with reference to the American Indian
tribes. They are the "primitive" peoples among whom the traditions that are
long dead among the "civilized" Europeans are still alive. Thus, in a brief
survey of some scholarly accomplishments of his day, he writes, "The study
of the living tradition of Zuni, Maki, and Navajo has contributed material so

unexpectedly, that it may be said never until this day has the Indian mind been really comprehensible" (1895, 235–36).

An ironic twist that has been lost on us occurred in the volume Tristram P. Coffin edited in 1968, which deals with folklore in modern America.[5] It bears the telling title *Our Living Traditions: An Introduction to American Folklore.* The first-person plural possessive pronoun *our* implicitly contrasts with its third-person counterpart *their,* and the latter could well have referred to the American Indians whom Newell originally mentioned as the bearers of "living traditions" and who are totally excluded from this volume.[6]

At the end of the nineteenth century, both Hartland in England and Newell in America reflect the assumption that traditions that are merely survivals in the "civilized" world have been and continue to be very much alive in the "primitive" and "semi-civilized" cultures. In their discourse, *living tradition* refers, in particular, to the customs, rituals, and literatures of oral societies. With the accumulation of research and change of perspectives in the twentieth century came the discovery that those traditions thought to be long dead in the "civilized" world are, in fact, very much alive, and it is this idea that Coffin's title conveys. While the shift in perspectives is certainly positive, the balance seems to have tilted too far to the other side. The traditions of the Native Americans are mentioned only in passing; in fact, in that now remote period of 1968, even ethnic groups were considered, as the title of Américo Paredes's (1968) essay succinctly expresses, only "tributaries to the mainstream." Their folklore is a survival "not of a dim Stone Age past but of the Old Country, whence the immigrant ancestors came" (Paredes 1968, 71). Our "living tradition" is inclusive, albeit reluctantly, of the ethnic group's traditions, but totally excludes those of the American Indians, who just half a century ago served as the prime example of a dynamic living tradition.

In all these semantic shifts and variations, *tradition* has remained the lore of a particular social entity. It refers to the knowledge of customs, rituals, beliefs, and oral literature as defined and practiced by a particular group and as transmitted within its confines from generation to generation.

Tradition as Canon

For American folklorists, tradition is not merely the collective group lore, but much more: It is the cultural canon of folk society. In Western and Oriental societies, the literate class has shaped, codified, and controlled the literary canons. In charge of education, they have fostered a system of aesthetic and ethnic cultural values, and sanctioned texts as the literary and religious canons by which their peoples lived and in which they believed (von Hallberg 1983–84). They have established the Great Tradition that emanates from the major urban centers (R. Redfield 1956). Because of the association of canons with literacy and social hierarchy, the appellation "high culture" has often been ascribed to this core of a cultural system, thereby attributing to it an adventitious value.[7]

From the perspective of the literati, who foster and control cultural canons, oral literature is, by definition, noncanonic. Taking this view, Barbara Herrnstein Smith, a literary theorist, lumps together "modern texts, especially highly innovative ones, and such culturally exotic works as oral or tribal literature, popular literature, and 'ethnic' literature" (8–9)—all of which are noncanonic. Together with such works, oral literature has subversive potential that, in particular political situations, would deliberately undermine the basic tenets of the canon as perceived and defined by the central social institutions.

However, Barbara Herrnstein Smith (1983) also recognizes that the same cultural functions and factors that shape the canons in literary societies can affect the formation of canons in nonliterate societies. She proposes that "the antiquity and longevity of domestic proverbs, popular tales, children's verbal games, and the entire phenomenon of what we call 'folklore,' which occurs through the same or corresponding mechanisms of cultural selection and reproduction as those described above specifically for 'texts,' demonstrate that the 'endurance' of a verbal artifact (if not its achievement of *academic* canonical status as a 'work of literature'—many folklore works do, however, perform all the functions described above as characteristic of canonical works *as such*) may be more or less independent of institutions controlled by those with political power" (30).

In folklore studies as well, longevity and endurance are criteria for canon definition. Those narratives, songs, proverbs, and riddles that have withstood the test of time and have become the main mental staple of a society are conceived as the cultural canon and have been regarded as *the* tradition. Folklorists have internalized, but not necessarily articulated, such a conception of *tradition*. Our use of the term, however, clearly reflects the idea of tradition as a folk canon. For example, advising the collector of regional songs and ballads, Edward Ives writes, "Even the question of acceptance into tradition must be seen in its local context, and the collector should pay close attention to the song that occurs in only one version in order to attempt to determine why it did *not* enter tradition" (1983, 210).

Ives, who has recorded the repertoire of individual singers (1964, 1971, 1973), is cognizant of the problems the concept of tradition poses for him in this context; hence, more than other folklorists, he displays some self-consciousness in using the term. He indicates that

> students of folksongs have been talking about "the tradition" and how songs either "entered" it, were "altered" by it, or perhaps "rejected" by it for so long and with such confidence that we have come to think of it as something that's really there, when of course it is nothing but a convenient abstraction. Reification is nothing new, and a full-scale discussion of how we have reified "tradition" would in fact be nothing more than a battle report from one front of the great "culture war." . . . Others have written well on this subject, and without minimizing its importance in the least, I will skirt it by adopting Melville Herskovits's compromise as my starting point. That is, if we are careful never to forget that tradition is a concept having no independent reality, we can frequently learn things by *assuming* that reality for the time being. In short, we may flesh out our ghost, just as long as we deny his existence. (Ives 1978, 371–72)

Ives engages unnecessarily in Herskovits's version of an "as if" philosophy, in which he knowingly treats an abstract concept in a fictive fashion, as if it has a tangible existence (Vaihinger 1952). By defining the question of tradition as a problem in the correspondence between concepts and reality, Ives misses the nature of the incongruity that perplexes him. In theory, he adopts Herskovits's definition, which, as we shall shortly see, identifies tradition with culture, but in practice, as his choice of words makes patently clear, he conceives of tradition as a canon of folk society, into which it is possible to gain acceptance, or to enter, or conversely, by which it is possible to be rejected. In such a discourse, tradition becomes the distinct socially recognized canon of oral literary texts.

Such a concept of tradition also underlies Tristram P. Coffin's reference to the texts in Francis James Child, *The English and Scottish Popular Ballads* (Boston: Houghton Mifflin, 1882–89) as "the British traditional ballad" (Coffin 1963; see also Toelken 1967). The definite article in Child's title that conveys the notion of a canon has been transformed to the adjective *traditional*. However, while Coffin refers to a canon established by a scholar, Ives and other folklorists who use the term in this sense consider tradition to be the oral literary canon of folk society itself.

As any other canon, *tradition* is subject to pressures by and infringements from apocryphal trends and texts. They effect changes, modifications, and variations in the oral canon, which, by its very nature, lacks any written text as stabilizing reference. Implicit in American folklore scholarship is a tripartite model of the "enemies" of "tradition"; that model has become one of the fundamental assumptions guiding research and theory, but rarely, if ever, has it been fully articulated.

Accordingly, *tradition* has three offenders, two external and one internal, and it is possible to present them in a set of three dichotomous pairs:

a. little tradition vs. great tradition;
b. tradition vs. popular culture;
c. tradition vs. creativity.

Little tradition vs. great tradition. The anthropologist Robert Redfield coined the terms and formulated the relationship between the little tradition and the great tradition. He had begun to develop the model for the "structure of tradition" (Singer 1959, 192) at least by the beginning of the fifties, but its most prominent articulation appears in his book *Peasant Society and Culture.*[8] Redfield sets up the relationship between the tradition of a folk society and the tradition of a civilization, referring in the process to a variety of terms that have been and still are in use. The two canons are, thus, distinct paradigms that share the qualities of "tradition" but that have distinct social and historical references. As he states, he has chosen the pair *great tradition* and *little tradition* from such others as *high culture* and *low culture, folk and classical cultures,* or *popular and learned traditions*: "In a civilization there is a great tradition of the reflective few, and there is the little tradition of the largely unreflective many. The great tradition works itself out and keeps itself going in the lives of the unlettered in their village communities. The tradition of the philosopher, theologian, and literary man is a tradition consciously cultivated and handed down; that of the little people is for the most part taken for granted and not submitted to much scrutiny or considered refinement and improvement" (R. Redfield 1956, 70).

In spite of the obvious direct relevance of such a formulation to folklore studies, American folklorists were slow to react to this model. Negative evidence is as important as positive testimony would have been. The *Journal of American Folklore* did not publish a review of the book; in his comprehensive essay "A Theory for American Folklore," which appeared in 1959, Richard M. Dorson refers to Robert Redfield only in passing, mentioning an earlier article rather than his then recently published volume (1959, 212). Redfield's model could have been valuable to Dorson, who uses similar terms when he subtitles his own conceptual framework "Folklore and American Civilization" (1959, 203). Similarly, the leading folklorist-anthropologist of the fifties, William Bascom, was under the influence of his former teacher and colleague, Melville Herskovits, and had hardly any use for Redfield's model, particularly since its application to West Africa, Bascom's areal interest, was not immediately apparent. Ake Hultkrantz, a scholar equally at home in American and

European folklore and ethnography, lists Redfield's book in the bibliography of his *General Ethnological Concepts* (1960), but ignores the coinage of *little tradition* and *great tradition* and their theoretical implications in his extensive discussion of *tradition* (229–31).

When Redfield's term finally appeared in a publication of the American Folklore Society, it was in a volume dedicated to his memory, *Traditional India: Structure and Change*, edited by the anthropologist and Indianist Milton Singer and published as volume 10 in the Bibliographical and Special Series of the American Folklore Society (Singer 1959). Singer states that his "own thinking has been greatly stimulated by Robert Redfield," and he quotes at length from a lecture Redfield delivered on February 6, 1958, at the Center for Advanced Study in the Behavioral Sciences at Stanford, California (Singer 1959, x, xxii). Singer emphasizes that Redfield's model was "the leading idea which was the point of departure for [his] research in India and which gives unity to the present symposium" (x). His own contribution, "The Great Tradition in a Metropolitan Center: Madras," is a clear application of Redfield's model (Singer 1959, 141–82). But the publication of this volume under the auspices of the American Folklore Society may be misleading. In spite of the fact that many of the essays relate directly to folklore subjects, the contributors are primarily linguists, anthropologists, and Indianists. Their relationship to folklore studies in the United States is negligible at best.

Two (or three) more years would have to pass before the terms and the concepts would make their premiere in the *Journal of American Folklore* in a theoretical essay by the leading folklore scholar Francis Lee Utley, "Folk Literature: An Operational Definition" (1961). Utley refers to Redfield's model as a familiar concept, its sense of novelty worn off in the short lifespan of scholarly innovation. References to Redfield's works are scattered throughout the essay (195, 196, 203, 205), and Utley makes specific use of Redfield's model of tradition while criticizing Samuel Bayard's (1953) definition of folklore. Utley comments that "the gravest difficulty with [Bayard's] choice of a definition by content rather than by method or process is that he leaves little creativity for what Robert Redfield would call 'the great tradition' as opposed to 'the little tradition'" (1961, 195). Utley then continues to argue that as scientists, folklorists should be aware of their debt to the "great tradition" of Western thought and criticism. But it is clear that the two terms established themselves in folklore studies without much printed evidence of a theoretical struggle, shifting their position from a programmatic hypothetical proposal to a descriptive cultural-historical model.

In Redfield's own model, there is a continuum rather than opposition between the two traditions: "[They] are interdependent. Great tradition and little tradition have long affected each other and continue to do so" (R. Red-field 1956, 71) on multiple levels:

> The relations between Muslim teacher and pupil, between Brahman priest and layman, between Chinese scholar and Chinese peasant—all such as these that are of importance in bringing about communication of great tradition to the peasant or that, perhaps without anyone's intention, cause the peasant tradition to affect the doctrine of the learned—constitute the social structure of the culture, the structure of tradition. From this point of view a civilization is an organization of specialists, of a kind of role-occupiers in characteristic relations to one another and to lay people and performing characteristic functions concerned with the transmission of tradition. (R. Redfield 1956, 101–2)

However, when Utley transposes the two canons to folklore studies, they oppose each other. From a folkloristic perspective, the great tradition has a potential capability to influence and change the little tradition destructively. Folklorists have recognized that through imitation and aspiration for more comfortable economic conditions, the folk society could modify and undermine its own culture. Therefore, while they accept the midcentury model that Redfield has developed, they interpret it in terms of the European model that Hans Naumann made known through the term *gesunkenes Kulturgut* (1929). In spite of the criticism of this concept (Bausinger 1966; Freudenthal 1955), it is well established in folklore scholarship to express the notion that cultural materials originate in the upper classes and filter down to the lower classes. While the original controversy had tempered by midcentury, the opposition between the two classes and their traditions has been imprinted on folklore theoretical schema. Consequently, in folklore, the great tradition looms large over the little tradition as a source of ideas, customs, themes, and forms that belong to a more powerful, and often more valued, canon.

Tradition vs. popular culture. If the great tradition is the little tradition's big brother, popular culture is its rival sister. Dorson summarizes this perception, stating that "the enemy of folklore is the media that blankets mass culture: the large circulation newspapers and magazines we read, the movie and television screens we watch, and the recording industry whose discs we listen to. . . . What is distributed to the millions, after an elaborate, expensive packaging process, does seem the antithesis of the slow drip of invisible tradition" (1978, 37).

In American folklore writings, this conception of an antagonistic relationship between tradition and mass culture has, in fact, taken ambivalent turns. On the one hand, there has been a resentful attitude toward a popular culture that capitalized on traditional resources; the term *fakelore* epitomizes both the ridicule and the despise in which folklorists hold the mass-marketing of tradition (Dorson 1950). On the other hand, American folklorists have slowly realized that in modern industrialized society, mass culture may well be their next research target, since in its variety of forms and genres, the mass media provides the modern world with the equivalent of folk tradition. "This train of thought," Dorson says, "readily leads toward the acceptance of a mass culture species of folklore" (1978, 42).

But resentment persists even in acceptance. From a folkloristic point of view, popular culture simply has a negative value when compared with tradition. The basic assumptions on which students of folklore have constructed their conception of popular culture are well formulated by Dwight Mac-Donald, one of America's most articulate critics of the mass media. He proposes that for its development, mass culture requires a fully matured cultural tradition:

> The connection, however, is not that of the leaf and the branch but rather that of the caterpillar and the leaf. *Kitsch* [the German term for mass culture] "mines" high culture the way improvident frontierism mines the soil, extracting its riches and putting nothing back. Also, as *kitsch* develops, it begins to draw on its own past, and some of it evolves so far away from High Culture as to appear quite disconnected from it.
>
> It is also true that Mass Culture is to some extent a continuation of the old Folk Art which until the Industrial Revolution was the culture of the common people, but here, too, the differences are more striking than the similarities. Folk Art grew from below, it was a spontaneous, autochthonous expression of the people, shaped by themselves, pretty much without the benefit of High Culture, to suit their own needs. Mass Culture is imposed from above. It is fabricated by technicians hired by businessmen; its audience are passive consumers, their participation limited to choice between buying and not buying. (MacDonald 1957, 60)

For MacDonald, *High Culture* and *Folk Art* are analogous with Redfield's concepts of *great traditions* and *little traditions*. But while Redfield intends to construct a theoretical descriptive model, MacDonald develops a theory for criticism; consequently, his terms are value laden—the positive value of genuineness is attributed to both high and folk arts, whereas the mass media is shallow and manipulative.

Such a criticism of mass culture corresponds to the ideas that the fellows of the Frankfurt Institute of Social Research have developed. In commenting on their critical theory in relation to popular culture, Martin Jay (1973) states that, despite its Marxist tendencies, the Institute valued tradition: Adorno pointed to the traditional component in Schonberg's "seemingly revolutionary music," while in Benjamin's view, tradition was part of an "art work's aura." But by *tradition*, the Institute meant something very different from "the continuation of 'progress.'" Instead, "tradition referred to the type of integrated experience the Institute members called *Erfahrung*, which was being destroyed by so-called progress" (215).

Among the Institute members, Leo Lowenthal (1957) wrote more directly about popular literature in America and, along with MacDonald, he conceives of popular culture as a negative force that gnaws at the positive values fostered by either folk or high art. He argues that "the decline of the individual in the mechanized working processes of modern civilization brings about the emergence of mass culture, which replaces folk art or 'high' art. A product of popular culture has none of the features of genuine art, but in all its media popular culture proves to have its own genuine characteristics: standardization, stereotypy, conservatism, mendacity, manipulated consumer goods" (55).

Barely articulated but always existing, these assumptions about the relationship between folk tradition and popular culture have been one of the basic tenets of folklore's own worldview. Margaret Redfield, Robert Redfield's wife, resonates the same sentiments, referring directly to MacDonald's essay and arguing that "folk utterances are more comparable to the classical traditional expressions of civilization than they are to the products of the modern mass media since both folk and enduring civilized art support the implicit basic values of their society. . . . Folklore may be distinguished from modern popular expressive utterance then in that, formed by tradition, it has a quality of genuine art" (M. Redfield 1956, 361).[9]

For her, *tradition* serves as a canon, a heritage, and a process of transmission which, in itself, positively affects artistic creations. Roger Abrahams and Susan Kalčik reiterate the existence of such an assumption in folklore studies by observing that "folklorists have assumed an ideal *folk* group, uncontaminated by the incursions of mass culture and its accompanying media of record (such as print and phonograph records). Dorson's distinction between folklore and fakelore gave a name to the fear that the existence of folk culture was threatened, that nothing was so inimical to folk culture as blatant and sweetened-up imitations of folk performances" (Abrahams and Kalčik 1978, 228).

We state our premises almost in passing, but folklorists' own words, even more than their comments on folklore scholarship, reflect their romantic conception of tradition, in verbs and adjectives that only indirectly relate to the main discussion. For example, Archie Green notes that folklorists "perceive commerce . . . as debasing traditional life," and then comments on "a low-keyed debate [that] has occurred between two sets of folklorists: those who have perceived canned music and cheap records as corrosive agents, destroying the past, robbing people of deep treasures; and those who have welcomed discs as exciting documents of folklife, indeed, as instruments in folk culture's counterhegemonic role" (1983, 434).

Similarly, Henry Glassie, Morrisean folklorist that he is, states the dichotomy between popular culture and tradition in blatant terms. In analyzing the style of a hypothetical local architect, he notes, "Fashionable detail proves the builder was aware of the latest modes. Traditional basic form shows he was unwilling to surrender to them. The conflict of *fashion and tradition*, national and local culture, is resolved in the building of real houses" (1983, 379; my emphasis). Glassie places tradition opposite to fashion (i.e., popular culture) and national culture (i.e., great tradition), but it is the verb *to surrender* that reveals his ideas about tradition and the forces that surround it.

In the United States, perhaps more than in Latin America, Asia, or Africa, the national culture consists of passing fashions more than of long-term tradition; hence folklorists could conceive of the relationship between popular culture and folk tradition almost in terms of a morality play, in which the winds of fashions sweep across the land, but the genuine folk does not surrender to their whims. The extent to which this conception is a fundamental tenet of American folklore scholarship is apparent also in a negative manner. The verb *to surrender* or any of its synonyms is not used to describe the conflict between, say, tradition and creativity.

Tradition vs. creativity. Tradition and creativity have become an uneasy pair between which opposition and dependency never resolve. While tradition is the canon of the group, creativity is the act of the individual folk artist. Each is essential to the other, yet the relations between them are marred by change and constraint. While creativity is necessary for the survival of tradition, it brings about its change, modifying the continuity of the past into the present. Tradition is the frame within which the creative folk artist can perform but from which he must not deviate. The paradox of this relationship becomes apparent in the analysis of individual and collective creativity in ballad and riddle traditions, respectively.

Bertrand Bronson, for example, proposes that a reduction in creativity results in stability but ends up in tradition stagnation. With the spread of literacy, such a process could take place because "literacy has drawn off into other channels a large proportion of the creative energy which once went into ballads. The later generations of ballad singers have for the most part lacked the gifts to do more than perpetuate in a relative unenlightened fashion the verses they had received" (1969, 61). Thus the very creative energy that changes the canon is required to keep tradition alive. The "creative energy" to which Bronson refers, is, of course, not an abstract entity, but a general term that implies many individual singers who maintain the tradition with their verbal creativity.

In explaining the decline in the riddling tradition of northeastern Scotland, Kenneth Goldstein points to the withering of social and cultural ethnic resources for riddling creativity. He explains this phenomenon by suggesting that the only way to maintain the vitality of riddling tradition is by the continued introduction of new riddles, either by invention from within the society or introduction from without. To the degree that these societies draw new materials and new audiences from the outside, the riddling tradition can remain vital, and therefore those societies with a large network of outside contacts will have a more vital riddling tradition than those with a more limited series of outside contacts (Goldstein 1963, 333). The infusion of new riddles from external sources into the canon is the process that keeps the tradition vital.

As interdependent concepts, *tradition* and *creativity* appear in American folklore studies as a contrastive pair. Daniel Crowley (1966, 1–7) employs them as opposites in his discussion of storytelling in Bahamian folklore as does David Evans (1982) to describe the folk blues in his recent study.

The respective domains of tradition and creativity and the perpetual tension between them become apparent in the set of research questions Stith Thompson (1953, 592) formulates: "What . . . is the relation of the individual to the tradition which he carries on . . . how compulsive is the tradition of his social group and how much freedom is there for the expression of individuality? What is the relation of the bearer of oral tradition to his group? How specialized is he, and what characteristics has he, artistic or personal, that cause approval or disapproval by his fellows? How is tradition, oral or material, modified by cultural patterns?" Thompson's formulation partially reflects the basic assumptions of the historic-geographic method and its "law of self-correction," according to which any deviation from the canonic form, either through creativity or by default, is self-corrected by the traditions the group maintains (Thompson 1946, 437).

But such a conception of creativity and tradition is not a part only of folklore literary studies. Anthropological folklorists have maintained a similar view. William Bascom (1953, 286; 1955, 248), for example, approaches the problem of creativity by distinguishing between the variations that individual narrators introduced and the concern with the actual origin of tales, focusing, however, on the former issue. Crowley (1966, 137) accepts these tenets of creativity and concludes that in actuality, few individual narrators bring anything new into their tradition.

In folklore, as well as in literary criticism, creativity is attributed to the individual and tradition to the group. However, the basic concerns in these two fields diametrically oppose each other. In literary criticism, individual creativity is the starting point from which there is an attempt to examine the poet's relation to tradition; in folklore, in contrast, tradition is the norm, and research concerns itself with the discoveries of deviation from, and innovation within, the canon.

Canon formation. In the past, the contrast between tradition and creativity implied a dichotomy between stability and activity, permanence and change, past and present; but in recent years, the concept of tradition itself has changed status and become an object of conscious creativity. Folklorists, anthropologists, and historians have come to the conclusion that society does not treat tradition passively; often, it creates its own tradition through the selection of historical events and heroes, and even through the invention of a past (Hobsbawm and Ranger 1983). Tradition, then, could well be a constructed canon, projected into the past in order to legitimize the present. Since the past serves as such a powerful authority in culture, no society could afford to let it just be; it must add to it, subtract from it, mold it in its own image. Raymond Williams describes this process, naming it a *selective tradition*. He argues,

> Theoretically, a period is recorded; in practice this record is absorbed into a selective tradition; and both are different from the culture as lived by.
>
> It is very important to try to understand the operation of a selective tradition. To some extent, the selection begins within the period itself; from the whole body of activities, certain things are selected for value and emphasis. In general this selection will reflect the organization of the period as a whole, though this does not mean that the values and emphases will later be confirmed.... The lived culture would not only have been fined down to selected documents; it would be used, in its reduced form, partly as a contribution (inevitably quite small) to the general line of human growth; partly for historical reconstruction; partly, again, as a way of having done with us, of naming and placing a particular stage of the past. The selective tradition thus creates, at one level, a general human culture; at another level, the historical record of a particular society; at a third level, most difficult to accept and assess, a rejection of considerable areas of what was once a living culture....
>
> The traditional culture of a society will always tend to correspond to its *contemporary* systems of interests and values, for it is not an absolute body of work but a continual selection and interpretation. In theory, and to a limited extent in practice, those institutions which are formally concerned with keeping the tradition alive (in particular the institutions of education and scholarship) are committed to the tradition as a whole, and not to some selection from it according to contemporary interests. The importance of this commitment is very great, because we see again and again, in the workings of a selective tradition,

reversals and re-discoveries, returns to work apparently abandoned as dead, and clearly this is only possible if there are institutions whose business it is to keep large areas of past culture, if not alive, at least available. . . .

In a society as a whole, and in all its particular activities, the cultural tradition can be seen as a continual selection and re-selection of ancestors. (Williams 1961, 50–52)

Williams obviously discusses the formation of tradition in a literate society and in a literary, even academic, context. However, the subjectivity of tradition is an idea with which folklorists and anthropologists could concur, though until recently, other terms, like history or myth, have served to describe this process.

Within the context of American folklore studies, the notion of conscious formation of tradition as a canon sanctioned by the past emerged, to the best of my knowledge, only in the seventies. Defending tradition as an essential folklore concept, Dell Hymes has changed its meaning. He proposes to "root the notion not in time but in social life," and to use the notion "not simply as naming objects, traditions, but also, and more fundamentally, as naming a process" (1975, 353). But the process that he names is no longer the process of delivery, or handing down of themes, symbols, or forms, but of selecting and constructing a narrative that would become part of a canon, even a pantheon, projected into present and future life from an imagined or real past. While defending tradition, Hymes, in fact, changes the focus from tradition to the quality of being traditional, to traditionality. The verb *to traditionalize* that he uses first with, and later without, quotation marks, names the process of attributing the quality of the traditional to selected experiences and personalities on the basis of correspondence with cultural or personal values and goals. Hymes has thus proposed to replace the notion of tradition as a given canon of folk society with Williams's idea of a selective tradition as a major concept for folklore.

Both Williams and Hymes insist that the construction of tradition as a symbolic past has social purposes, one of which is the creation of an identity for a group. It is in recognition of this function that Jocelyn Linnekin defines *tradition* as a "conscious model of past lifeways that people use in the construction of their identity." For her, the idea that tradition is a cultural inheritance is illusory. "Tradition is a self-conscious category [and hence] inevitably 'invented'" (1983, 241). According to Linnekin and Handler, such a definition departs from the naturalistic conception of tradition that has prevailed in sociology and anthropology and is being replaced by a cognitive and symbolic conception according to which *tradition* is "a model of the past and is inseparable from the interpretation of tradition in the present" (Handler and Linnekin 1984, 276).

Once introduced into the scholarly discourse of folklore, such a conception of tradition implies a significant departure from past notions. The awareness of the possibility for new traditions, and change and discontinuity within old ones, has been an integral part of folklore as the science of tradition. But this time, it is not tradition as lore that is changing in response to social and economic conditions, nor is it an idea of tradition that is created to contrast with fashion, modernity, or even the great tradition; rather, it is a tradition that constitutes a canon that fosters the social and cultural definitions of a group.

Tradition as Process

It is possible to appreciate more fully the significance of this change in meaning by clarifying the former notion of tradition as process. In folklore, as well as in other disciplines, the process of tradition implies the dynamics of transmission of cultural heritage from generation to generation. Such a meaning closely retains the semantics of the Latin verb *tradere*, to deliver, to hand down, as evident in the phrase *oral tradition*, which has often been the defining feature of folklore. Archer Taylor (1946), folklorist-philologue that he was, employed the term in this meaning in his definition of *folklore* as that material that is handed on by tradition, either by word of mouth or custom and practice.

As a transmission process, tradition has clearly been associated with the past. Folklorists, however, have extended the tradition process from temporal to social and spatial dimensions. "There are," as two ballad scholars pointed out, "two kinds of traditions to be distinguished: *tradition in time* and *tradition in space*" (Eckstrom and Barry 1930). In folklore scholarship, both were essential in the examination of the social dynamics of transmission and in the analysis of the geographical diffusion of tales and songs.

As a process of transmission, *oral tradition* also refers to the nonliterate stage in the history of literate societies and to the precanonic period in the history of religious movements that later canonized their teachings in scriptures. This use is not confined to American folklore studies; rather, it is central in theology and in biblical scholarship, reflecting emic distinctions in some historical societies (see, e.g., Congar 1967; Gerhardsson 1961; Nielsen 1954; and Pelikan 1984).

As a process in history, *tradition* also occurs in Milman Parry's studies of the Homeric epics and the modern Yugoslavian oral bards. Later on, as his students, and students of students, developed a distinct school within American folklore and classical studies, *oral literature* and *oral poetry* have become the key terms, but in Parry's own writings, *tradition* occupies a central position. He titled his 1928 MA thesis "L'épithet traditionelle dans Homère: Essai sur un problème de style homérique" (Parry 1971, 1–190), with the clear understanding that the term refers to a transmission process that also becomes a composition process. Five years later, when he wrote his essay "The Traditional Metaphor in Homer" (Parry 1971, 365–75), orality and traditionality had become almost interchangeable terms for Parry, as is evident from the following paragraph written in 1932: "That the Homeric poems were oral is shown by their diction, which, being formulaic, can only be traditional and oral. Putting the two sets of facts together, we see that the variety of words and forms which so long puzzled Homeric scholars is the natural and necessary condition of the Homeric diction. Being oral it must be traditional, and being traditional it must have in it old words and forms" (Parry 1971, 339).

Tradition as Mass

When tradition is the process, folklore is its object, but when oral transmission is the quintessential quality of folklore, the two concepts—folklore and tradition—inevitably switch positions, and tradition becomes the material and folklore its vehicle. Richard Bauman (1971) describes this view (considering it as representing the former, rather than the "new," perspective of folklore). He suggests that in those terms, "Folklore is the product through creation or recreation of the whole group and its forebearers, and an expression of their common character. It is spoken of in terms of traditions, with tradition conceived of as a superorganic temporal continuum; the folk are 'tradition bearers,' that is, they carry the folklore traditions on through time and space like so much baggage" (33).

Bauman is well aware of the contradiction between the concept of tradition as superorganic and its metaphor as baggage; after all, the two notions seesawed in folklore discourse with the respective rise and fall of the anthropological and the literary approaches. In social scientific terms, tradition could be conceived as a superorganic force, whereas from literary perspectives, tradition is embodied in the literary forms that singers and narrators transmit to each other.

This literary view of tradition as a load evolved from Carl von Sydow's metaphor of narrators as tradition bearers. He sought to replace the Romantic idea that "the traditions of the peasantry are . . . the common property of the whole peasantry, to be found everywhere 'in the depths of the soul of the people'" (1948, 12) with an empirical approach to the dynamics of tradition within a community. Therefore, he suggests that "each tradition has its own bearers," who constitute only "a very small number of the population of the whole parish." It is "the active bearers who keep the tradition alive and transmit it" (12). Von Sydow regards tradition not as superorganic but rather as an organic mass that changes with the people who bear it. If folklorists wish "to understand the life of tradition, its origin and development, its dissemination and transmission (they) must . . . give heed to these circles and the various kinds of bearers of tradition" (12). If, then, from a social-scientific point of view, tradition could be a superorganic force, in terms of literary folklore, tradition becomes a carried torch. But even among literary folklorists, there has not been a homogenous view: While Taylor regarded tradition as the transmission process, von Sydow considered it as the transmitted mass.

In the United States, von Sydow's conception of tradition has had but a limited influence on research; perhaps in the classroom, teachers discuss his theory, but in print, the references to his approach are rather scarce. Several things could account for that. First, in the United States, narrative distribution studies that follow the historic-geographic method, and to which von Sydow's concept of the tradition bearer is most relevant, are few in number (Goldberg 1984). Second, his concepts of active and passive tradition bearers are in agreement with the anthropological-sociological concept of role that American folklorists accepted, and hence von Sydow's notion would be redundant. Third, most studies of individual narrators and singers focus on their oral literary repertoire and social function, and not on their contribution to the dissemination of tales and songs. Fourth, such a situation possibly results from Stith Thompson's attitude toward von Sydow; while Thompson recognized von Sydow's scholarly significance, he has paid more attention to von Sydow's polemical character (Thompson 1951b).

Among American-educated folklorists, Kenneth Goldstein and Barre Toelken are perhaps the only ones who have integrated von Sydow's concept of tradition into their work. In Goldstein's (1964) guide for folklore fieldwork, the concept of tradition as mass is dominant. In fact, the phrase *tradition bearer* is the only reference to tradition in the index; it is a term Goldstein uses interchangeably with *informant* instead of *narrator* or *singer*. Similarly, Barre Toelken, in his textbook *The Dynamics of Folklore* (1979), makes extensive use of the term (157–59, 292–93). Goldstein is also the single folklorist in America, to the best of my knowledge, who sought to further refine the concepts of active and passive tradition bearers. In his essay "On the Application of the

Concepts of Active and Inactive Traditions to the Study of Repertory" (1971), Goldstein proposes that the dichotomy between the two is not permanent and does not necessarily reflect personal verbal ability; rather, the activation of tradition is dependent on situational circumstances. Even those few references to the concept of tradition as mass represent a shift in focus from the tradition to its bearers; from a concern with a horizontal dissemination of themes and genres to a paradigmatic pattern of tradition that, as repertoire, exists in the minds and lives of folklore performers.

Tradition as Culture

American folklorists, particularly those with an anthropological orientation, tend to regard tradition not as mass, but as culture. Herskovits states this assumption simply and without further elaboration: "One synonym for culture is *tradition*" (1948, 17). His definition of folklore is predicated on such a view of tradition, and other anthropologists follow suit. Therefore, virtually all the anthropologists who contribute to the assembly of definitions in the *Funk and Wagnalls Standard Dictionary of Folklore, Mythology and Legend*, William R. Bascom, George M. Foster, M. Harman, Melville J. Herskovits, Katherine Luomala, and Richard A. Waterman, omit the term *tradition* from theirs. Marion Smith, the only exception, refers specifically to "oral literary tradition"; hence, while using the term *tradition*, she does not depart from the anthropological conception of folklore as "literary art of a culture," or as "verbal art." Obviously, when the two terms *culture* and *tradition* occur in the same phrase, such as "traditional culture" or "cultural traditions," the expression is not necessarily redundant; *tradition* or *culture* modify each other in terms of time and substance, respectively. Anthropological folklorists in America have modified Hartland's initial formulation. For him, folklore is "the science of tradition"; for them, it can be only the science of part of tradition—anthropology bites off the larger slice.

Such a use has also extended to folklorists with an initial literary orientation. When, for example, Américo Paredes and Ellen J. Stekert titled the volume they edited *The Urban Experience and Folk Tradition*, they referred to folk culture in the city. Although throughout the volume (in the foreword and introduction by the editors, and in the separate essays and the discussions that follow), the term *tradition* occurs in a variety of contexts, having a variety of meanings, as an overarching concept, *tradition* (even in its plural form, *traditions)* essentially connotes the rural and ethnic cultures in an urban environment. Such a use is particularly apparent in Ellen Stekert's prefatory remarks:

> The papers that follow represent both old and new approaches to the study of urban traditions. Their approach is old in that they focus on traditions brought to the city and acted on by the metropolis. Traditions that have originated and developed in the urban milieu are explored only fleetingly. The papers also reflect past approaches to urban traditions in that they treat the lore of the groups low on the socioeconomic ladder. There is no direct treatment, for example, of traditions held by the white Anglo-Saxon, Protestant middle class, a group that has been called, for better or worse, the "dominant culture." (Stekert 1970, iii)

The last reference to dominant culture interprets all previous references to traditions of social groups, considering the two to be equivalent terms. This focus on the social basis of folklore among anthropologically oriented folklore research in the United States compels the use of *tradition* as *culture*. Similarly, in defining folklore itself, Alan Dundes employs the term *tradition* in its Herskovitsian sense, as a synonym of culture. He argues, "It does not matter what the linking factor is—it could be a common occupation, language, or religion—but what is important is that a group formed for whatever reason will have some tradition which it calls its own. . . . A member of the group may not know all the other members, but he will probably know the common core of traditions belonging to the group, traditions which help the group have a sense of group identity" (Dundes 1965, 2).

Through this approach, *tradition* in folklore, like *culture* in anthropology, has become a defining and identifying aspect of social life. There is a direct and mutual relation between a group and its tradition. Through experience, interaction, language, and history, a society builds up a tradition that, in turn, functions as its complex identity mark.

Tradition as Langue

Once tradition is viewed as culture, it could become subject to the same theoretical problems and methodological dilemmas as the concept of culture (Kroeber and Kluckhohn, 1952). Bauman's reference to tradition as a "superorganic temporal continuum" resonates with a seven-decade-old anthropological debate about culture as superorganic (Kroeber 1917; Sapir 1917). The definitions of *tradition* implicit in folklore scholarly discourse have not necessarily followed all the twists and turns the definitions of *culture* have, yet some of them made their impact on folklore theory, and it is possible to detect parallel trends, not necessarily contemporaneous, in the conceptions of culture and tradition in anthropology and folklore, respectively.

The notion of culture as an abstract, but not superorganic, set of standards, rules, and symbols that govern human conduct in society and guide individuals in their decision making has direct relevance to current folklore explorations. In response to the challenge to the centrality of tradition in the definition of folklore (Ben-Amos 1971, 13–14), Kay Cothran proposes to redefine the concept: "Tradition—not antiquity and orality, but 'our ways, our means, our categories, our system'" (Cothran 1973, 7; Brunvand 1979, 445). By evoking notions both of identity and system, she redefines *tradition* as "the rules by means of which a given context is made sensible, by means of which further contexts are made possible" (Cothran 1973, 7; Brunvand 1979, 445). Such a shift does not restore tradition to its venerable position in folklore thought, but offers a new concept for an old term. In fact, this very shift had been in process for some time when Kay Cothran named and identified a new paradigm for *tradition*.

This paradigm (according to which *tradition*, like *langue* for de Saussure, is an abstract system of rules that generates the performance and speaking of folklore) has been implicit in the theoretical writings of Roger Abrahams. He suggests that "it seems most convenient to come to some working definition of folklore that takes both of these dimensions—tradition and performance— into account" (Abrahams 1971, 29). By stating these two terms as a contrastive pair, Abrahams makes an implicit analogy to the Saussurian pair of concepts *langue* and *parole*, or to the Chomskyan pair of terms *competence* and *performance*, in which *tradition* becomes the abstract system of knowledge that generates the actual performances.

This idea has been long in developing in the writings of Roger Abrahams; at first, *tradition* occurred as a synonym for *stability*, *lore*, and only vaguely for *cultural rules*. In his first theoretical essay, Abrahams states, "The study of folklore itself inherently contains one pair of oppositions, the analysis of which can cast some light on the lore itself and its creation and transmission: the conflict between stability (tradition) and change. Any study of a body of collected lore should contain at least some discussion of the place of improvisation and the improviser within the group from which the material has come. Improvisation can be a traditional mode itself. Though folklore is by its nature traditional, therefore conservative, the influence of conscious change, or innovation is not alien or inimical to any group" (Abrahams 1963, 101; Brunvand 1979, 394).

Five years later, in 1968, *tradition* becomes a comprehensive term, equivalent to de Saussure's *langage*, composed of both *langue* and *parole*. Performance becomes one pole of the contrasting pair *within tradition*, taking the position previously occupied by change and improvisation. Abrahams contends that "the full analysis of a tradition or genre calls for the study of organizational elements of both items and performance" (1968, 145). While *performance* itself begins to have a clear definition—Abrahams suggests that "items of expressive folklore . . . come to life only through that special kind of organized and habitual action called 'performance'" (145)—*tradition* remains an elusive term, implicit in the domain in which items of folklore are dormant and from which they come to life.

Ambiguous and vague as they are, these statements of the rhetorical theory of folklore are precursors of Abrahams's enactment-centered theory. When in 1977 he writes that "folklorists have always been concerned with the most vital expressions of culture: folktales and myth, riddles and proverbs, festivals and rituals . . . expressions of tradition [which] mark those moments when valued relationships are enacted" (79), the phrase *expressions of tradition* is not merely a grammatical transformation of the common folklore idiom *traditional expressions*. It is also a reflection of Abrahams's conception of tradition as an abstract system of rules and symbols that exists as a guiding pattern and as a storehouse of themes and forms that can be enacted during appropriate situations by capable performers.

Tradition as Performance

On the surface, it may appear that Abrahams's conception of tradition resolves a logical predicament for performance-oriented folklorists. After all, he enables students of "the science of tradition" to retain tradition as a central concept of their discipline, while developing a rhetorical theory of folklore that is, by definition, synchronic. By following Abrahams's and Cothran's reconceptualization of tradition, it becomes possible to have our cake and eat it too: to use atemporally a concept that connotes time past. Tradition becomes a dimension of folklore that constantly exists regardless of the actual performance. It is folklore in potential. It is knowledge that is secured in the minds and memories of the people only to be performed on appropriate occasions; the sense of appropriateness in itself is subject to rules of tradition.

This pair of terms, *tradition* and *performance*, also resolves the problem concerning the very ontology of folklore forms that Robert Georges (1959) has raised. He has argued forcefully that in terms of folklore, there are no narratives, only narrations; that the only existence of the tale is in the telling. But by following Abrahams's suggestion, it is possible to place narratives in the domain of tradition, and to consider narrations as part of cultural performances.

Apparently, however, the solution has not been completely satisfactory; in spite of the separation between stable and labile aspects of folklore in folkloristic thought from Hartland to Holbek, tradition itself has undergone historical changes. Even faster than grammatical rules, the rules of tradition, be it lore, canon, or a heritage, respond to their society and change over time. In order to resolve the dilemma that a changing tradition poses to folklorists, Barre Toelken, without directly addressing the issue, proposes to subsume *tradition* to *change*. Consequently, he suggests that "*all folklore* participates in a distinctive, dynamic process. Constant change, *variation within tradition* [my emphasis], whether intentional or inadvertent, is viewed here simply as a central fact of life for folklore, and rather than presenting it in opposed terms of conscious artistic manipulation or forgetfulness [Toelken has] sought to accept it as a defining feature that grows out of context, performance, attitude, cultural tastes and the like" (Toelken 1979, 10).

Toelken switches the terms that make up Abrahams's model of folklore; instead of the two terms *tradition* and *performance* opposing each other, he considers the very qualities and processes that are inherent in performance to be integral features of tradition. In his attempt to describe his own view of tradition, Toelken is caught up in a contradiction not of his own making. He suggests a definition of folklore as "tradition-based communicative units informally exchanged in dynamic variation through space and time" (1979, 32), and then elaborates: "*Tradition* is here understood to mean not some static, immutable force from the past, but those pre-existing culture-specific materials and options that bear on the personal tastes and talents. . . . [I]n the use of *tradition* . . . such matters as content and style have been for the most part passed on but not invented by the performer" (32).

But tradition cannot be both dynamic (i.e., "not some static, immutable") force and pre-existing, culture-specific material. Dynamic variations occur in performance, in speaking, singing, music making, painting, and sculpting. The attempt to overcome the bipolarity of tradition and performance, stability and change, structure and transformation, inevitably forces on Toelken a concept of tradition as performance itself.

Conclusion

The seven strands of *tradition* are exposed not for choice nor for preference; none is more adequate than the other, none is more proper than the other. Together, they reveal the meanings *tradition* has had in American folklore studies, and together these meanings constitute the history of the term. As a keyword, it has served students of different periods and different persuasions.

All retained the term but preferred to shift and twist the meanings for their own theoretical and methodological purposes. Like *selective tradition* itself, *tradition* has accumulated its own traditional meanings through a process of selection and combination of ideas and references. *Tradition* has survived criticism and remained a symbol of and for folklore. It has been one of the principal metaphors to guide us in the choate world of experiences and ideas. As a metaphor that has been in such common use, *tradition* has also accumulated a patina of meanings with its own luster. But behind the shine, there is also an accumulation of frustrations, ambiguities, trends, and directions for which the history of folklore could be a guiding map.[10]

Notes

1. See Leach and Fried (1949). Out of twenty-one definitions of folklore, only six, all by anthropologists, do not employ the term *tradition* in one form or another. Such an omission is consistent with the anthropological approach that regards *tradition* as coterminous with *culture*. See Rioux (1950, 192–98). Anthropologists, however, do employ the term *tradition* and its various forms in reference to folklore for nondefinitional purposes (Beckwith 1931, 2–6, 12, 41–44).

2. Lauri Honko's comments on the status of the term *tradition* are relevant to this issue. He said at the 22nd Congress of Nordic Ethnology and Folkloristics: "First of all, it is a question of the actual concept [of] *tradition*. The congress centers on 'traditional research,' but, strangely enough, nobody has drawn attention to the fact that we have not dealt with the question of 'What is tradition?'"

3. She opts for the use of the term *style* to avoid the emotive load that *tradition* connotes.

4. For example, when W. Edson Richmond describes the most recent trends in folklore theory, he implicitly describes, in the negative, the approaches that have prevailed until just a few years ago by saying, "No longer do folklorists confine their studies solely to those things which are perpetuated orally or by precept; no longer do folklorists concern themselves only with backward classes or the less cultured classes of more advanced peoples" (Richmond 1983, xii; see also Eisenstadt 1969).

5. In his review of *Our Living Traditions*, Ken Periman (1969, 83) wishes that the book would have "more material dealing with the Southwest, with the heritage of the Hispanos and the Indians of the region," not realizing that his wish is incompatible with the basic assumption of the book.

6. In his review of the book, the anthropologist Melville Jacobes pointed out the absence of any reference to Native American traditions in this volume; see Melville Jacobes, "Review of *Our Living Traditions: An Introduction to American Folklore* by Tristram Potter Coffin," *American Anthropologist* n.s., 72, no. 2 (1970): 434–35.

7. Often, this term is used to contrast with *popular culture* (see Sammons 1977, 114–34). There is now a growing interest in popular culture and literature, and among the studies available, see Bigsby (1976); Burke (1978); Danforth (1983); Neubereg (1976); M. Redfield (1956); and Slater (1982).

8. This phrase occurs in a lecture he delivered on February 6, 1958, at the Center for Advanced Study in the Behavioral Sciences, Stanford, California (Singer 1959, xxii), published in R. Redfield (1962, 1:392–414).

9. The notion that mass media affects oral tradition negatively is not particularly American. For example, Brazilian folklorists also see "the mass media as antithetical to folk creation, insisting that it destroys, or, at best, imposes a certain sameness on art forms such as the literatura de cordel" (Slater 1982, 51). Slater refers in particular to the writings of Gustavo Barroso, who insists that tradition is "at the gates of death because the radio will surely kill it." Similarly, Loring M. Danforth (1983) points out that Greek folklorists have a negative reaction to the entry of Greek shadow theater into the world of mass and popular culture.

10. An earlier version of this essay was presented at the Culture, Tradition, Identity Conference that took place at Indiana University, Bloomington, Indiana, on March 26–28, 1984. The comments of many participants helped me in preparing the present form, and I would like to thank them all; in particular, I am grateful to Linda Dégh for suggesting the topic, and to Alan Dundes and Lucy Long for bibliographical references.

Bibliography

Abrahams, Roger D. 1963. "Folklore in Culture: Notes toward an Analytic Method." *University of Texas Studies in Literature and Language* 5:98–110. Reprinted in Brunvand (1979, 390–403).

———. 1968. "Introductory Remarks to a Rhetorical Theory of Folklore." *Journal of American Folklore* 81, no. 320:143–58.

———. 1971. "Personal Power and Social Restraint in the Definition of Folklore." *Journal of American Folklore* 84, no. 331:16–30. Reprinted in Paredes and Bauman (1972, 16–30).

———. 1977. "Toward an Enactment-Centered Theory of Folklore." In *Frontiers of Folklore*, edited by William R. Bascom, 79–120. AAAS Selected Symposia Series 5. Boulder, CO: West View, for the American Association for the Advancement of Science.

Abrahams, Roger D., and Susan Kalčik. 1978. "Folklore and Cultural Pluralism." In *Folklore in the Modern World*, edited by Richard M. Dorson, 223–36. World Anthropology. The Hague: Mouton.

Acton, H. B. 1952–53. "Tradition and Some Other Forms of Order: The Presidential Address." *Proceedings of the Aristotelian Society*, n.s. 53:1–28.

Barnard, F. M. 1965. *Herder's Social and Political Thought: From Enlightenment to Nationalism*. Oxford: Clarendon.

Bascom, William. 1953. "Folklore and Anthropology." *Journal of American Folklore* 66, no. 262:283–90.

———. 1955. "Verbal Art." *Journal of American Folklore* 68, no. 269:245–52.

Bauman, Richard. 1971. "Differential Identity and the Social Base of Folklore." *Journal of American Folklore* 84, no. 331:31–41 Reprinted in Paredes and Bauman (1972, 31–41).

Bausinger, Hermann. 1966. "Folklore und gesunkenes Kulturgut." *Deutsche Jahrbuch für Volkskunde* 1:15–25.

Bayard, Samuel. 1953. "The Materials of Folklore." *Journal of American Folklore* 66, no. 259:1–17.

Beckwith, Martha Warren. 1931. *Folklore in America: Its Scope and Method*. Poughkeepsie, NY: The Folklore Foundation, Vassar College.

Ben-Amos, Dan. 1971. "Toward a Definition of Folklore in Context." *Journal of American Folklore* 84, no. 331:3–15. Reprinted in Paredes and Bauman (1972, 3–15).

Bigsby, C. W. E., ed. 1976. *Approaches to Popular Culture*. London: Edward Arnold.

Boberg, Inger M. 1953. *Folkemindeforskningens Historie*. København: Einar Munksgaards.

Bronson, Bertrand Harris. 1969. *The Ballad as Song*. Berkeley: University of California Press.

Brunvand, Jan Harold. 1968. *The Study of American Folklore: An Introduction*. New York: W. W. Norton.

———. 1978. *The Study of American Folklore: An Introduction*. 2nd ed. New York: W. W. Norton.

———. 1979. *Readings in American Folklore*. New York: W. W. Norton.

Burke, Peter. 1978. *Popular Culture in Early Modern Europe*. New York: Harper and Row.

Burrow, J. W. 1966. *Evolution and Society: A Study in Victorian Social Theory*. Cambridge: Cambridge University Press.

Bury, J. B. 1932. *The Idea of Progress: An Inquiry into its Origin and Growth*. New York: Macmillan.

Cantlie, Audrey. 1979. "The Concept of Tradition." In *Tradition and Politics in South Asia*, edited by R. J. Moore, 1–16. New Delhi: Vikas.

Cocchiara, Guiseppe. 1981. *The History of Folklore in Europe*. Translated by. John N. McDaniel. Philadelphia: Institute for the Study of Human Issues.

Coffin, Tristram P. 1963. *The British Traditional Ballad in North America*. American Folklore Society. Bibliographical and special series, vol. 2. Philadelphia: American Folklore Society.

———, ed. 1968. *Our Living Traditions: An Introduction to American Folklore*. New York: Basic Books.

Coleman, Samuel. 1968. "Is There Reason in Tradition?" In *Politics and Experience*, edited by Preston King and B. C. Parekh, 239–82. Cambridge: Cambridge University Press.

Congar, Yves M. J. 1967. *Tradition and Traditions*. New York: MacMillan.

Cothran, Kay. 1973. "Participation in Tradition." *Keystone Folklore* 18, nos. 1–2:7–1. Reprinted in Brunvand (1979, 444–48).

Crowley, Daniel J. 1966. *I Could Talk Old-Story Good: Creativity in Bahamian Folklore*. Folklore Studies 17. Berkeley and Los Angeles: University of California Press.

Danforth, Loring M. 1983. "Tradition and Change in Greek Shadow Theater." *Journal of American Folklore* 96, no. 381:281–309.

Diamond, Stanley, ed. 1980. *Anthropology: Ancestors and Heirs*. Studies in Anthropology 5. The Hague: Mouton.

Doren, Charles Van. 1967. *The Idea of Progress*. Concepts of Western Thought Series. New York: Frederick A. Praeger.

Dorson, Richard M. 1950. "Folklore and Fake Lore." *American Mercury* 70:335–43.

———. 1951. "The Great Team of English Folklorists." *Journal of American Folklore* 64, no. 251:1–10.

———. 1959. "A Theory for American Folklore." *Journal of American Folklore* 72, no. 285:197–215.

———, ed. 1961. *Folklore Research Around the World: A North American Point of View*. Bloomington: Indiana University Press.

———. 1968a. *The British Folklorists: A History*. Chicago: University of Chicago Press.

———, ed. 1968b. *Peasant Customs and Savage Myths: Selections from the British Folklorists*. 2 vols. Chicago: University of Chicago Press.

———. 1978. "Folklore in the Modern World." In *Folklore in the Modern World*, edited by Richard M. Dorson, 11–51. World Anthropology. The Hague: Mouton.

Dundes, Alan. 1965. *The Study of Folklore*. Englewood Cliffs, NJ: Prentice-Hall.

E[ckstrom], F[anny] H., and P[hillips] B[arry]. 1930. "What Is Tradition?" *Bulletin of the Folksong Society of the Northeast* 1:2.

Eisenstadt, S. N. 1969. "Some Observations on the Dynamics of Traditions." *Comparative Studies in Society and History* 11, no. 4:451–75.

———. 1973a. "Post-Traditional Societies and the Continuity and Reconstruction of Tradition." *Daedalus* 102, no. 1:1–28;

———. 1973b. *Tradition, Change, and Modernity.* New York: John Wiley.

Ergang, Robert Reinhold. 1966. *Herder and the Foundations of German Nationalism.* New York: Octagon Books. Originally published in *Studies in History, Economics, and Public Law,* no. 341. New York: Columbia University Press, 1931.

Evans, David. 1982. *Big Road Blues: Tradition and Creativity in the Folk Blues.* Berkeley: University of California Press.

Freudenthal, Herbert. 1955. *Die Wissenschaftstheorie der deutschen Volkskunde,* Schriften des niedersachsischen Heimatbundes, Neue Folge Bd. 25. Hannover: Niedersächsischer Heimatbund.

Gayton A. H. 1947. "Plan of Work and Summary Reports." *Journal of American Folklore* 60, no. 238:351–55.

Georges, Robert A. 1969. "Toward an Understanding of Storytelling Events." *Journal of American Folklore* 82, no. 326:313–28.

Gerhardsson, Birger. 1961. *Memory and Manuscript: Oral Tradition and Written Transmission in Rabbinic Judaism and Early Christianity.* Acta Seminarii Neotestamentici Upsaliensis 22. Lund: C. W. K. Gleerup.

Glassie, Henry. 1983. "Folkloristic Study of the American Artifact: Objects and Objectives." In *Handbook of American Folklore,* edited by Richard M. Dorson and Inta Gale Carpenter, 376–83. Bloomington: Indiana University Press.

Goldberg, Christine. 1984. "The Historic-Geographic Method: Past and Future." *Journal of Folklore Research* 21, no. 1: 1–18.

Goldstein, Kenneth S. 1963. "Riddling Traditions in Northeastern Scotland." *Journal of American Folklore* 76, no. 302:330–36.

———. 1964. *A Guide for Field Workers in Folklore.* Memoirs of the American Folklore Society, vol. 52. Hatboro, PA: Folklore Associates.

———. 1971. "On the Application of the Concepts of Active and Inactive Traditions to the Study of Repertory." *Journal of American Folklore* 84, no. 331:62–7. Reprinted in Paredes and Bauman (1972, 62–67).

Green, Archie. 1983. "Sound Recordings, Use and Challenge." In *Handbook of American Folklore,* edited by Richard M. Dorson and Inta Gale Carpenter, 434–40. Bloomington: Indiana University Press.

Halbett, Garth. 1967. *Wittgenstein's Definition of Meaning as Use.* New York: Fordham University Press.

Hallberg, Robert von, ed. 1983–84. "Canons." *Critical Inquiry* 10, no. 1:1–223; no. 2:321–47; no. 3:462–542.

Handler, Richard, and Jocelyn Linnekin. 1984. "Tradition, Genuine or Spurious." *Journal of American Folklore* 97, no. 385:273–90.

Hartland, E. Sidney. 1885. "The Science of Folk-Lore." *The Folk-Lore Journal* 3, no. 2:115–21.

———. 1891. *The Science of Fairy Tales: An Inquiry into Fairy Mythology.* London: Walter Scott.

———. 1899. *Folklore: What Is It and What Is the Good of It?* Popular Studies in Mythology, Romance and Folklore, no. 2. London: David Nutt. Reprinted in *Peasant Customs and Savage Myths: Selections from the British Folklorists,* ed. Richard M. Dorson (Chicago: Chicago University Press, 1968), 1:233.

Hautala, Jouko. 1969. *Finnish Folklore Research, 1828–1918.* Helsinki: Societas Scientiarum Fennica.

Herskovits, Melville J. 1948. *Man and His Works: The Science of Cultural Anthropology.* New York: Knopf.

Herzfeld, Michael. 1982. *Ours Once More: Folklore, Ideology, and the Making of Modern Greece.* Austin: University of Texas Press.

96 | *Folklore Concepts*

Hobsbawm, Eric, and Terence Ranger, eds. 1983. *The Invention of Tradition*. Cambridge: Cambridge University Press.

Holbek, Bengt. 1983. "Final Discussion: On the Analytical Value of the Concept of Tradition." In "Nordic Research in Popular Prose Narrative," edited by Lauri Honko and Pekka Laaksonen, 240–42. *Studia Fennica* 27. Helsinki: Suomalainen Kirjallisuuden Seura.

Honko, Lauri. 1983. "Research Traditions in Tradition Research." *Studia Fennica* 27:13–22.

——— et al. 1983. "On the Analytical Value of the Concept of Tradition." *Studia Fennica* 27: 233–49.

Hultkrantz, Ake. 1960. *International Dictionary of Regional European Ethnology and Folklore. Volume 1: General Ethnological Concepts*. Copenhagen: Rosenkilde and Bagger.

Hyman, Stanley Edgar. 1955. "T. S. Eliot and Tradition in Criticism." In *The Armed Vision: A Study in the Methods of Modern Literary Criticism*, 73–105. New York: Vintage Books.

Hymes, Dell. 1975. "Folklore's Nature and the Sun's Myth." *Journal of American Folklore* 88, no. 350:345–69.

Ives, Edward D. 1964. *Larry Gorman: The Man Who Made the Songs*. Bloomington: Indiana University Press.

———. 1971. *Lawrence Doyle: The Farmer-Poet of Prince Edward Island*. Maine Studies, no. 92. Orono: University of Maine Press.

———. 1978. *Joe Scott: The Woodsman-Songmaker*. Urbana: University of Illinois Press.

———. 1983. "The Study of Regional Songs and Ballads." In *Handbook of American Folklore*, edited by Richard M. Dorson and Inta Gale Carpenter, 208–15. Bloomington: Indiana University Press.

Jacobes, Melville. "Review of *Our Living Traditions: An Introduction to American Folklore* by Tristram Potter Coffin." *American Anthropologist* n.s., 72, no. 2 (1970): 434–35.

Jay, Martin. 1973. *The Dialectical Imagination: A History of the Frankfurt School and the Institute of Social Research, 1923–1950*. Boston: Little Brown.

Kroeber, A. L. 1917. "The Superorganic." *American Anthropologist* 19, no. 2:163–213.

Kroeber, A. L., and Clyde Kluckhohn. 1952. *Culture: Critical Review of Concepts and Definitions*. Cambridge, MA: Peabody Museum.

Leach, Maria, and Jerome Fried., eds. 1949. "Folklore." In *Funk and Wagnalls Standard Dictionary of Folklore, Mythology and Legend*, 1:398–403. New York: Funk and Wagnalls.

Lerner, Daniel. 1958. *The Passing of Traditional Society: Modernizing the Middle East*. Glencoe, IL: Free Press.

Linnekin, Jocelyn. 1983. "Defining Tradition: Variations on the Hawaiian Identity." *American Ethnologist* 10, no. 2: 241–52.

Lowenthal, Leo. 1957. "Historical Perspectives of Popular Culture." In *Mass Culture: The Popular Arts in America*, edited by Bernard Rosenberg and David Manning White, 46–57. New York: Free Press.

MacDonald, Dwight. 1957. "A Theory of Mass Culture." In *Mass Culture: The Popular Arts in America*, edited by Bernard Rosenberg and David Manning White, 59–73. New York: Free Press.

Naumann, Hans. 1929. *Grundzüge der deutschen Volkskunde*. 2nd ed. Leipzig: Quell and Meyer. Originally published in 1922.

Neuberg, Victor E. 1977. *Popular Literature: A History and Guide*. Harmondsworth: Penguin.

[Newell, William W.] 1888a. "The Necessity of Collecting the Traditions of the Native Races." *Journal of American Folklore* 1, no. 2:162–63.

———. 1888b. "On the Field and Work of a Journal of American Folk-Lore." *Journal of American Folk-Lore* l, no. 1:3–7.

——. 1895. "Folk-Lore Study and Folk-Lore Societies." *Journal of American Folklore* 8, no. 30:231–42.

Nielsen, Eduard. 1954. *Oral Tradition*. London: SCM Press.

Paredes, Américo. 1968. "Tributaries to the Mainstream: The Ethnic Groups." In *Our Living Traditions: An Introduction to American Folklore*, edited by Tristram P. Coffin, 70–80. New York: Basic Books.

Paredes, Américo, and Richard Bauman, eds. 1972. *Toward New Perspectives in Folklore*. American Folklore Society Bibliographical and Special Series, vol. 23. Austin: University of Texas Press.

Paredes, Américo, and Ellen J. Stekert. 1971. *The Urban Experience and Folk Tradition*. American Folklore Society, Bibliographical and Special Series, vol. 22. Austin: University of Texas Press.

Parry, Adam, ed. 1971. *The Making of Homeric Verse: The Collected Papers of Milman Parry*. Oxford: Clarendon.

Pelikan, Jaroslav. 1984. *The Vindication of Tradition*. New Haven: Yale University Press.

Periman, Ken. 1969. "Review of *Our Living Traditions: An Introduction to American Folklore*, edited by Tristram P. Coffin. New York: Basic Books, 1968." *Journal of American Folklore* 82, no. 323:83–84.

Pocock, J. G. A. 1968. "Time, Institutions and Action: An Essay of Traditions and Their Understanding." In *Politics and Experience: Essays Presented to Professor Michael Oakeshott on the Occasion of His Retirement*, edited by Preston King and B. C. Parekh, 209–38. London: Cambridge University Press.

Pollard, Sidney. 1968. *The Idea of Progress: History Society*. Harmondsworth: Penguin.

Rearick, Charles. 1974. *Beyond the Enlightenment: Historians and Folklore in Nineteenth-Century France*. Bloomington: Indiana University Press.

Redfield, Margaret. 1956. "The Expressive Utterance, Folk and Popular." *Journal of American Folklore* 69, no. 274:357–62.

——, ed. 1962. *Human Nature and the Study of Society: The Papers of Robert Redfield*. 1:392–414. Chicago: University of Chicago Press.

Redfield, Robert. 1956. *Peasant Society and Culture: An Anthropological Approach to Civilization*. Chicago: University of Chicago Press.

——. 1962. "Civilizations as Cultural Structures." In *Human Nature and the Study of Society: The Papers of Robert Redfield*, edited by Margaret Park Redfield, 1:392–414. Chicago: University of Chicago Press. Originally delivered as a lecture on February 6, 1956, at the Center for Advanced Study in the Behavioral Sciences, Stanford, California.

Richmond, W. Edson. 1983. "Introduction." In *Handbook of American Folklore*, edited by Richard M. Dorson and Inta Gale Carpenter, xi–xix. Bloomington: Indiana University Press.

Rioux, Marcel. 1950. "Folk and Folklore." *Journal of American Folklore* 63, no. 248:192–98.

Royce, Anya Peterson. 1982. *Ethnic Identity: Strategies of Diversity*. Bloomington: Indiana University Press.

Rudolph, Lloyd I., and Susanne H. 1967. *The Modernity of Tradition*. Chicago: University of Chicago Press.

Rudolph, Susanne H. 1979. "Beyond Modernity and Tradition: Theoretical and Ideological Aspects of Comparative Social Sciences." In *Tradition and Politics in South Asia*, edited by R. J. Moore, 17–31. New Delhi: Vikas.

Sammons, Jeffrey L. 1977. *Literary Sociology and Practical Criticism*. Bloomington: Indiana University Press.

Sapir, E. 1917. "Do We Need a 'Superorganic'?" *American Anthropologist* 19, no. 3:441–47.

Seeger, Charles. 1950. "Oral Tradition in Music." In *The Funk and Wagnalls Standard Dictionary of Folklore, Mythology, and Legend,* edited by Maria Leach and Jerome Fried, 2:825–29. New York: Funk and Wagnalls.

Shils, Edward. 1981. *Tradition.* Chicago: University of Chicago Press.

Singer, Milton B. 1959. *Traditional India, Structure and Change.* American Folklore Society, Bibliographical and Special Series, vol. 10. Philadelphia: American Folklore Society. Previously published as a special issue, *Journal of American Folklore* 71, no. 281 (1958): 191–518.

———. 1972. *When a Great Tradition Modernizes: An Anthropological Approach to Indian Civilization.* New York: Praeger.

Slater, Candace. 1982. "The Hairy Leg Strikes: The Individual Artist and the Brazilian Literatura de Cordel." *Journal of American Folklore* 95, no. 375:51–89.

Smith, Barbara H. 1983. "Contingencies of Value." *Critical Inquiry* 10, no. 1:1–35.

Stekert, Ellen J. 1970. "Foreword." *Journal of American Folklore* 83, no. 328:iii–iv. Reprinted in Paredes and Stekert (1971, 11–12).

Stromback, Dag. 1971. *Leading Folklorists of the North: Biographical Studies.* Oslo: Universitetsforlaget.

Taylor, Archer. 1946. "The Problems of Folklore." *Journal of American Folklore* 59, no. 232:101–7.

Thompson, Stith. 1946. *The Folktale.* New York: Holt, Rinehart and Winston.

———. 1951a. "Folklore at Midcentury." *Midwest Folklore* 1, no. 1:5–12.

———. 1951b. Review of *"Selected Papers on Folklore Published on the Occasion of His 70th Birthday. By C. W. v. Sydow.* Copenhagen: Rosenkilde and Bagger, 1948. Pp. 259." *Journal of American Folklore* 64, no. 253:332–33.

———. 1953. "Advances in Folklore Studies." In *Anthropology Today: An Encyclopedic Inventory,* edited by A. L. Kroeber, 587–96. Chicago: University of Chicago Press.

Toelken, Barre. 1967. "An Oral Canon for Child Ballads: Construction and Application." *Journal of the Folklore Institute* 4, no. 1:75–101.

———. 1979. *The Dynamics of Folklore.* Boston: Houghton-Mifflin.

Utley, Francis Lee. 1961. "Folk Literature: An Operational Definition." *Journal of American Folklore* 74, no. 293:193–206. Reprinted in Dundes (1965, 7–24).

Vaihinger, Hans. 1952. *The Philosophy of "As If."* Translated by C. K. Ogden. London: Routledge and Kegan Paul.

Wager, W. Warren. 1972. *Good Tidings: The Belief in Progress from Darwin to Marcuse.* Bloomington: Indiana University Press.

Williams, Raymond. 1961. *The Long Revolution.* London: Chatto and Windus.

Wilson, William A. 1976. *Folklore and Nationalism in Modern Finland.* Bloomington: Indiana University Press.

Wittgenstein, Ludwig. 1953. *Philosophical Investigations.* Translated by G. E. M. Anscombe. New York: MacMillan.

6

A HISTORY OF FOLKLORE
STUDIES—WHY DO WE NEED IT?

To PARAPHRASE WILLIAM JAMES (1907, 198), A NEW theory has three stages:
first it is attacked as absurd; then it is admitted to be true, but obvious and
insignificant; finally, it is seen as indeed important, but not new at all.[1] Then
both its adversaries and champions regard it as an integral part of the history
of ideas and diligently trace the genealogy of its intellectual ancestors and
philosophical kin. The new surge of interest in the history of folklore studies
attests that at long last, our discipline has reached this third developmental
stage (Bell 1973; Dorson 1968a; Dwyer-Schick 1979; Henderson 1975; McNeil
1980; Reuss 1971; Senn 1974, 1975, 1981; Stromback 1971). If nobody else does so,
at least students of folklore claim an intellectual and scholarly tradition for
their discipline that sanctions its scientific identity and confirms its position
in academe.

However, aside from fulfilling this need (which is no less psychological
than scholarly), the inevitable question still lingers: Why do we need a history of folklore? Why should we expose past debates, forgotten failures, and
wished-to-be-forgotten errors, and air them in print again, particularly when
the present tasks of folklore research are rapidly mounting and there are never
enough of us to shoulder them?

No doubt, it would be simplest to dismiss this question with the mountain climber's answer: "Because it is there." Like the top of the mountain, the
history of folklore exists, covered with the clouds of time, awesome, looming
from a growing distance. The discovery of facts and the penetrating scrutiny
of the past could be a challenge to the scholar like the conquest of the peak
and the view from the top are to mountain climbers. But such an answer
reveals the possible hidden shortcomings of historical research rather than
expounds its value. The examination of the history of folklore might provide
simply a new outlet for the obsession with collecting for which our profession

is reputed and ridiculed (Dundes 1962). It could divert the energy of enterprising folklorists from collecting tales, songs, proverbs, and log cabins to the gathering of historical facts. Tediously and laboriously, we would unveil whatever our predecessors tried to conceal, peep into their drawers of correspondence, and collect and classify the facts about past collecting and classifying. By merely transferring earlier methods in folklore research into this newly emerging subject, folklorists could easily fall into the trap of the "chronic fallacy" (Fischer 1970, 152), listing facts that relate to each other only in calendric succession. The resulting narrative would be a chronicle but not a history of folklore (see Croce 1921, 11–26; Collingwood 1946, 202–3; Danto 1965, 112–42; White 1965, 222–70).

After all, folklore scholarship did not succeed, in many respects, in avoiding the pitfalls of method that are analogous to mere chronicling. The accumulations of texts and the construction of indexes have proven usable chroniclers, not historians, of oral tradition. We organize our data according to an arbitrary thematic system that often has nothing to do with the inherent relationships between themes and motifs in the texts themselves. Thompson's statement of purpose is the best testimony regarding the nature of his monumental index. He says, "As a method in folklore, motif-indexing is merely spadework for future research. It is hardly research itself. We are not studying any one of the motifs that are being listed. *The work has the same relation to future folklore research as a dictionary has to the writer of literature, or the map to the explorer who needs to keep his bearing*" (Thompson 1955, 9; my emphasis). Yet, while chronology has been condemned as unfit for the presentation, explanation, and analysis of history, the very equivalent of this method in folklore has long been thought to be one of the cornerstones of scholarship. The formative years of folklore have been devoted to the construction of research tools such as classification systems, indexes, bibliographies, and annotated collections. These were designed to enable the folklorist to be professional, and at the same time, to guard his subject matter from other scholars from all walks of academe, who raided it for their own purposes. But the consuming concern with techniques and instruments resulted in the inevitable neglect of the theories and philosophical issues that originally generated interest in folklore. Consequently, folklore has become a craft, not a science.

Symptomatically, when in a new textbook Dorson wishes to identify the features that set the folklorist apart from "the anthropologist, the historian, the literary critic, the sociologist, the psychologist, and the political scientist," he discusses the folklorist's *skills*: fieldwork, the use of museums, and the uses of indexes (Dorson 1972b, 5–7). This is particularly revealing since

Dorson sets out to discuss not so much the techniques as the theories of the discipline. The title of the paper "Current Folklore Theories" (Dorson 1963), which is an earlier version of his introduction to the volume of *Folklore and Folklife: An Introduction*, clearly indicates this intention. However, it soon becomes apparent that while the theories of folklore are all borrowed from other disciplines, the techniques are all its own. In fact, in the earlier version of the essay, Dorson identifies some of the theories by the name of the discipline from which they are derived, such as "Anthropological Theory" and "Psychological Theory," and the others—"Comparative Folklore Theories," "National Folklore Theories," and "Structural Folklore Theories"—are closely associated with fields such as history, political science, and linguistics and literature, even if not so named in the title. In the later version of the essay that also incorporates more recent folklore scholarship, Dorson names the theories according to the methods they employ, such as "historical-geographical"; the purpose they serve, such as "historical reconstruction"; or the external use to which they are put, as, for example, "ideological." The ability to neglect the previous conception of folklore theories and to embrace a newer view of them may in itself reflect the maturation process of folklore as a discipline. However, folklorists, and apparently Dorson among them, hardly recognize the new phase to which they themselves have brought the field of folklore. They continue, inadvertently, to condemn their chosen field of study by emphasizing its technical aspects, rather than discussing its salient ideas and unique theoretical problems. On another occasion, instead of defining folklore, Dorson proposes that "we may do better defining the folklorist, and then say that what he studies is folklore. Our premise is that he possesses a set of skills setting him apart from his departmental neighbors in literatures and languages, anthropology, linguistics, history and sociology. No one of these skills may be unique but in totality they do describe the *Gestalt* of a particular kind of scholar" (1968b, 2).

The emphasis on craftsmanship rather than ideas and theories, which underlies our own teaching, became apparent to me in our own program at the University of Pennsylvania. On several occasions, I have tried to include in the PhD qualifying examinations questions about the aims of folklore studies and their relationships to the general understanding of human nature and social conduct. The questions were rejected every single time either by my chairman, who excluded them from the examination, finding them too obscure, or by my students, who simply avoided them.

The intellectual double bind of mastering research tools with no applicable theoretical issues yields frustration, dissatisfaction, and an enormous academic inferiority complex. The attitude of students of folklore toward other disciplines clearly demonstrates this. More than any other group of scholars, folklorists advocate and practice interdisciplinary work. They search for ideas, issues, and theoretical frameworks in anthropology, linguistics, literary criticism, cultural geography, and other social science and humanistic studies. Certainly, the trend toward the breaking down of barriers between disciplines is commendable; however, when it involves only one-sided action, it is a symptom of a low status in the university and not a reflection of liberal scholarly tendencies. A measure for the prestige of academic fields could be made, as Uriel G. Foa suggests, by analyzing "the frequency with which scientists in one discipline quote papers from other disciplines, and relate these findings to the relative status of the discipline involved" (1967, 149). My impression is that folklorists would be likely to quote publications in other fields the most and to be quoted by scholars from these disciplines the least.

The awareness of the low status of folklore among other disciplines results in a tendency to look for scapegoats to blame for this frustrating situation. The most prominent among these is none other than the elusive, allegedly undefinable name of our discipline: folklore. On this very point, a friend wrote me expressing what seems to me a general feeling that is discussed but rarely written down: "Folkloristics, unlike semiotics today (or linguistics twenty years ago) is not emerging; it has emerged; and folkloristics, unlike semiotics or linguistics, is not likely to attract financial backers on the basis of the 'charisma' or connotations of the word *folkloristics* (or *folklore studies* or even *folklore and mythology studies*) alone" (Personal communication, October 8, 1972).[2] Finding fault with the term is like blaming the dress when it is the bride who is actually ugly. Linguistics or semiotics, fashionable as the terms might be, address themselves to subjects and issues that have long occupied human thought. If we are to develop folklore from craft to science, a change of name could at most be likened to the magical practices that we study. This would not suffice. We must infuse our discipline with ideas, be able to pose problems in general terms, and seek solutions on the basis of research. The need for such a change in the course of our studies and the conception of our discipline is particularly urgent now, in the postinstrumentalization era of folklore; yet in order to regenerate folklore research, we have to reach no further than the preinstrumentalization stage of the discipline, examining the ideas that initially gave rise to the interest in folklore.

The roots of folklore studies reside in the fertile ground of the seventeenth- and early eighteenth-century's thought and art; some extend back in time even further. Romanticism and nationalism, the literary and political movements with which folklore is commonly associated, were but the last phases in its emergence. The Russian formalist Mikhail Bakhtin observes correctly that "the narrow concept of popular character and folklore was born in the pre-Romantic period and was basically completed by von Herder and the Romantics" (1968, 4) Although the speculative solutions of the Renaissance and the Enlightenment philosophers need no revival at present, the fundamental questions they posed about the nature of belief and history, language and the imagination, and man, nature, and society are crucial to our inquiry today. The challenge they provide to folklore studies should be met with modern concepts, methods, and theoretical formulations. The study of the history of folklore would then restore to the discipline the perspective of ideas we lost in developing the tools for research.

Of course, the epoch that began with the Brothers Grimm's recording of tales from oral tradition and ended with Thompson's monumental indexing of these and other available texts was not unified. The students of folklore during that era had their share of ideas and theories, but the emphasis of scholarship was on creating tools for folklore. Now that the tools exist, there is again a demand and a desire among folklorists to meet the challenge of ideas and to reexamine established premises. The study of the history of folklore studies could extend the range of theoretical issues with which we deal well beyond the formative years into the preparadigmatic period of the discipline and bring into modern studies problems we sidetracked because of the concern with techniques. It also could lift folklore as a discipline from the position of academic marginality and relocate it in the midst of the main core of the intellectual discourse about the nature of man.

Some folklorists have sought other means to achieve this last goal. The current interest in applied folklore (Sweterlitsch 1971) is nothing but an honest attempt to make our research relevant to the urgent social issues of today, to find practical ends for theoretical investigation. Thus, if applied folklore relates our studies to the needs of society, the quest into the history of folklore reestablishes the ties between our discipline and the major ideas of men about man.

But the history of folklore does not only fulfill present needs. It is a subject of study in and of itself. The complex social relationships between the students of folklore and their subjects, the intersection of different disciplines, and popular and political movements in our field constitute a still hardly explored chapter in the history of science. The solution to the deceptively simple question "Who studies whom?" becomes a complex narrative when there is an accounting for the historical variables of period, country, and ethnic groups. The impression that the biographies of the Grimm brothers and the history of British folklore yield is that folklore is basically intellectual slumming; the middle- and upper-class people study those whom they regard as socially inferior (Dorson 1968a; Ginschel 1967; Michaelis-Jena 1970; Peppard 1971). The motivation that initiates these social relationships is not necessarily related to class consciousness or to a derogatory attitude toward the subjects of research. On many occasions, because of the romantic-nationalistic premises on which folklore research is founded, scholars express adulation for the simple, unsophisticated narrators and singers. But by and large, in that area, we lack details and cannot yet establish general patterns of behavior examining the social relations and attitudes of folklorists to their informants. So far, we have at our disposal anecdotal information, and in such cases the exception rather than the rule stands out, as, for example, a second-generation Jewish immigrant from Brooklyn who studies not his own culture, but that of the Scottish poor. The sociology of our own discipline has, thus, an historical dimension. Its exploration has direct bearing on the ideas and theories we formulate, because in many cases, these are direct consequences of research situations and field experiences (Nash and Wintrob 1972).

The social interaction between the student and his subject is but a single parameter of relations; we cannot, and should not, conceive of the activity of the researcher in terms of the class structure of a society. Academic disciplines and traditions have affected our approaches to the study of folklore and constitute a changing network of relationships that deserve study as well. The papers from a panel on folklore history have direct bearing on this aspect of the history of folklore, and they reflect some of the major developments in the field in the United States.[3] Naturally, they do not represent all the formative trends in the early days of folklore scholarship. Missing, for example, are discussions of the activities in the recording and study of folklore along ethnic, regional, and occupational boundaries. The impressive quantity of folklore publications that followed the Federal Writers' Project involvement in recording oral traditions has affected the course of folklore as an academic discipline and both directly and indirectly shaped the interests of many American folklorists (Mangione 1972, 265–85; Botkin 1939, 7–14; 1946, 252–63). Similarly, the negative and positive influence that popularization has had on the recognition of folklore as an academic discipline deserves a fuller analysis (Dorson 1962). As recent studies clearly demonstrate, folklore, perhaps to a greater extent than any other social science and humanistic discipline, is interrelated with nonacademic trends of thought and action. The ideas of Herder that initially stimulated folklore research in Europe and affected the literary awareness of "the folk" in America in modern times were transformed into ideologies of political movements on the right and the left (Bluestein 1972; Denisoff 1971, 1972; Emmerich 1971; Reuss 1971). The complex historical relations between social propaganda and methodological research should be faced and thoroughly analyzed in historical terms.

M. Carole Henderson (1975) touches on this problem in the Canadian context. She aptly demonstrates that folklore studies constitute an open system, which is susceptible to the influence of social and political events. The folklore paradigm should be examined within the larger social context of scientific research (Kuhn 1962; Masterman 1970).

Yet most of the papers in this panel revolve around the very process of paradigm formation in folklore; that is, they narrate the attempts to lay the foundations for research in terms of the identification and selection of a unique subject matter, the construction of a theoretical framework, and the proposal of methodological procedures. They also describe the process of institutionalization of folklore in social and academic contexts. The significance of this last aspect of the organization of scientific activity did not escape the founding fathers of folklore in America. They well understood that control over institutions would allow them to regulate, systematize, and administrate research and publication; hence the fierce clashes of personalities that Michael Bell (1973) and Regna Darnell (1973) describe in their respective papers illustrate the conflict between scientific trends and trends of thought. Their papers tell the creation story of folklore in America, describing the battles between intellectual ancestors and demigods. But strangely enough, unlike the mythical narratives to which we are all accustomed, the defeated camp survived the battle and ended up dominating the field for many years to come.

As Bell and Darnell relate, the American Folklore Society held a central position during the struggle over the direction of research and served as a power base for Boas and Newell, from which they conducted their respective intellectual battles. Each had his own vested interest in the Society. On the one hand, Boas fought the anthropological establishment of Boston and Washington and promoted his own theories and students through the Society (Stocking 1968, 195–233). On the other hand, Newell challenged the purely literary direction of the Chicago Folklore Society headed by Bassett. The combined forces of Boas and Newell left on the American Folklore Society the imprint of anthropological theories. Thoresen (1973) shows in his paper that this orientation enabled Kroeber to carry out anthropological-folkloristic research that was at the time at the vanguard of social and scientific theory.

Like many other disciplines in the United States, folklore had not one, but two forms of institutionalization: the learned societies and the university departments and centers. Boas and Newell controlled the Society, but their ambition, particularly that of Boas, was to establish authority over university research and teaching. Indeed, in due time, Boas achieved his goal in anthropology, but folklore lagged behind and only many years later gained a stronghold at the university. Actually, there is a gap of over fifty years between the founding of the American Folklore Society in 1888 and the establishment of the first degree-granting program in folklore at Indiana University in 1949 (see Anon. 1949, 193; Baker 1971; Boggs 1940, 1945; Dorson 1950, 1951, 1963, 1972a).

Nevertheless, sporadic instruction in folklore, with differing degrees of intensity and concentration, took place at various universities throughout that period. Many of these courses, however, reflected the literary orientation that Bassett and the Chicago Folklore Society advocated, rather than the anthropological direction that Newell and Boas pursued. The support of the literary camp came from a third party, hardly involved in the battle between the societies, namely Francis J. Child, a Chaucerian who is remembered mostly because of the ballads he canonized. Most of the university courses are related directly and indirectly to his teaching at Harvard at the end of the nineteenth century and the courses offered by his disciple, George Lyman Kittredge, following in the footsteps of his teacher. As Linda Morely has suggested to our panel, Child arrived at folklore studies and ballad research through his interest in medieval English literature, and the literary approach continued to dominate the writings and teachings in folklore of both scholars. When Stith Thompson and Archer Taylor studied with Kittredge at Harvard during the second decade of the twentieth century, they continued in the tradition already established there. Their transference of scholarly allegiance to the Finnish method in folklore research presented no conflict, since the historic-geographic approach likewise was partly an outgrowth of literary interest in folklore tradition. These two scholars exerted major influence on the direction of folklore teaching at American universities, and they established instruction on literary, not anthropological, foundations. Thus, while the anthropological approach remained dominant in the American Folklore Society itself for many years, it was the literary approach, heralded by Bassett and the Chicago Folklore Society, that was the dominant force at the universities. The impact of this tradition can be noticed still today, as most folklore courses are given in literature rather than anthropology departments (Baker 1971).

The struggle over the control of the centers of scholarly activities should not overshadow the role of the individual in the advancement of a discipline. It provides but a partial picture of the scholarly activity of a period, especially a performative one. By the selection of his subject, the contribution of Phillips Barry to folklore, Alvey (1973) is able to underscore this very point. He demonstrates the import of the rebelling, nonconformist scholar, the individual who has obligations to none and is free of responsibility to institutions and their scientific norms. Phillips Barry was able thus to explore new theories and methods, to challenge authorities, and to speculate imaginatively, thereby breaking new grounds for research.

The biographical focus of most of the papers presented at this panel does not and should not disguise the purpose of explorations into the history of folklore studies, namely the examination of the theories and ideas that underlie the research activities in different periods of folklore scholarship. While the unfolding of a biography could easily drift into anecdotal narration, when properly developed, it provides a description of intellectual development not as thought but as an experience (Gruber 1966; Holton 1970).[4] A study of that genre, as the present examples illustrate, underscores the intellectual activity of the past as a human involvement, affected by the intricacies of personal interactions, the frustrations of failure, and the elation with success. These essays offer keys to the understanding of a context much larger than themselves; at the same time, they constitute modalities of intellectual growth that both individually and collectively shaped the forms of folklore scholarship.

Notes

1. My paraphrase does not match the wit and wisdom of the original text, the last sentence of which reads, "Finally it is seen so important that its adversaries claim that they themselves discovered it."

2. Letter of October 8, 1972.

3. A panel on "The Historiography of Folklore" at the 1972 Annual Meeting of the American Folklore Society in Austin Texas.

4. See also see the special issue "The Making of Modern Science: Biographical Studies," *Daedalus* 99, no. 4 (Fall 1970).

Bibliography

Alvey, Gerald. 1973. "Phillips Barry and Anglo-American Folksong Scholarship." *Journal of the Folklore Institute* 10, no. 1/2:67–95.

Anon. 1949. "Folklore News." *Journal of American Folklore* 62, no. 244:193–95.

Baker, Ronald L. 1971. "Folklore Courses and Programs in American Colleges and Universities." *Journal of American Folklore* 84, no. 332:221–29.

Bakhtin, Mikhail. 1968. *Rabelais and His World*. Translated by Helene Iswolsky. Cambridge, MA: MIT Press.

Bell, Michael J. 1973. "William Wells Newell and the Foundation of American Folklore Scholarship." *Journal of the Folklore Institute* 10, no. 1/2:7–21.

Bluestein, Gene. 1972. *The Voice of the Folk: Folklore and American Literary Theory*. Amherst, MA: University of Massachusetts Press.

Boggs, Ralph Steele. 1940. "Folklore in University Curricula in the United States." *Southern Folklore Quarterly* 4:93–109.

———. 1945. "The Development of Folklore in a University." In *Studies in Language and Literature*, ed. George R. Coffman, 106–11. University of North Carolina Sesquicentennial Publications. Chapel Hill: University of North Carolina Press.

Botkin, A. 1939. "WPA and Folklore Research: 'Bread and Song.'" *Southern Folklore Quarterly* 3:7–14.

———. 1946. "Living Lore on the New York City Writers' Project." *New York Folklore Quarterly* 2:252–63.

Croce, Benedetto. 1921. *History: Its Theory and Practice*. Translated by Douglas Ainslie. New York: Harcourt, Brace and Co.

Collingwood, R. G. 1946. *The Idea of History*. London: Clarendon.

Danto, Arthur C. 1965. *Analytical Philosophy of History*. Cambridge: Cambridge University Press.

Darnell, Regna. 1973. "American Anthropology and the Development of Folklore Scholarship: 1890–1920." *Journal of the Folklore Institute* 10, nos. 1/2:223–39.

Denisoff, R. Serge. 1971. *Great Day Coming: Folk Music and the American Left*. Music in American Life. Urbana: University of Illinois Press.

———. 1972. *Sing a Song of Social Significance*. Bowling Green: Bowling Green University Popular Press.

Dorson, Richard M. 1950. "The Growth of Folklore Courses." *Journal of American Folklore* 63, no. 249:345–59.

———. 1951. "Folklore Studies in the United States Today." *Folklore* 62, no. 3:353–66.

Dorson, Richard M. 1962. "Folklore and the National Defense Education Act." *Journal of American Folklore* 75, no. 296:160–64.

———. 1963a. "The American Folklore Scene, 1963." *Folklore* 74, no. 3:433–49.

———. 1963b. "Current Folklore Theories." *Current Anthropology* 4, no. 1:93–112.

———. 1968a. *The British Folklorists: A History*. Chicago: University of Chicago Press.

———. 1968b. "The Techniques of the Folklorist." *Louisiana Folklore Miscellany* 11:1–23. Reprinted in Dorson (1972c, 11–32).

———. 1972a. "The Academic Future of Folklore." *Journal of American Folklore Supplement*, 104–10. Reprinted in Dorson (1972b, 295–304).

———, ed. 1972b. *Folklore and Folklife: An Introduction*. Chicago: University of Chicago Press.

———. 1972c *Folklore: Selected Essays*. Bloomington: Indiana University Press.

Dundes, Alan. 1962. "On the Psychology of Collecting Folklore." *Tennessee Folklore Society Bulletin* 28: 65–74.

Dwyer-Schick, Susan. 1979. "The American Folklore Society and Folklore Research in America, 1888–1940." PhD diss. University of Pennsylvania.

Emmerich, Wolfgang. 1971. *Zur Kritik der Volkstiimsideologie*. Frankfurt am Main: Suhrkamp Verlag.

Fischer, David H. 1970. *Historians' Fallacies: Toward a Logic of Historical Thought*. New York: Harper and Row.

Foa, Uriel G. 1967. "Differentiation in Cross-Cultural Communication." In *Communication: Concepts and Perspectives*, edited by Lee Thayer, 135–51. Washington: Spartan Books; London: Macmillan.

Ginschel, Gunhild. 1967. *Der junge Jacob Grimm, 1805–1819.* Deutsche Akademie der Wissenschaften zu Berlin, Veroffentlichungen der Sprachwissenschaftlichen Kommission 7 Berlin: Akademie.

Gruber, Jacob. 1966. "In Search of Experience: Biography as an Instrument for the History of Anthropology." In *Pioneers of American Anthropology: The Uses of Biography*, edited by June Helm, 5–27. The American Ethnological Society Monograph 43. Seattle: University of Washington Press.

Henderson, M. Carole. 1975. "Many Voices: A Study of Folklore Activities in Canada and Their Role in Canadian Folklore." PhD diss. University of Pennsylvania.

Holton, Gerald. 1970. "Introduction to the Issue: 'The Making of Modern Science, a Biographical Approach." In "The Making of Modern Science: Biographical Studies." Special issue, *Dædalus* 99, no. 4:723–29.

James, William. 1907. *Pragmatism: A New Name for Some Old Ways of Thinking.* New York: Longmans, Green and Co.

Kuhn, Thomas S. 1970. *The Structure of Scientific Revolutions.* 2nd ed. Chicago: University of Chicago Press.

McNeil, William K. 1980. "A History of American Folklore Scholarship before 1908." PhD diss. Indiana University.

Mangione, Jerre. 1972. *The Dream and the Deal: The Federal Writers' Project, 1935–1943.* Boston: Little, Brown and Company.

Masterman, Margaret. 1970. "The Nature of a Paradigm." In *Criticism and the Growth of Knowledge*, edited by Imre Lakatos and Alan Musgrave, 59–89. Cambridge: Cambridge University Press.

Michaelis-Jena, Ruth. 1970. *The Brothers Grimm.* New York: Praeger.

Nash, Dennison, and Ronald Wintrob. 1972. "The Emergence of Self-Consciousness in Ethnography." *Current Anthropology* 13, no. 5:527–42.

Peppard, Murray B. 1971. *Paths Through the Forest: A Biography of the Brothers Grimm.* New York: Holt, Rinehart and Winston.

Reuss, Richard A. 1971. "American Folklore and Left-Wing Politics, 1927–57." PhD diss. Indiana University.

Senn, Harry A. 1974. "Arnold Van Gennep: Structuralist and Apologist for the Study of Folklore in France." *Folklore* 85, no. 4:229–43.

———. 1975. "Gaston Paris as Folklorist (1867–1895): The Rise and Decline of French Folklore Studies." *Journal of the Folklore Institute* 12, no. 1:47–56.

———. 1981. "Folklore Beginnings in France: Académie Celtique, 1804–1813." *Journal of the Folklore Institute* 18, no. 1:23–33.

Stocking, George W. Jr. 1968. *Race, Culture and Evolution: Essays in the History of Anthropology.* New York: Free Press.

Stromback, Dag., ed. 1971. *Leading Folklorists of the North: Biographical Studies.* Oslo: Universitetsfolaget.

Sweterlitsch, Dick, ed. 1971. *Papers on Applied Folklore.* Folklore Forum Bibliographic and Special Series, no. 8. Bloomington: Folklore Institute, Indiana University.

Thompson, Stith. 1955. *Narrative Motif-Analysis as a Folklore Method*, FFC, 161. Helsinki: Suomalainen Tiedeakatemia.

Thoresen, Timothy H. H. 1973. "Folkloristics in A. L. Kroeber's Early Theory of Culture." *Journal of the Folklore Institute* 10, no. 1/2:41–55.

White, Morton. 1965. *Foundations of Historical Knowledge.* New York: Harper and Row.

7

THE CONCEPT OF MOTIF IN FOLKLORE

Introduction

Motif has become a distinctive concept in folklore. The ability to use Stith Thompson's *Motif Index of Folk Literature* is, according to Richard Dorson (1972, 6), a skill that is indispensable to the folklorist and the defining trait that separates him from all other students of culture. Yet, in spite of the deep impression that the term has made on our discipline, the concept that it represents has remained vague and varied, subject to abuse and rebuke, and has often been regarded as an obstacle rather than a vehicle for research (Greenway 1964, 291–2; Dundes 1962; Jacobs 1966, 423; Grambo 1976, 251).[1] However, there are now hints that suggest renewed interest in the idea of motif. Some of them come from the same ranks of the structural-formalist folklorists who were the most hostile critics of this concept; others expand its application to biblical studies and classical and medieval epics (Bynum 1978, 79–81; Doložel 1972; Duggan 1973, 160–212; Grambo 1976; Meletinsky et al. 1974, 73–139; Meletinsky 1977; Nagler 1974, 64–130; Warshaver 1972). Before these novel voices are lost in the waves of trends and countertrends, and lest their sound turns into a whimper, we should review the emergence and fall of the concept of motif in folklore, examine the reasons why the historic-geographic school adopted the concept in the first place, compare it with the historically available alternatives, and analyze the qualities that made motif a superior concept. Once the diverse usages and meanings of the concept of motif outside folklore are clarified, it will be possible to examine the transformation of the concept within the discipline of folklore itself. As a result of such a theoretical historical survey, we will be in a better position to assess the importance and usefulness of the concept of motif in current folklore studies and to respond effectively to future developments in this direction.

Minimal Narrative Units and the Historic-Geographic Method

The historic-geographic method evolved in Finland as a nationalistic and imperial response to nineteenth-century speculative controversies about folktale origins (Krohn 1971, 4–5, 174–47; Hautala 1969; Wilson 1976, 53–66). It purported to depose specific countries, such as India, Greece (Benfey 1859; Deslongchamps 1838; Thompson 1946, 15–16, 373–79),[2] or the Middle East (Cosquin 1922), or specific stages of evolution—either savagery, barbarism, or civilized life (Hartland 1891; Lang 1884, xli–lxx; MacCulloch 1905)—from their privileged position as the sole source of all folktales. In order to achieve these objectives, the historic-geographic school set as its research goal the discovery, or rather recovery, of the original form (*Ur*-form) of each known folktale as it was created in a distinct time and place, tracing back the migration routes and thematic transformations of its narrative elements.

Essential for the success of this research method was first, the identification and classification of all internationally known tales, and second, the delineation, definition, and classification of minimal narrative-units. While the first task was to provide a common frame of reference for the historic-geographic study of narratives (Jason 1970, 1972; Ketner 1976; Krohn 1971, 28–33, 126–34; Thompson 1946, 415, 426), the second task, our present concern, was to offer the basic analytical tools with which it would have been possible to pursue the search for the original forms of the folktale.

Implicit in this analytical procedure is the notion that narratives are formed and change in terms of elementary episodes that over time combine into elaborate tales. Stories, like Locke's ideas, are distinguishable as simple and complex, and the former necessarily evolve into the latter. The primary search on the *Ur*-form trail should unravel this process through a minute analysis of content variations that exist in the texts along the way. The complete tale is too complex and cannot be subjected to the reconstruction of its past unless it is divided into minimal narrative units beforehand. Karl Spiess stated in 1917, and later, in 1924, Kaarle Krohn quoted him with approval, that "the folktale as a whole is too variable in its design to serve as an object for comparison; in addition, the fact that the relationship is often restricted to completely isolated characteristics indicates that those characteristics lead, so to speak, an independent existence, detaching themselves with relative ease from one context and, with equal ease, entering another. They are firmly outlined, have a well-delineated size, and are of a material content that can be characterized with a few words. Therefore, they are manageable enough to be used for comparison studies" (Krohn 1971, 29–30, quoted from Spiess 1917, 37).

Spiess calls these narrative characteristics *motif* (*Motiv*) or *trait* (*Zug*), which are "the smallest thematic units of the *Märchen*" (1917, 37). In spite of Krohn's general agreement with Spiess's methodological approach, they differ in their fundamental idea concerning the ontology of narrative motifs and complete stories and the relationship between them. Spiess regards motifs as context-free units that have an independent existence and therefore have the capacity to enter into innumerable narrative relations. The complex tales represent variations on such combinations between motifs and groups of motifs, and hence, while there is a limited number of motifs, the number of tales is infinite (cf. Hahn 1864, 43).[3]

In contrast, Kaarle Krohn assumes that "every *Märchen* prototype has its own special motifs" (1971, 31) and therefore, the combination of narrative traits has an historical priority over the minimal units themselves. The tale as a whole, however complex it may be, emerges in a distinct time and place. Any resulting similarity between tales is due to historical changes and the transference of motifs from one story to another. Krohn proposes, at least as "a working hypothesis . . . the assumption that virtually every motif originally belonged to some one particular prototype from which it has migrated" (31, 105–6). In either case, the smallest narrative entity remains the basic analytical unit in the pursuit of historical folktale forms.

Different as they are, these two theories about *Märchen* origins established the importance of the minimal narrative unit as an analytical concept in historical-comparative folk tale research. Krohn's *Die folkloristische Arbeitsmethode*—which was both a summative and a programmatic research statement of the Finnish school—fixed the isolatable narrative trait as the research vehicle for the recovery and the reconstruction of prototypical folklore forms and the tracing of their historical changes. Furthermore, as a research program, *Folklore Methodology* aimed at an even more ambitious goal—namely, the establishment of scientific principles for historical folklore research.

For that purpose, the method had two immediate requirements. First, there was a need for a precise, unambiguous definition of the folktale minimal narrative unit, and second, there was a need for a classification system that would enable the organized registration of all these units as they appear in narratives the world over. Theoretically, such a catalogue should have been a list of basic narrative elements that vary as tales diffuse. In practice, Krohn recognized that variations occur not necessarily within the most basic elements, but rather within major narrative divisions such as "episodes" or "formulas." Within them, it is possible to isolate even smaller divisions "that can be called 'factors' (*Momente*). . . . Each small part of a major component contains in turn several *primary* or *foundation* traits that are more precisely characterized by *secondary elements* or *details*" (Krohn 1971, 31). Although Krohn specifically avoids the term *motif* for that purpose, the distinction between it and the smaller narrative divisions is not completely clear, and on occasion, he considers them synonymous (1971, 126–27).

Regardless of vagueness in terminology, for cross-cultural purposes, the primary research need was therefore a list of minimal units to which tales are analyzable on any level and that occur in more than one story. Stith Thompson's *Motif Index of Folk Literature* was to answer this particular need. Thompson based the plan of his *Motif Index* on the assumption, accepted since Linnaeus, that a classification system is the primary prerequisite for transforming any knowledge into a scientific discipline. For that purpose, he employed the concept of the *motif* that was already in use in folklore and was also current in literary and art criticism and scholarship.

The "Story Radicals" of Sabine Baring-Gould

Looked at historically, the concept of motif was not the only one that could have served the purposes of historical-geographic narrative research. Back in 1866, the Reverend Sabine Baring-Gould (1834–1924), a popular and prolific writer (Addison 1947; Baring-Gould 1922, 1925; Purcell 1957) who was "said to have more books to his credit in the British Museum catalogue than any man alive" (Dorson 1968, 295), borrowed the concept of *root* from comparative philology (see Jespersen 1922, 367–95; Pedersen 1931, 1–30; and Robin 1964, 206–13)[4] and proposed it as a minimal narrative unit. "Every language," he argued, "has its primary roots and these roots united together, expanded, somewhat altered with wear-and-tear, become words. The number of radices is fixed. It is small; the words formed from them are innumerable and continually changing. . . . Much the same may be said of household tales. In all nations belonging to the same stock there exist stories resembling each other in many particulars, and differing from each other in others; yet with an unmistakable radical unity about them, which makes it easy to reduce them to a primeval root. Who can doubt" he says, concluding his statement with an example, "that *jardin* and *garden* are identical in significance, though they differ somewhat in spelling and in pronunciation? Sometimes in the same nation one radical had developed into several distinct ideas; as garden and warden: so with stories, they may not resemble each other in much that is superficial, yet a critical eye can often perceive their radical identity" (Baring-Gould 1866, 299–300).

On the basis of these assumptions, Baring-Gould proposed a classification system for story radicals that he lifted, with minimal changes, from
J. G. von Hahn, *Griechische und albanesisclze Märchen* (1864).[5] He divides the
"story radicals" into two groups of "family stories" and "various" themes. The
social relationships are the main concern in the first group, and the supernatural world in the second.

   I. Family Stories
      A. Relating to Husband and Wife
      B. Relating to Parents and Children
      C. Relating to Brothers and Sisters
      D. Relating to Persons Betrothed

   II. Various
      A. Men and the Unseen World
      B. Men Matched with Men
      C. Men and Beast
      D. Luck Depending on the Preservation of Palladium (a statue of Pallas Athene
         whose preservation was believed to ensure the safety of Troy)

This classification system and the concept of story radicals had little
impact on folklore scholarship. William Ralston and Joseph Jacobs revised
and modified his classification (Jacobs 1887, 1914; Ralston 1878, 77–78), but
since neither Stith Thompson nor any of the Finnish scholars relate their own
efforts to Baring-Gould's work, his contribution to narrative analysis and
classification remains, with rare exceptions, mostly unnoticed (Dorson 1965,
xvii; 1968, 295–97, 390). In fact, Baring-Gould's system had a closer affinity in
concept and theory to the Finnish scholars than they later realized or admitted. First, the very effort to construct a closed classification system implies
the idea that there is a finite number of narrative elements, a principle that
Baring-Gould made explicit. Secondly, his notion of "story radicals" as the
narrative kernel anticipates Krohn's ideas about the formation of tales and
the association of motifs with particular stories. Both consider narratives to
develop out of an initial core, the continuous existence of which in all of its
versions is responsible for the similarity between them. Third, the distinction
between thematic centrality and marginality enables Baring-Gould to avoid
the theoretical differences that could be later discerned in the respective ideas
of Krohn and Spiess. Baring-Gould reserved narrative stability for the story
root and admitted free thematic variations into the periphery of the story.

   In spite of these theoretical affinities, the notion of "story radicals" was
not suitable for the needs of historical comparative research. The focus on the
central thematic unit that many narrative versions share in common diverted

attention from the peripheral and volatile story elements that vary from one version to another, yet could offer clues to the tale's history. The appropriate minimal narrative unit should be able to include both constant and variable themes. Change itself should be an optional rather than an obligatory aspect of the unit. The concept of motif, it appears, fulfilled these qualifications.

Motif in German Romanticism

Like the idea of folklore itself, the concept of motif emerged in the writings of the German Romantics. Respectively, the two notions drew on the nationalistic and the aesthetic-psychological currents in Romantic thoughts. The term *motif* (*Motiv*) refers to the motivating elements in the plot, to the causes that activate the characters and advance the narrative. For example, Jean Paul (Johann Paul Richter, 1763–1825) considers motifs, along with plot and character, as the principal elements in the epic, the drama, and the novel. He regards motif as a literary-psychological factor, the motivation that contributes to the plot is development (Paul 1804, §68). Similarly, Johanne August Eberhard (1739–1809) distinguishes between elements (*Gliedern*) and motifs (*Motiven*) as the two categories into which fantasy orders images. Motifs then represent the dynamic relations, the actions and their causes, between elements (Eberhard 1803–5, 1:98).

The term *motif* occurs in the correspondence between Goethe and Schiller (Chamberlain 1910, 2:48, 2:132, 2:146, 2:151, 2:152, 2:181, 2:191, 2:193, 2:271), and the essay "On Epic and Dramatic Poetry" that grew out of this exchange includes a systematic delineation of the kinds of motifs in terms of their effects on the plot. Accordingly, there are five kinds of motifs:

1. Progressive, which advance the action . . .
2. Retrogressive, which draw the action away from its goal . . .
3. Retarding, which delay the progress of the action . . .
4. Retrospective, which introduce into the poem events which happened before the time of the poem.
5. Prospective, which anticipate what will happen after the time of the poem. (Goethe 1921, 101)

The principal criterion for Goethe's classification is that the motifs function within a literary context, without any reference to their themes or genres. Although he attempts to differentiate between epic and drama, the motifs themselves, their subject or form, do not serve as a distinctive feature that separates one form from the other. Rather, they can occur in both genres, since the sole distinction between them is the relation of narrative to time: "An epic poet narrates an event as completely past, while the dramatist presents it as completely present" (Goethe 1921, 100).

However, functional description is still not a substantive definition. Goethe is not clear as to precisely what he means by the term *motif*. In his letters and conversations, the term *motif* appears to have dual, though related, meanings of theme and motivation. He refers to the "death by thirst" motif, to "astrological motifs," and he describes the situation in the *Odyssey* involving the agitation of a woman's heart by the arrival of a stranger as "the loveliest motif" (Goethe 1921, 152,188–93, 48). In *Wilhelm Meister's Apprenticeship*, in a discussion of Hamlet, Wilhelm says, "My project therefore is, not at all to change those first-mentioned grand situations, or at least as much as possible to spare them, both collectively and individually; but with respect to these external, single, dissipated and dissipating *motives* [my emphasis], to cast them all at once away, and substitute a solitary one instead of them" (Goethe 1962, 280).

And later on, in the discussion between Wilhelm Meister and Serio, Wilhelm says, "Hamlet returns; for his wandering through the churchyard perhaps some lucky motive may be thought of" (Goethe 1962, 280). While in these usages of the term *motif* the notion of motivation is implicit, in other cases, the term refers to a specific theme. On February 25, 1824, Eckermann noted, echoing the words of Goethe, "To-day Goethe showed me two very remarkable poems, both highly moral in their tendency, but in their several *motives* so unreservedly natural and true, that they are of the kind which the world styles immoral" (Oxenford 1874, 63). About a year later, on January 18, 1825, Eckermann quotes Goethe, commenting on some poems of a poetess they knew and about whom he wrote an essay: "I have in a few words, characterized these poems according to their chief subjects, and I think you will be pleased with the valuable *motives*." After reading such characterizations as "Modesty of a Servian Girl," "conflict in the mind of a lover," and "The lover comes from abroad, watches her by day, surprises her at night," Eckermann remarked, "These mere motives excited in me such lively emotions, that I felt as if I were reading the poems themselves, and had no desire for the details." Goethe comments in his reply, "No one dreams that the true power of a poem consists in the situation—in the *motives*. And for this very reason, thousands of poems are written, where the *motive* is nothing at all, and which merely through feeling and sounding verse reflect a sort of existence" (Oxenford 1874, 107). In this instance, Goethe employs the term *motif* not only as meaning a theme, but also as a succinct description of a situation. In that sense, he probably reflects an idea of the Italian playwright Carlo Gozzi (1720–1806), who contended that there are thirty-six basic plots to all tragedies. Frederic Soret (1795–1865) noted a comment that Goethe made in a conversation on February 14, 1830: "Gozzi would maintain that there are only six-and-thirty tragical situations. Schiller took the greatest pains to find more, but he did not find even so many as Gozzi" (Oxenford 1874, 439).[6]

All these variations in use and meaning, in fact, do not contradict but complement each other. In Goethe's letters, conversations, and essays, the term *motif* refers to a dramatic situation and its reductive description. The succinct summation of a situation must encapsulate its essential characteristic, and this could be accomplished only by referring to the motivating force, the active cause that moves the characters in the plot. In that sense, motif is not the minimal narrative unit, but the reduction of a narrative to a minimum.

From this perspective, the ultimate motive for action becomes identical with the abstract idea that is dominant in a narrative situation or even, by extension, in the entire work. In the context of Goethe's search for thematic and formal unity in art, the concept of motif relates to the fundamental idea that provides unity to an epic, a drama, or a novel. This notion has become the accepted meaning of *motif*, so much so that a dictionary of aesthetics from that period describes the term as "the mainspring of the plot, the primary cause of the gradually self-realizing operation that the poet . . . must make in order to establish unity" (Jeitteles 1835–37, 2, 98).

As developed by the German Romantics, there is an inherent polarity in the concept of motif, connoting both the minimal and the maximal, the concrete and the abstract aspects of any work. The minimal narrative unit becomes, in this case, the indispensable motive for action, without which the entire story is rendered meaningless. By the virtue of its import, this motive also encapsulates the essential meaning of the work, and hence conveys the abstract idea that the author wishes to express in his poem or story. Since the motive could theoretically be also hidden or implicit, there is no necessary textual representation for the motive, and it could be inferred from the relations between actions and characters, or reconstructed on the basis of interpretation. If art is a world unto itself, then the Romantic motif is its grain of sand.

Ruskin's Aesthetics and the Motif

John Ruskin extricates the concept of motif from the ambiguity in which the polarity of meanings trapped it, but in the process, he reverses the term's connotations. Motif is no longer a minimal unit, either narrative or visual. Rather, for him, motif is "a leading emotional purpose" (Ruskin 1872, 175) of any work of art. He shifts the focus of motif from initial to final causes, and explains art teleologically by its ultimate purpose. Unlike the Romantic notion of motif, the minimal unit does not encapsulate the core idea of a single situation or a whole work, but contributes to its expression. He asserts that "the minutest portion of a great composition is helpful to the whole." In defiance of the imagined reader's incredulity, he states emphatically, "it is inconceivable. But it is a fact" (175).

In accordance with such an approach, every discernible minimal part, be it a line, a color, or a form, contributes to the emotive effect the artwork would have on its viewers. An artist achieves the leading purpose of his artwork by selecting the appropriate "minutest details" and harmoniously relating them to form a whole. "Undulating lines, for instance are expressive of action; and would be false in effect if the motive of the picture was one of repose. Horizontal and angular lines are expressive of rest and strength; and would destroy a design whose purpose was to express disquiet and feebleness. It is therefore necessary to ascertain the motive before descending to the detail" (Ruskin 1872, 175).

Ruskin shifts meanings around, and consequently, he puts even a greater emphasis on the import of the minimal unit. Like Goethe, he considers the motif in terms of its function within the context of the individual artwork, though he relates it to the artistic purpose rather than to the plot progression. He is concerned with aesthetic evaluation and therefore would examine the minimal units in terms of their correlation to each other and correspondence with the purpose of the whole. However, in spite of such specific analysis, Ruskin implicitly assumes that the minimal units have an absolute and general meaning. They are the morphemes of a universal visual language, extending beyond culture and relative perception, and having a definite effect in any context. Motives vary, but the minimal units are constant, limited in number and distinct in their meaning. They enter into unlimited combinations, but to be aesthetically effective, any composition must rely on the meanings inherent in these forms and lines.

Some sixty years later, the art historian Erwin Panofsky (1892–1968) would renew the concept of visual motifs, restoring the term to its earlier meaning of a minimal unit and formulating an analytical framework that was suggestive, though rarely applied systematically (Panofsky 1939, 18–31). But before such development became possible, it was necessary to transfer the term *motif* from the vocabulary of literary criticism and aesthetic evaluation to the terminology and concerns of literary research.

Motif: From Aesthetic Evaluation to Literary Research

The two scholars who laid the foundation for the analytical use of the concept of motif in literature, art, and subsequently folklore research, were Wilhelm

Scherer (1841–86) and Wilhelm Dilthey (1833–1911). Wilhelm Scherer was "the most influential German literary historian in the later [nineteenth] century" (Wellek 1955–92, 4, 297). He proposed applying Comte's positivism to literary history. Like Henry T. Buckle (1821–62) in England (Buckle 1859–66) and Hyppolyte Taine (1828–93) in France (Taine 1863–64, 1865), Scherer sought to establish the relations between society and literature on an empirical basis. According to him, such a study required a precise and rigorous analysis of "heritage, experience, and learning" (*Erbertes, Erlebtes, Erlerntes*)—three concepts that parallel Taine's *la race, le milieu et le moment*—as the three determining factors that influence art and literature of a nation at any given period.[7]

Through the examination of traditional culture, historical experience, and social and religious ideas, Scherer sought to establish empirically the unique character of a nation as it is manifested in language, poetry, and literary history. As a student—and the first biographer—of Jacob Grimm (Scherer 1864, 1865a, 1865b, 1865c), Scherer regarded philology as the science that comprises all the cultural manifestations of a nation, and he wished to demonstrate the validity of this view by the study of German literary history in particular (Scherer 1886). His interest in the uniqueness of a national group logically required the identification of all elements that do not fit the ideal model of the group as inherently foreign to the national ethos. Consequently, there was a need to trace their origin to external sources. In the context of such an endeavor, the concept of motif had a crucial role. Scherer maintained that "the history of the motif was to be pursued carefully, especially with regards to borrowing and parallels" (Wirth 1937, 7; see Scherer 1875, 1–10), since in this way, it would be possible to sift out the alien from the indigenous cultural elements.

Such research requires a clear idea and a precise definition of the nature of motif. For Scherer, who was interested in cultural mores and their literary manifestation, "the doctrine of motifs was primarily a doctrine of cultural ethics" (Scherer 1888, 213). The motif itself was an idea, a topic, a theme, and a subject (212), an abstract notion that had a literary formulation. In narratives and songs, motif was "an elementary unitary part of a poetic theme" (Scherer 1888, 212; see Wellek 1965, 4, 299). But since, according to Scherer, poetry essentially challenges the possible and the probable through "the relationship between action and character" (1888, 214) it is implicit in his "doctrine of motifs" that the unitary part of a theme is such a relationship. The central idea of a literary work that becomes apparent through the relations between actions and characters is, by definition, the main motif (*Hauptmotive*) of a poem, a story, or a drama. But in realization of the fact that a single motif cannot encapsulate the ethical principles of a work in completion, Scherer recognizes also the existence of supplementary motifs (*Nebenmotiven*) that support the principle literary action.

Scherer proposes a classification system of motifs that is based on the possible relationship between action and character. Only an outline, this classification system includes the following categories:

> Relations between Human Beings
> > Unnatural love
> > Natural love to a girl; reciprocal and nonreciprocal
> > [Natural love] to a wife
> > [Natural love] to another man's wife
>
> Marriage
> > Selfishness of man
> > [Selfishness] of wife
> > Devotion of man
> > [Devotion] of wife
> > A wife who refuses her husband (Aristophanes' *Lysistrata*)
> > Mock-marriage
> > Wife accused unjustly
>
> Relations between parents and children
> > King Lear
> > Orestes the mother-killer (Aeschylus, *The Libation Bearers*, 892–1062; *The Eumenides*, 585–613; Euripides, *Orestes*).
> > The father who sacrifices his child (Abraham and Isaac) or executes him (Brutus in Virgil, *Aeneid* 6:817–823)
> > The mother who kills her children (Gretchen in Goethe, *Faust*)
> > Brother-murder (Cain and Abel)
>
> Illicit Liaisons
> Mother-marriage (Oedipus)
> Incest
> Adulterous affair (Phaedra)
> > Brother and sister who unknowingly fall in love with each other (Goethe's "Brother and Sister")
>
> Friendship
> > Friends who pledge their lives for each other (Damon)[8]
> > Good intention with bad results (Carlos in "Clavigo") (Goethe *Clavigo*)
>
> Master and Servant
> > The slave in the Roman theatre
> > The flatterer
> > Don Quixote and Sancho Panza
>
> Mutual sacrifice
> > Servant for the master
> > Wolfdietrich for the people
>
> Relations between individuals, however not between one another, but between a single person and a group, a community, a social circle and their general interests:
> > The hero in his relations with the state, or the people (Codrus, Arminius).[9]

Relations between one people and another:
   Iliad
Relations toward property:
   The miser
Relations toward spiritual matters:
   Toward science (the unsatisfied researcher: Faust)
   Toward justice (Michael Kohlhaas).[10]
   These latest motifs belong to the part of relations of men toward themselves.
Relations to God
   Religious heroes
   Jesus Christ as a literary subject
   Muhammad (Scherer 1888, 214–16)

Such a system, in which social relations are the crucial taxonomic principle, can theoretically serve as an analytical framework for the empirical relationship between literature and society. In different stages of human development, or in different nations, there should be a different distribution of literary motifs reflecting social reality. Unlike the Reverend Sabine Baring-Gould, who used a similar criterion in constructing his classification system, but who designed it for the sole purpose of literary comparisons, Scherer's conception of motifs and their classification, inconsistencies disregarded, allows the delineation of smaller units and the examination of their preponderance in a body of literature.

Scherer assumes motifs to be clearly delineated literary units, each expressing a unitary idea and each corresponding to the cultural-historical heritage, experience, and learning that generate a national literature. In this way, his "doctrine of motifs" is a doctrine of culture, comprising all values as they are represented in literature. According to his view, there is a correspondence between society and literature, and hence it is possible, even necessary, to consider literature as a social document that reflects social-cultural changes. The use of the motif in such an analysis makes it possible to separate indigenous ideas from alien elements.

The Motif in Wilhelm Dilthey's Poetics

In its assumptions and goals, the poetics of Wilhelm Dilthey contrasts sharply with Scherer's theory of literature. Though they were contemporaries, even acquaintances during their student days, and though they both attended Jacob Grimm's lectures in Berlin (Dilthey 1886; Salm 1968, 6), their reaction to the intellectual scholarly trends of the nineteenth century could not have been farther apart. While Scherer applied to literary studies research models developed in the natural and social sciences, Dilthey insisted on the comprehension of "human life in its own terms" (Friess 1929, 11), emphasizing the priority of subject matter over methodology. Only in this way it would be possible, according to him, to account for the complexity, often unobservable, of human life. Still seeking generalizations based on empirical grounds, Dilthey asserts,

> Starting from the most universal concepts of a general methodology the human studies must work towards more definite procedures and principles within their own sphere by trying them out on their own subject-matter, just as the physical sciences have done. We do not show ourselves genuine disciples of the great scientific thinkers simply by transferring their methods to our sphere; we must adjust our knowledge to the nature of our subject-matter and thus treat it as the scientists treated theirs. We conquer nature by submitting to it. The human studies differ from the sciences because the latter deal with facts which present themselves to consciousness as external and separate phenomena, while the former deal with the living connections of reality experienced in the mind. It follows that the sciences arrive at connections with nature through inferences by means of a combination of hypotheses while the human sciences are based on directly given mental connections. We explain nature but we understand mental life. Inner experience grasps the processes by which we accomplish something as well as the combination of individual functions of mental life into a whole. The experience of the whole context comes first; only later do we distinguish its individual parts. This means that the methods of studying mental life, history and society differ greatly from those used to acquire knowledge of nature. (Dilthey 1976,89)

Consistent with his general approach, Dilthey formulates outlines for poetics in which motif functions along with other concepts such as theme (*Stoff*), poetic mood (*poetische Stimmung*), plot (*Fabel*), character (*Charakter*), action (*Handlwzg*), and means of presentation (*Darstellungs-mittel*). The understanding of literature becomes possible through the analysis of all these elements within a particular work. Such an examination illuminates the working of the creative imagination in its psychological dimensions, and would bring insights into the inner mental life of the artist.

Dilthey develops the general concept of motif in terms of a holistic view of the literary work and does not employ the concept for purposes of cultural comparisons, nor does he engage the motif in the cultural-historical reconstruction of the course of evolution.

Unlike Scherer, Dilthey conceives of the poetic process in psychological rather than social evolutionary terms. He does not assume a direct correspondence between the realities of social ethics and cultural beliefs and the realities of literary works. Rather, he considers artistic creativity as a selective process that incorporates into literature only a limited number of situations that are qualitatively unique. Once such situations are within a poetic context, their meaning may change in adjustment to their position within the artistic work and to their relations with the other elements that are active in literature, such as theme, plot, character, and action.

Like his Romantic predecessors, Dilthey considers motifs in terms of dramatic situations. This is the force that both motivates and unifies the action. Like them, he assumes the existence of only a limited number of motifs, and makes provision, like Scherer did, for the occurrence of dominant and supplementary motifs in the same work. But in a clear departure from earlier conceptions of motif, he assumes these situations to be not products of the fictive imagination, but rather actions rooted in life experience.

According to Dilthey, a motif is a situation of life (*Lebensverhiiltnis*) that becomes art. Such a transformation of themes occurs through the effects of various contrasting poetic moods and it is dependent on the artist's ability to grasp the meanings and emotions that the life situation signifies. The motif, then, is a situation of life that has undergone artistic transformation and is subject to the meanings and logical consequences that are brought to bear on it by a unifying poetic motivating force. Dilthey says, "Several motifs are operating with a larger poetic work. Among them one must have the dominant motivating force toward the establishment of a unity within the entire work. The number of possible motives is limited, and it is the task of comparative literary history to describe the development of individual motives" (Dilthey 1922–36, 6:216; see also Makkreel 1975, 194–96; and Müller-Vollmer 1963, 173–74).[11]

In Dilthey's poetics, motif functions in a dual capacity, as a life experience and as its artistic transformation. On the one hand, it is a situation of life that has the potentiality of becoming poetry; on the other hand, it is a situation of life that has already undergone artistic transformation and has acquired additional significance. The concept of motif as an experience is conceived as effecting the psychological process of artistic creativity, while as a literary element, motif is understood in its relationship to other concepts of poetics, as well as to other motifs.

By formulating a theory of poetics that contains this dual function of motif, Dilthey sets up a framework for historical poetics that transcends national, social, and linguistic boundaries, yet remains empirical and substantive. He rationalizes the comparative study of motifs. The quest into the changing artistic perception of reality provides a psychological basis for historical poetics, and the comparative motif analysis demonstrates the differing artistic transformations of similar situations.

Motif as a Folklore Concept

Theoretically, Dilthey's concept of motif and his framework for comparative historical studies would have been most appropriate for the purposes of folklore research and the needs of *Ur*-form reconstruction. The cross-cultural and historical study of individual motifs, either as constant narrative cores or as variable elements in them, is, after all, the basis of the historical-geographical method. Dilthey's recognition of the potential universality of motifs provides for flexibility in the comparative pursuit of original forms. No doubt, a synthesis between compatible aspects of Scherer's and Dilthey's theories of poetry could have been a further methodological improvement. The notion that a motif is an idea expressed in the relations between actions and characters offered a greater degree of precision than the concept of motif as a "situation of life."

In fact, however, neither theory of poetics had a direct effect on folklore research. Only the concept of motif remained to haunt and stimulate students of folktales. During the end of the nineteenth and the beginning of the twentieth centuries, the term *motif* gained popularity, and with it, many of the meanings already discussed, until it lost its analytical value. "The motif," wrote Julius Petersen, "is, in general the most overused, and therefore unclear concept that is employed in the analysis of poetry. No other word has been brought, for no apparent reason, to such use. It is possible to call it a 'sponge word' because it has absorbed and was burdened with all kinds of expressions" (Petersen 1937, 45; cf. Bastide 1962; Boudon 1971; Viet 1965).

No wonder, then, that with the existence of such a conceptual muddle, Stith Thompson pointedly stated on the conclusion of his revision of the *Motif Index of Folk Literature* that this work "is not based on any philosophical principles at all, but mainly on practical experience, on trial and error" (1955, 7). But the avoidance of issues does not make them disappear. The preference for practical solutions over philosophical principles certainly has some useful value, but it is also responsible, partially at least, for the "sterility" and "pointlessness" that Stanley Edgar Hyman finds in the method in general (1948, 485, 495).

Unfortunately, although Thompson opted for a short-term solution to the immediate needs of folklore scholarship, he nevertheless produced a book destined to longevity because, in spite of its flaws, it is an indispensable encyclopedic reference work. He himself regarded his *Motif-Index of Folk Literature* as a mere tool for future research, not research per se, saying, "The work has the same relation to future folklore research as a dictionary has to the writer of literature, or the map to the explorer who needs to keep his bearing"

(Thompson 1955, 9).[12] But the analogy is erroneous. Motifs are not the folk-lore equivalents of words in a language. They are not the items that make up folklore, but only constructed entities that Thompson and his students abstracted and named within a particular body of narrative tradition. While words, or better, morphemes have symbolic meanings in a spoken or written language, motifs are constructed symbols in the language of metafolklore— that is, the discourse of scholars about folklore. Motifs are signs for elements that exist in tales, but not the narrative elements themselves. The delineation and the naming of these narrative units depends completely on the classifica-tion system that Thompson formulated. When Thompson begins to assume that motifs "persist in tradition" (Thompson 1946, 415) he is like Cassirer's "primitive man" who believes in the actual existence of the forces he names (Cassirer 1946, 44–62).

An example could clarify this point. Motif B291.2.1, "Horse as messenger," chosen at random, is a conceptual abstraction based on numerous actions performed by the animal, but in itself is not a minimal narrative unit, occur-ring in any folktale. The motif so named refers to an idea that is expressed in various actions or could be inferred from them, but it does not function in narratives as a word does in a language. Certainly, among the many motifs, there are differing degrees of abstraction, ranging from a summary of specific incidents, such as F1041.1.13.2, "Woman dies of shame at seeing naked man (husband)," to a very general idea, G303.3.3, "The devil in animal form," but in all cases, contra Thompson, the motifs are not the minimal units that tales are made of.

Indeed, Thompson defines motif as "the smallest element in a tale," albeit he adds two modifications, "[(a)] having a power to persist in tradition. In order to have this power it must have [(b)] something unusual and striking about it" (1946, 415). Size is a necessary but no longer sufficient criterion in delineating motifs. In order for this unit to have any value in comparative studies and in the historical reconstruction of tales, it is necessary to add a qualitative requirement to the existing quantitative measure. Only with recurrence in the tradition of at least a single culture, but preferably many cultures, could a theme become part of a historical-geographical study. The continuous existence of a narrative element depends further on a psychologi-cal factor, namely its effect on the narrators and the listeners.

Thompson not only defines but explains the existence of motifs. Basically, he views motif not as the minimal narrative unit, but as the minimal unit in tradition that has the capacity to become part of a narrative. This element is not bound by the particular story in which it appears, since, according to

Thompson's definition, it must occur in several tales before being recognized as motif. Thus the same terms that define the motif also explain its existence.

At this particular point, Thompson implicitly departs from Arthur Christensen's definition of *motif*, in which the psychological aspect contributes to the formulation of a notion of a dynamic, evolving motif (1925, 5). According to Christensen, a motif is the simplest part into which it is possible to analyze a narration, whether historical or fictitious. These narrative elements are episodes that captivate the audience by their strangeness or by their tragic or comic effects. Oddity is thus the inherent quality of the motif that makes its persistence in social memory and tradition possible, an explanation that Thompson adopted. Once a narrative element ceases being at odds with the culture of narrators and audience, it is no longer a motif, and vice versa, episodes that become strange and unusual to the listeners acquire the quality of oddity and transform into motifs:

> We call *motifs* such meaningful elements that are "catching," according to an undefinable psychological law, and which are detached with greater or lesser ease from their primitive connection in order to enter into new combinations. If one compares the narrations of primitive people with the tales of the peoples of a superior civilization, it is possible to see that the primitive narrations that are supposed to be historical accounts, resemble a true story which is composed of elements of simple narrations, in which the motifs properly speaking are absent. At the age of totemism, the talking animals, the magic acts, the transformation of man into animals, the sexual relationships between man and animals were as ordinary and as natural events as in other periods were episodes of war and hunting. However, a trait that at that period was a simple element of a narration, could have become a motif in another degree of civilization in which the transformation and the magical acts and so forth, are considered extraordinary things. (Christensen 1925, 5–6)[13]

Such a shifting concept of motif, in which episodes can change their narrative status depending on their cultural context, was not suitable for a compendium of a universal scope. Therefore, while Thompson incorporated Christensen's idea of strangeness into his definition of motif, he eliminated the principle of cultural relativity that is implied by this feature.

Once having formulated his definition, Thompson (1946) distinguishes among the entire body of motifs three classes of actors, objects, and actions. "First are the actors in a tale—gods, or unusual animals, or marvelous creatures like witches, ogres, or fairies, or even conventionalized human characters like the favorite youngest child or the cruel stepmother. Second come certain items in the background of the action—magic objects, unusual customs, strange beliefs and the like. In the third place there are single incidents—and these comprise the great majority of motifs" (415–6). Alan Dundes has already pointed out that "if motifs can be actors, items, and incidents, then they are hardly units. They are not measures of a single quantity. . . . In addition, the classes of motifs are not even mutually exclusive. Can one conceive of an incident which does not include either an actor or an item, if not both?" (Dundes 1962, 97; see also Grambo 1976, 243–56).

In fact, Thompson's distinction of motif classes appears to be an a posteriori observation rather than an initial basis for classification. In his attempt to introduce order into "the traditional narrative material of the whole earth" (1955–58, 1:10). Thompson follows two separate models of biological and bibliographical classifications. He deliberately avoids the alphabetical ordering of narrative elements as arbitrary, linguistically narrow, and hence of limited use.[14] The classification system that he proposes should have provided folklore with a scientific foundation, like the Linnaean classification had done for biology. At the same time, his notation method, like that of the Library of Congress, should have facilitated registration and retrieval of motifs.

However, the method of classification that resulted from this intended synthesis is no more scientific than any previous system. Most important, the analogy to the biological order of things is a mere illusion. Through his classification, Linnaeus actually discovered an existing order and existing relations in nature. His classification is based on features that are inherent in the species of animals and plants. In contrast, bibliographical classification involves an imposition of order on reality. It is an arbitrary order that depends not on the qualities of the subject, but on external means, like the availability and the shape of signs, like the alphabet that has no intrinsic relation to the subject matter of oral tradition. Utility, convenience and criticism notwithstanding, at the hands of Thompson, the motif was transformed from a minimal unit of narration into a minimal unit of classification. He shifted the concerns with units from their function in the formation and transmission of narratives, and from their relations within the tale context, to a focus on their position in a classification system.

While the attempt to categorize motifs in to classes began with Goethe, as soon as the term gained some conceptual significance, the initial system involved the formulation of relations between minimal units within a narrative or dramatic form. In the course of the nineteenth century, when the diffusion of literary themes and their bearing on culture and society occupied central positions in scholarship, motifs became research tools in the service of broader goals. Thompson never lost the focus of these global aims of folklore scholarship (1964), but in the process of preparing the way for their attainment, the means overtook the ends, creating issues and problems that are still in search of solution.

Motif as a Minimal Folk Narrative Element

The most puzzling and most elusive of these are still the most fundamental problems—namely, the very idea of a minimal narrative unit, its ontology, and its position within a narrative, a poem, a play, or within a tradition at large (Eisler 1929, 2,184–89).[15] Comparative studies and the historic-geographic search for *Ur*-forms cast the motif in a dual perspective. On the one hand, it is the fundamental theme of a story, the primary moving force within a distinct plot; but on the other hand, it is the most elemental narrative particle that has the power to move from one story to another. Motif is "the smallest element of narrative that has the capacity (strength) to exist in transmission" (Lüthi 1962, 18). This definition implies the complete decontextualization of narrative elements. Motifs become the perennial moving elements in inter- and intra-spheres of tradition. They have an equal capacity to enter in and out of narrative combinations. The categorization of motifs as major and supplementary that appeared in previous studies becomes related not to meaning but to the transitory capacity of these narrative elements.

According to Anna Birgitta Rooth, for example, the principal motifs are the least detachable and cannot be omitted from the composition without affecting the essential structure of the story. In contrast, "the detail motifs are those of minor importance; they cleave to the principal motifs but may be eliminated without causing any notable alteration in the plot." A combination of a principal and several detail motifs constitutes a motif complex, which is "the smallest unit of composition within a tale." In Rooth's distinction, only a motif complex, not a motif alone, "may be regarded as being independent, even self-sufficient. The motif is only a single clement in this structure; hence it can neither be preserved nor related in isolation . . . it is at all times dependent on one or more motifs with which it can form a motif-complex or unit" (Rooth 1951, 32–33, see also 237–40).

Similarly, Boris Tomashevsky distinguishes between two types of motifs, those "which cannot be omitted are *bound motifs;* those which may be omitted without disturbing the whole causal chronological course of events are *free motifs*" (1965, 67).

This idea of motifs in musical chairs requires the designation not only of free and bound motifs, but also the consideration of motifs that are in free variation with each other—that is, those that can serve as substitutes in similar narrative contexts. For them, Christensen suggests the term *corresponding motifs* (1925, 6).

The bonds between the moving motifs and their narrative contexts depend on the logical position of the element within the whole. Essence and meaning are no longer a consideration in formulating the relations between a motif and a narrative situation. The idea of motif as an element wandering in the realms of literature cannot involve any semantic connections between an isolatable narrative particle and the entire work.

Consequently, it is necessary to make a terminological and conceptual distinction between actions and meanings. There is no necessary direct relationship between motifs and ideas, actions and meanings. Christensen (1925) distinguishes between the concrete and the abstract aspects of the smallest narrative elements, referring to the first as *motif* and to the second as *theme*: "By the word theme [Christensen] understands the fundamental idea expressed by a motif or a combination of motifs . . . there are tales that have a theme and others that do not. . . . In other tales the theme is secondary, the interest lies mainly in the amusing character of the motifs or the combination of motifs. The more the tale approaches an historical account (voyage adventure, historic legend, local etiology) the more weak is the theme; the more the tale approaches a fable, the more dominant is the theme" (8). It becomes apparent that according to this distinction, the themes are the morals of stories, the messages communicated by tales, whereas motifs are sheer plots and actions; themes are the meanings of motifs, the abstract notions that concrete actions convey. Ina-Maria Greverus echoes this distinction when she states that the theme is abstracted from the content, and that in this way, she avoids the confusion between motif and theme: "By theme I understand the basic thought that is derived from a tale and that the tale embraces. These basic thoughts are realised in the narrative substance. The substance consists of the smaller subject-units, the motifs" (1965, 135).

The analytical separation between motifs and themes is implicitly an attempt to resolve the double bind of the Romantic concept of motif, designating the minimal narrative unit as motif and its essential and maximal meaning as theme. A folktale, and for that matter any work of art, can have a dominant theme, but many motifs. In that light, it is possible also to understand Veselovskij, who, at the end of the nineteenth century, regarded themes as a complex of motifs. In the spirit of his time, he viewed motifs as formulae by which early man answered metaphysical questions about nature. Such formulae have the capacity to expand and grow through a conscious artistic selection, combination, and schematization and then become a complete theme. Veselovskij regards the theme as the artistic rather than the philosophical abstraction of a motif (Veselovskij 1940, 493–95),[16] similar to the Wagnerian notion of the relations between motifs and a grand theme in music (Apel 1969, 465–66, 545–66).

From this perspective, repetition becomes an essential feature in the relationship between motif and idea. But this is no longer a repetition that occurs in narrative transmission and is due to the special capacity of motif to survive the hardship of time. Rather, the conceptualization of a minimal narrative unit as a motif results from a deliberate, meaningful repetition of the same episode, even metaphor, in different contexts of the same general tradition or a single work. The very occurrence of the motif in variable literary contexts constitutes its significance and function. The motif serves to interrelate different narrative contexts, reflect them on each other, and unify them into a notional, if not a narrative, whole. This idea echoes the Romantic motif insofar as "the fundamental motif becomes synonymous with 'the underlying idea'" (Nygren 1953, 37), albeit with two basic exceptions. First, this motif is not a necessary moving force for actions within a situation; at most, it becomes a rhetorical force used by the speaker or the writer. Second, reoccurrence in at least two distinct historical occasions is one of its essential features. This idea of motif has been articulated in religious studies and, discussing its place in Old Testament studies, Shemaryahu Talmon offers the following definition:

> A literary motif is a representative complex theme which recurs within the framework of the Old Testament in variable forms and connections. It is rooted in an actual situation of anthropological or historical nature. In its secondary literary setting, the motif gives expression to ideas and experiences inherent in the original situation, and is employed to reactualize in the audience the reactions of the participants in that original situation. The motif represents the essential meaning of the situation, not the situation itself. It is not a mere reiteration of the sensations involved, but rather a heightened and intensified representation of them. (Talmon 1966, 39; cf. Warshaver 1972, 51n33)

By the virtue of its multiple connections, such a motif is no longer a minimal or elementary unit, but rather a "representative complex theme" that has historical dimensions. Its significance becomes apparent in the phenomenological study of religion, as it is, as Peter Berger defined it, "a specific pattern or gestalt of religious experience that can be traced in a historical development" (1954, 478). The meaning of such a motif is completely dependent on its primary and subsequent contexts, and it derives its rhetorical effect from its inherent intertextuality.

The notion of a rhetorical motif contrasts sharply with the idea of the wandering motif that the historic-geographic school espouses. It implies meaning and intention, and deliberate manipulation of symbols versus free-floating themes, with neither control nor guidance, that move from one tale to another, from one language to the next over time. The idea that motifs roam through folk literature with no constraints at all was a necessary assumption for the start of a search for an *Ur*-form. Yet critical observation correlating forms with theme indicated that, even in this apparently cluttered world, order exists. Motifs appear in particular positions in a narrative or are associated with distinct genres. In other words, there is an intrinsic literary regulatory system that governs the migration of motifs, and their transference from one text to another follows some discoverable principles; their diffusion is not erratic, nor necessarily influenced by social and cultural contacts (Boas 1891, 1914), but has a folkloric-literary basis. For example, Robert Petsch (1929) distinguishes between frame motive (*Ralzmenmotive*), core motive (*Kermnotive*), and completing motive (*Fiillmotive*) that supplement and conclude narrative characteristics. Each of these motifs has its sphere of action within a narrative to which it is confined. Motifs that occupy different positions within narratives are not interchangeable with each other. In other words, there is a positional formal definition for each motif that governs its movements within literary spheres.

Albert Wesselski, who criticized the entire historic-geographic method, suggested the existence of a thematic-formal correspondence in folktale, according to which motifs occur in particular genres and no others. The basis of his distinction is the attitude of the people toward the narratives, a criterion that has served to describe genres. Hence he distinguishes between myth motifs (*Mytlzemnotive*), which are believed to be facts but are not; realistic motifs (*Gemeinsclzaftsmotive*), which are believed to be and are facts; and culture motifs (*Kulturmotive*), which are neither believed to be nor are facts. Each of the narrative folk genres—the *Märchen*, the novella, the *Sage*—has its own kinds of motif, which are not interchangeable, except under shifting cultural conditions that involve a decline or increase of belief in certain ideas that have thematic representation (Kiefer 1939, 38–58; Wesselski 1925, xvii; 1931, 12, 33–37). Wesselski's distinction is not merely an alternative motif classification; his approach has important implication to the theories of narrative formation and motif migration. Each genre, according to him, has a limited number and kind of appropriate motifs, and the transgression of these literary formal boundaries requires first a change in cultural attitudes toward these themes.

Although Wesselski was a literary scholar, he challenges the historic-geographic concept of motif as an anthropologist would, introducing cultural attitudes as a necessary dimension in delineating minimal narrative units. In the analysis of verbal art, questions of culture, meaning, and their representation often suffer from conventions in the understanding of symbols in verbal narratives. In contrast, the analysis of visual art, with its tangible forms and the iconic basis of its symbols, brings the relationship between units of meaning and units of form into a sharper focus; such an analysis could, in turn, illuminate some of the difficulties that folklorists have encountered in their attempts to delineate a minimal narrative unit.

In his attempt to formulate iconography systematically, Erwin Panofsky employed the same pair of terms, *motif* and *theme*, that folklore and literary scholars have used for many years. In doing so, he first distinguished between the universal and cultural forms as primary and secondary subject matter, respectively. The universal configurations are either factual or expressive forms that are recognized by all, cross-culturally. Shapes of men, animals, and plants are factual forms; expressive gestures such as a smile or mournful decline of the head are universal as well. In contrast, the secondary or conventional subject matter consists of the particular gestures associated with specific figures in each culture, or a period, such as the various positions and gestures associated with different saints in medieval paintings. The primary and universal forms are visual motifs and the secondary and particular subjects are themes. In the association between a gesture and a specific person, "we connect artistic *motifs* and combinations of artistic *motifs* (compositions) with themes or concepts. Motifs thus recognized as carriers of a secondary or conventional meaning may be called *images*" (Panofsky 1939, 6, see also 3–17).

By introducing the distinction between motifs and themes in terms of the universal and cultural, Panofsky reverses the relations between the concrete and the abstract aspects of the elementary artistic unit. If followed in folklore, the delineation between bound and free motifs, and the designation of some motifs as corresponding with each other, would be formulated in new terms: the motifs, as classes of actors, objects and actions, would remain constant, and hence more abstract and universal, and the themes would be variable and culturally specific.

But methodologically, such a formulation would have defeated the purposes of discovering the process of narrative formation and migration at which the historical-geographic method aimed and would have pushed motifs over the brink of history into the domain of structural and symbolic analysis.

Conclusion

In his work, Stith Thompson deliberately ignored these issues and possibilities. For him, they represented an interference with the practical need of his classification plan. However, now there is a revived interest in the concept of motif. The question of minimal narrative units becomes viable again in the light of structural studies, text grammar analysis, and inquiry into the symbolic meaning of narrative. Meletinsky suggests that "the next step [in folktale research] must be the analysis of motifs in the perspective of structuralism. One has to take into consideration here that the distribution of motifs within the theme is structurally also reducible to the above mentioned formula. But if this formula itself represents a specific mechanism for the synthesis of folktales, then the motif is the most essential element of that analysis" (Meletinsky 1974, 51; see also Prince 1973).

It well might be. But a renewed interest in the motif cannot be confined to the concept as it is presented in the *Motif Index of Folk Literature*. It must relate to the entire gamut of ideas and controversies that were part of its development from Romanticism to structuralism.

Notes

1. The criticism ranges from concern with the adequacy and utility of the classification plan to the adequacy of the motif as an analytical unit to questioning the very worthiness of motif analysis. Most of the criticism emerges in the early sixties, after the publication of the revised edition of the *Motif-Index* in 1958.

2. In his theory of the Indian origin of folktales, Benfey concedes to Greece the position of the cradle of animal tales and fables, given the historical priority of Aesop.

3. Hahn recognizes the similarity between narratives of different peoples, and hence, while he retains the idea of the potentiality of traits for infinite combination, in actuality, he observes, these combinations are rather limited.

4. I would like to thank John Fought for these references.

5. While Baring-Gould does not acknowledge his indebtedness to J. G. von Hahn, the relationship between these two schemes did not escape William Ralston, who writes: 'The most elaborate attempt at a classification of folk-tales yet made is that due to J. G. von Hahn, who prefixed to his collection of Greek and Albanian Tales (1864) a scheme for the reduction of such stories to their original elements, and their arrangement in divisions and groups. His plan was afterwards employed and modified by Mr. Baring Gould, whose classifications of 'Story Radicals' is appended to Mr. Henderson's 'Folklore of the Northern Counties'" (Ralston 1878, 76).

6. For a study on the influence of Gozzi on the German Romantics, see Rusack (1930), and on the idea of the limited number of tragic dramatic situations, see Potti (1917).

7. The deterministic tradition in literary and folklore scholarship was not limited to the nineteenth century and has continued well into current scholarship. One of the latest efforts in that direction is Jason (1969).

8. Damon and Phintias (erroneously Pythias), the two friends from Syracuse. When Damon was condemned to death, he asked permission to go and see his wife and children before he died. At first, the request was denied, but on his way to execution, he encountered his friend Pythias, who was ready to die in his stead if he did not return in time. Damon went to visit his family and, in spite of obstacles, came back just in time. Both were forgiven. See Cicero, *Tusculan Disputations*, bk. 5, chap. 63, sec. 12. The classical story was dramatized by Richard Edward, *Damon and Phithias* (1571), and John Banim, *Damon and Pythias* (1825). See *Gesta Romanorum*, tale 108.

9. Codrus, the last king of Athens. When he learned, during the Dorian invasion of the Peloponnesus, that the Delphic Oracle prophesized that the Athenians would be defeated if his life was spared, he deliberately courted death at the enemy camp. When the Dorians learned about his death, they retreated. See, for example, Pausanias, *Description of Greece*, bk. 1, chap. 19, sec. 5; bk. 7, chap. 25, sec. 2; bk. 8, chap. 52, sec. 1; Arminius (c. 18 or 16 BC–AD 19 or 21); Tacitus, *Annals*, bk. 1, chaps. 63–68; bk. 2, chaps. 9–18; known in later ages as Hermann der Cheruske. As a chief of the Cherussi, he led a revolt against the Roman forces in AD 9 on his return from service at Rome to his native home in northern Germany. He is celebrated in many German Romantic novels and plays.

10. A hero in a novel by Heinrich von Kleist (1777–1811) that was based on an old chronicle and appeared in his *Ezrählungen* (1810). Kohlhaas is a hero who is driven to crime through circumstances and his strong sense of justice.

11. The idea in this quotation contradicts a previous statement of Dilthey, cited by Wellek, in which he denies the possibility of a genealogical sequence of poetic schools and hence states that "the changes which occur with a type or motif, cannot be arranged in fixed series" (see Dilthey *Gesammelte Schriften*, 6:124; and Wellek 1955–92, 4:324).

12. Compare with Munro S. Edmonson, who wrote that "Motifs in folklore are like the phonetic dimensions of linguistics or like patterns, themes, configurations, and values in general cultural theory. They are, to a first approximation, structural units" (Edmonson 1971, 47). He seems to interpret Thompson in a way that is not consistent with Thompson's own ideas about his work.

13. Compare with the notion of defamiliarization (*ostraneniye*) that the Russian formalist Victor Shklovsky develops in his essay "Art as Technique" (1965), and the concept of foregrounding that Czech structuralist Jan Mukarovsky proposes in his essay "Standard Language and Poetic Language" (1964).

14. Attempts to arrange ideas, motifs, or titles in alphabetical order were made by Friedrich Hebbel in a review of *Deutsche Sagen von Adolph Bude* (1839), available in Hebbel (1901–7, 10, 390–92) and in the work of Scherer's student (Brahm 1880, 145–167). In America, under the guidance of Franz Boas, his then students made a list of "catch-words" of American Indian tales (Kroeber 1908; Lowie 1908a, 1908b). Kroeber discussed the relationship between motives and types (p. 226) in a way that is similar to the use Thompson was later to employ.

15. For a bibliography, a survey, and a few selected discussions of the concept of motif in literature in general, see Alston (1967); Czerny (1959); Daemmrich (1987, 187–91); Frenzel (1966); Guckel (1965); Kalinowska (1961); Katann (1931); Kayser (1951, 61–78); Korner (1924); Krogmann (1932a, 1932b, 1965); Levin (1973); Mahr (1928, 9–15); and Schmitt (1959).

16. The essay on "Thematic Poetics," 493–596, in which Veselovskij discusses the relationship between motif and theme was published posthumously, edited by his students V. F. Sismarev and V. M. Zirmunskij. It is based on his manuscript and on students' notes taken in his lectures on thematics given in the years 1898–1903. I would like to thank G. Saul Morson for a summary of Veselovskij's essay and lengthy discussions about the subject. See also Propp (1968, 12–13) for a discussion of Veselovskij's ideas about motif and theme.

Bibliography

Addison, William, E. 1947. *The English Country Parson*. London: J. M. Dent and Sons.

Alston, William P. 1967. "Motives and Motivation." In *The Encyclopedia of Philosophy*, edited by Paul Edwards, 5:399–409. New York: Macmillan and Free Press.

Apel, Willi, ed. 1969. *Harvard Dictionary of Music*. Cambridge, MA: Harvard University Press.

Baring-Gould, Sabine. 1866. "Household Stories." In *Notes on the Folklore of the Northern Counties of England and the Borders*, by W. Henderson, 299–311. London: Longmans, Green.

———. 1922. *Early Reminiscences*. New York: E. P. Dutton.

———. 1925. *Further Reminiscences: 1864–1894*. New York: E. P. Dutton.

Bastide, Roger., ed. 1962. *Sens et usages du terme structure dans les sciences humaines et sociales*. The Hague: Mouton.

Berger, Peter L. 1954. 'The Sociological Study of Sectarianism." *Social Research* 21, no. 4:467–85.

Boas, Franz. 1891. "Dissemination of Tales among the Natives of North America." *Journal of American Folklore* 4, no. 12:13–20. Reprinted in Boas (1940, 437–45).

———. 1914. "Mythology and Folktales of the North American Indians." *Journal of American Folklore* 27, no. 106:374–410. Reprinted in Boas (1940, 451–90).

———. 1940. *Race, Language and Culture*. New York: Macmillan.

Boudin, Raymond. 1971. *The Uses of Structuralism*. Translated by Michalina Vaughan. London: Heineman.

Brahm, Otto. 1880. *Das Deutsche Ritterdrama des achtzehnten Jahrhunderts. Studien über Joseph August von Törring, seine Vorgänger und Nachfolger*. Strasbourg: K. J. Trübner.

Buckle Henry T. 1859–66. *History of Civilization in England*. 2 vols. New York: D. Appleton.

Bynum, David F. 1978. *The Daemon in the Wood: A Study of Oral Narrative Patterns*. Milman Parry Collection. Publications. Monograph Series 1. Cambridge, MA: Center for Study of Oral Literature, Harvard University.

Cassirer, Ernst. 1946. *Language and Myth*. Translated by Susanne K. Langer. New York: Harper and Bros.

Chamberlain, H. Stewart, ed. 1910. *Briefwechsel zwischen Schiller und Goethe*. Jena, Germany: E. Diederichs.

Christensen, Arthur. 1925. *Motif et Theme: Plan d'un dictionnaire des motifs et contes populaires, de légendes et de fables*. FFC, 59. Helsinki: Suomalainen Tiedeakatemia.

Cosquin, Emmanuel. 1922. *Études folkloriques, recherches sur les migrations des contes populaires et leur point de depart*. Paris: Champion.

Czerny, Z. 1959. "Contribution à une théorie comparée du motif dans les art." In *Stil-und Formprobleme in der Literatur. Vorträge des VII Kongress der Internationalen Vereinigung für modern Sprachen und Literaturen in Heidelberg, 1957*, edited by. Paul Böckmann, 38–50. Heidelberg: Carl Winter, Universitätsverlag.

Daemmrich, Horst S., and Ingrid. 1987. *Themes and Motifs in Western Literature: A Handbook*. Tübingen: Francke.

Deslongchamps, Auguste-Louis-Armand Loiseleur. 1838. *Essai sur les fables indiennes et sur leur introduction en Europe*. Paris: Techner.

Dilthey, Wilhelm. 1886. "Wilhelm Scherer zum persönlichen Gedächtnis." *Deutsche Rundschau* 49: 132–46.

———. 1922–36. *Gesammelte Schriften*. 11 vols. Leipzig: Teubner.

———. 1976. *Selected Writings*. Edited and translated by H. P. Rickman. New York: Cambridge University Press.

Dorson, Richard M. 1965. "Foreword." In *Folktales of England*, edited by Katherine M. Briggs and Ruth L. Tongue, v–xxii. Folktales of the World. Chicago: University of Chicago Press.

———. 1968. *The British Folklorists: A History*. Chicago: University of Chicago Press.

———. 1972. "Introduction: Concepts of Folklore and Folklife Studies." In *Folklore and Folklife: An Introduction*, edited by Richard M. Dorson, 1–50. Chicago: University of Chicago Press.

Doložel, Lubomir. 1972. "From Motifemes to Motifs." *Poetics* 1, no. 4:55–90.

Duggan, Joseph J. 1973. *The Song of Roland: Formulaic Style and Poetic Craft.* Berkeley, CA; University of California Press.

Dundes, Alan. 1962. "'From Etic to Ernie Units in the Structural Study of Folktales." *Journal of American Folklore* 75, no. 296:95–105.

Eberhard, Johanne August. 1803–5. *Handbuch der Aesthetik für gebildete Leser aus allen Ständen in Briefen herausgegeben.* Halle: Hemmerde und Schwetschke.

Eisler, Rudolf. 1929. *Wörterbuch der Philosophischen Begriffe Historisch-Quellenmässig Bearbeitet.* Edited by Karl Roretz. Berlin: E. S. Mittler and Sohn.

Eisler, Rudolf. 1929. *Wörterbuch der Philosophischen Begriffe Historisch-Quellenmässig Bearbeitet.* Edited by Karl Roretz. 2:184–89. Berlin: E. S. Mittler and Sohn.

Edmonson, Munro S. 1971. *Lore: An Introduction to the Science of Folklore and Literature.* New York: Holt, Rinehart and Winston.

Frenzel, Elisabeth. 1963. *Stoff-, Motiv- und Symbolforschung.* Stuttgart, J. B. Metzler.

———. 1966. *Stoff-und Motivgeschichte.* Grundlagen der Germanistik 3. Berlin: E. Schmidt.

Friess, Horace L. 1929. "Wilhelm Dilthey: A Review of His Collected Works as an Introduction to a Phase of Contemporary German Philosophy." *The Journal of Philosophy* 26, no. 1:5–25.

Goethe, Johann Wolfgang von. 1921. "On Epic and Dramatic Poetry." In *Goethe's Literary Essays*, 100–103. Edited by J. E. Spingarn. New York: Harcourt, Brace, and Company.

———. 1962. *Wilhelm Meister's Apprenticeship.* Translated by Thomas Carlyle. New York: Collier Books.

Grambo, Ronald. 1976. "The Conceptions of Variant and Motif, A Theoretical Approach." *Fabula* 17, no. 3:243–56.

Greenway, John. 1964. *Literature among the Primitives.* Hatboro, PA: Folklore Associates.

Greverus, Ina-Maria. 1965. "Thema, Typus und Motiv: Zur Determination in Erzälforschung." In *IV International Congress for Folk-Narrative Research in Athens (1.9–6.9. 1964): Lectures and Reports*, edited by Georgios A. Megas, 130–39. Laographia 22. Athens: n.p.

Guckel, Ausrele Venclovie. 1965. "The Motif: Theory and Practical Illustrations from the Novels of Fontane." PhD diss., University of Illinois at Urbana-Champaign.

Hahn, Johann Georg von. 1864. *Griechische und albanesische Märchen.* Leipzig: W. Engelmann.

Hartland, Edwin Sidney. 1891. *The Science of Fairy Tales: An Inquiry into Fairy Methodology.* The Contemporary Science Series. London: Walter Scott.

Hautala, Jouko. 1969. *Finnish Folklore Research, 1828–1918.* Helsinki: Societas Scientiarum Fennica.

Hebbel, Friedrich C. 1901–7. *Sämtliche Werk: historich-kritische Ausgabe.* Edited by R. M. Werner. 24 vols. Berlin: Behr.

Hyman, Stanley Edgar. 1948. "Some Bankrupt Treasuries." *The Kenyon Review* 10, no. 3:484–500.

Jacobs, Joseph. 1887. "Types" [sec.]. In "Folktales, Hero Tales, Drolls" [chap.], *The Handbook of Folklore*, edited by George L. Gomme, 117–35. Publications of the Folk-Lore Society 20. London: Folk-Lore Society.

———. 1914. "Appendix C: Some Types of Indo-European Folktales." In *The Handbook of Folklore*, rev. ed., edited by Charlotte Sophia Burne, 344–55. Publications of the Folk-Lore Society 73. London: Sidgwick and Jackson.

Jacobs, Melville. 1966. "A Look Ahead in Oral Literature Research." *Journal of American Folklore* 79, no. 313:413–27.

Jason, Heda. 1969. "A Multidimensional Approach to Oral Literature." *Current Anthropology* 10, no. 4:413–26.

————. 1970. "The Russian Criticism of the 'Finnish School' in Folktale and Scholarship." *Norveg* 14:285–94.

————. 1972. "Structural Analysis and the Concept of the 'Tale Type.'" *Arv* 28: 36–54.

Jeitteles, Ignaz. 1835–37. *Aesthetisches Lexicon: Ein alphabetisches Handbuch zur Theorie der Philosophie des Schönen und der Schönen Künste. Nebst erklärung der Kunstausdrücke aller aesthetischen Zweige.* Vienna: C. Gerold.

Jespersen, Otto. 1922. *Language, Its Nature, Development and Origin.* London: Allen and Unwin.

Kayser, Wolfgang Johannes. 1951. *Das sprachliche Kunstwerk; eine Einführung in die Literaturwissenschaft.* Bern: A. Francke.

Ketner, Kenneth Laine. 1976. "Identity and Existence in the Study of Human Tradition." *Folklore* 87, no. 2:192–200.

Kiefer, Emma Emily. 1939. *Albert Wesselski and Recent Folktale Theories.* Indiana University Publications, Folklore series 3. Bloomington: Indiana University.

Kleist, Heinrich von. 1810. *Ezrählungen.* Berlin: Realschulbuchhandlung.

Körner, Joseph. 1924. "Erlebnis—Motiv—Stoff." In *Vom Geiste neuer Literaturforschung: Festschrift für Oskar Walzel*, edited by Julius Wahle and Victor Klemperer, 80–90. Wildpark-Postdam: Akademische Verlagsgesellschaft Athenaion m.b.h.

Kroeber, A. L. 1908. "Catch-Words in American Mythology." *Journal of American Folklore* 21, no. 81:222–27.

Krogmann, Willy. 1932a. "Motivanalyse." *Zeitschrift für angewandte Psychologie*, 42:264–72.

————. 1932b."Motivübertragung und ihre Bedeutung für die Literarhistorische Forschung." *Neophilologus* 17:17–32.

————. 1965. "Motiv." In *Reallexicon der deutschen Literatur-geschichte*, edited by Werner Kohlschmidt and Wolfgang Mohr, 2:427–32. Berlin: De Gruyter.

Krohn, Kaarle. 1971. *Folklore Methodology: Formulated by Julius Krohn and expanded by Nordic Researchers.* Translated by Roger L. Welsch. Publications of the American Folklore Society Bibliographical and Special Series, vol. 21. Austin, TX: University of Texas Press. Originally published as *Die folkloristische Arbeitsmethode.* Oslo: Institute for Comparative Research in Human Culture, 1926.

Lang, Andrew. 1884. "Introduction." In *Grimm's Household Tales*, translated and edited by Margaret Hunt, xi–lxxv. London: George Bell and Sons.

Levin, Harry. 1973. "Motif." In *Dictionary of the History of Ideas*, edited by Philip P. Wiener, 3:235–44. New York: Charles Scribner's Sons.

Lowie, H. R. 1908. "Catch-Words for Mythological Motives." *Journal of American Folklore* 21, no. 80:24–27.

————. 1909. "Additional Catch-Words." *Journal of American Folklore* 22, no. 85:332–33.

Lüthi, Max. 1962. *Märchen.* Stuttgart: J. B. Meltzer.

————. 1972. "Europäische Volksliterature: Themen, Motive, Zielkräfte." In *Weltliterature und Volksliterature: Probleme und Gestalten*, edited by Albert Schaefer, 55–79. Munich: C. H. Beck.

Meletinsky, Eleazar. 1974. "Structural-Typological Study of Folktales." In *Soviet Structural Folkloristics*, edited by P. Maranda, 19–51. Approaches to Semiotics 42. The Hague: Mouton.

————. [Meletinski, Eléazar]. 1977. "Principes sémantiquus d'unnouvel index des motifs et des sujets." *Cahiers de Littérature Orale* 2:15–24.

Meletinsky, Eleazar, S. Nekludov, E. Novik, and D. Segal. 1974. "Problems of the Structural Analysis of Fairy Tales." In *Soviet Structural Folkloristics*, edited by P. Maranda, 73–139. Approaches to Semiotics 42. The Hague: Mouton.

MacCulloch, John Arnott. 1905. *Childhood of Fiction: A Study of Folk Tales and Primitive Thought*. New York: John Murray.

Mahr, August Carl. 1928. *Dramatische situationsbilder und -bildtypen: eine studie zur kinstgeschichte des dramas*. Stanford: Stanford University Press.

Makkreel, Rudolf A. 1975. *Dilthey: Philosopher of the Human Studies*. Princeton: Princeton University Press.

Mukarovsky, Jan. 1964. "Standard Language and Poetic Language." In *A Prague School Reader on Esthetics, Literary Structure, and Style*, translated and edited by Paul L. Garvin. Washington, DC: Georgetown University Press.

Müller-Vollmer, Kurt. 1963. *Towards a Phenomenological Theory of Literature: A Study of Wilhelm Dilthey's Poetik*. Stanford Studies in Germanics and Slavics 1. The Hague: Mouton.

Nagler, Michael N. 1974. *Spontaneity and Tradition: A Study in the Oral Art of Homer*. Berkeley, CA: University of California Press.

Nygren, Anders. 1953. *Agape and Eros*. Translated by Philip S. Watson. London: Society for Promoting Christian Knowledge.

Oxenford, John, trans. 1874. *Conversations of Goethe with Eckermann and Soret*. London: G. Bell and Sons.

Panofsky, Erwin. 1939. *Studies in Iconology: Humanistic Themes in the Art of the Renaissance*. New York: Harper and Row.

Paul, Jean. 1804. *Vorschule der Aesthetik*. 3 vols. Bibliothek der deutschen Literatur. Hamburg: F. Meiner.

Pedersen, Holger. 1931. *The Discovery of Language: Linguistic Science in the Nineteenth Century*. Translated by John W. Spargo. Cambridge, MA: Harvard University Press.

Petsch, Robert. 1929. "Motiv, Formel und Stoff." *Zeitschrift für deutsche Philologie* 54:378–94.

Potti, Georges. 1917. *The Thirty-six Dramatic Situations*. Translated by Lucile Ray. Ridgewood, NJ: Editor Company.

Prince, Gerald. 1973. *A Grammar of Stories: An Introduction*. De proprietatibus litteratum: Series minor 13. The Hague: Mouton.

Purcell, William E. 1957. *Onward Christian Soldiers: A Life of Sabine Baring-Gould, Parson, Squire, Novelist, Antiquary, 1834–1924*. London: Longmans, Green.

Ralston, W. R. 1878. "Notes on Folk-Tales." *The Folk-Lore Record* 1:71–98.

Robins, R. H. 1964. *General Linguistics: An Introductory Survey*. Bloomington: Indiana University Press.

Rooth, Anna Birgitta. 1951. *The Cinderella Cycle*. Lund: Gleerup.

Rusack, Hedwig Hoffmann. 1930. *Gozzi in Germany: A Survey of the Rise and Decline of the Gozzi Vogue in Germany and Austria with a Special Reference to the German Romantics*. Columbia University Germanic Studies. New York: Columbia University Press.

Ruskin, John. 1872. *Modern Painters*, vol. 5. New York: Wiley.

Salm, Peter. 1968. *Three Modes of Criticism: The Literary Theories of Scherer, Walzel, and Staiger*. Cleveland: Press of Case Western Reserve.

Scherer, Wilhelm. 1864. "Jacob Grimm." *Preussische Jahrbücher* 14:632–80.

——. 1865a. "Jacob Grimm." *Preussische Jahrbücher* 15:1–32.

——. 1865b. "Jacob Grimm." *Preussische Jahrbücher* 16:1–47, 99–139.

——. 1865c. *Jacob Grimm, zwei Artikel der preussischen Jahrbücher aus deren 14, 15, und 16 Bände besonders abgedruckt*. Berlin: Reimer.

——. 1875. *Geschichte der deutschen Dichtung im elften und zwölften Jahrhundert*. Quellen und Forschungen zur Sprach- und Kulturgeschichte der germanischen Völker 12. Strasbourg: K. J. Trübner.

———. 1886. *A History of German Literature*. Translated from the 3rd German edition by F. C. Conybeare. Edited by F. Max Müller. Oxford: Clarendon.

———. 1888. *Poetik*. Edited by Richard Moritz Meyer. Berlin: Weidmann.

Schmitt, Franz Anselm, ed. 1959. *Stoff- und Motivgeschichte der deutschen Literatur; eine Bibliographie*. Berlin: de Gruyter. 2nd ed. 1965; 3rd ed. 1976.

Shklovsky, Victor. 1965. "Art as Technique." In *Russian Formalist Criticism: Four Essays*, translated and edited by Lee T. Lemon and Marion J. Reis, 3–24. Lincoln, NE: University of Nebraska Press.

Spiess, Karl von. 1917. *Das deutsche Volksmärchen*. Leipzig: B. G. Teubner.

Taine, Hyppolyte. 1863–64. *Histoire de la littérature anglaise*. Paris: L. Hachette.

———. 1865. *Philosophie de l'art*. Paris: L. Hachette.

Talmon, Shemaryahu. 1966. "The 'Desert Motif' in the Bible and in Qumran Literature." In *Biblical Motifs: Origins and Transformations*, edited by Alexander Altmann, 31–63. Cambridge, MA: Harvard University Press.

Thompson, Stith. 1946. *The Folktale*. New York: Holt, Rinehart and Winston.

———. 1955. *Narrative Motif-Analysis as a Folklore Method*, FFC, 161. Helsinki: Suomalainen Tiedeakatemia.

———. 1955–58. *Motif-Index of Folk-Literature: A Classification of Narrative Elements in Folktales, Ballads, Myths, Fables, Medieval Romances, Exempla, fabliaux, Jest-Books and Local Legends*. Rev. edition. 6 vols. Bloomington: Indiana University Press.

———. 1964. "The Challenge of Folklore." *PMLA* 79, no. 4:357–65.

Tomashevsky, Boris. 1965. "Thematics." In *Russian Formalist Criticism: Four Essays*, translated and edited by Lee T. Lemon and Marion J. Reis, 61–98. Regents Critics Series. Lincoln: University of Nebraska Press.

Veselovskij, A. N. 1940. *Istoričeskaja poètika*. Edited by V. M. Zirmunskij. Leningrad: Khudozh litra.

Viet, Jean. 1969. *Les methodes structuralistes dans les sciences sociales*. 2nd ed. Paris: Mouton.

Warshaver, Gerald E. 1972. "A Comparative Study According to the Traditio-historical Method." *Folklore Forum* 5, no. 2: 38–54.

Wellek, René. 1955–92. *A History of Modern Criticism: 1750–1950*. 8 vols. New Haven: Yale University Press.

Wesselski, Albert. 1925. *Märchen des Mittlealters*. Berlin: Stuberauch.

———. 1931. *Versuch einer theorie des Märchens*. Hildesheim: Gerstenberg.

Wilson, William A. 1976. *Folklore and Nationalism in Modern Finland*. Bloomington: Indiana University Press.

Wirth, Otto. 1937. *Wilhelm Scherer, Joseph Nadler, and Wilhelm Dilthey as Literary Historians*. Chicago: Privately published, distributed by the University of Chicago Press.

8

CONTEXT IN CONTEXT

IN CONTEMPORARY USAGE, THE TERM *CONTEXT* REFERS TO a broadly defined background of a composition or a structure, as well as to the parts that precede and follow a given passage. In folklore studies, its use draws on theories and methods in anthropology, linguistics, socio-linguistics, sociology, psychology, and philosophy, and coincides with similar usages in literary theory, history, and cultural studies (cf. Goodwin and Duranti 1992). However, its immediate antecedent appeared in anthropological functional theory. In 1954, William Bascom proposed that any functional analysis required an adequate description of "the social context of folklore," including the time and place for the telling of specific forms; the identity of the narrators and the composition of the audience, as well as the relationship of the narrator to the text; the use of dramatic and rhetorical devices in performance; audience participation; and folk classification of traditional genres and the people's attitudes toward them (Bascom 1954, 334).

From this perspective, contextual analysis explores the contribution folklore makes to the functioning of society (Bascom 1953, 290). Initially, when Malinowski advanced his functional theory in anthropology, he sought to discover how the different aspects of culture, including folklore, maintained social cohesion. But when he addressed the issues of context of culture and context of situation, he turned to the question of meaning in primitive languages (Malinowski 1946, 307; 1965, 18). This subtle shift in focus from society to meaning has barely been acknowledged, yet it provides the clue for the kind of reception bestowed on contextual analysis in folklore studies. When the concept of context emerged in 1971 as an essential component of the redefinition of folklore as "artistic communication in small groups" (Ben-Amos 1971, 13) and as a unifying principle for the new perspectives (Paredes and Bauman 1972), folklorists reacted as if it were a new, rather than a familiar, scholarly term.[1] Its critics defined the concern with context as if it were in opposition to text (Jones 1979a, 1979b; Ward 1977, 1979; Wilgus 1973, 1986;), and its defenders identified the concept of context itself as new together with its ancillary terms of *communication, conventions, performance,* and *rhetoric* (Bascom 1977; Dorson 1972, 45–47). Both critics and defenders bypassed some more fundamental changes that contextual theory introduced into folklore.

From Explanation to Interpretation

The break with traditional scholarly practices involved not so much the consideration of the immanence of context—this has been recognized before— but the shift from explanation to interpretation in the analytical modality of folklore. This change had dual dimensions, analytical and pragmatic. A broad range of previous theories, from the nineteenth-century cultural evolution to modern formulaic theory, have sought to offer a causal explanation of the content, form, actions, and beliefs that compose the substance of folklore. These theories invariably involve the construction of models and the postulation of universal cultural—not natural—laws that serve as premises that cover attempts to rationalize or explain the persistence of folklore. Such an analytical modality prevails in schools of thought as different as the Müllerian "solar mythology" and the Cambridge-based "myth and ritual" theory. Even when the formulation of a new theory involves the refutation of a previous one, as in the case of formalism and the historic-geographic method, both the new and the rejected approaches nevertheless have shared the analytical modality of causal explanation.

In contrast, contextual analysis does not explain folklore; it interprets it, seeking meanings rather than causes (cf. Honko 1984). It does so by considering not only the text but the entire experience of folklore in society. Such an approach takes the concept of folklore as orally performed verbal art to its logical conclusions, insisting that any valid interpretation consider the entire cultural, social, and situational context. The meaning of a text is its meaning in context. The transference of any folklore text to a different literary, historical, or cultural context grants it a new meaning. Because of their transient nature, folklore texts do not have single meanings, and any repeated, historically conscious use connotes previous contexts as an integral part of their set of meanings. A valid interpretation is an interpretation of a text in context.

The Text versus Context Controversy: A False Dilemma?

In terms of contextual analysis, there is no dichotomy between text and context, nor is it necessary, unless heuristically advisable, to conceive of text and context as levels of communication or as a series of forms embedded in each other and in culture and society. Folklore exists in a contextual state.

By turning terms around, Paul Ricœur (1971a, 1971b) has proposed a kind of a nominalistic solution to the apparent dichotomy between text and context by conceiving and naming social action as text. In such a renaming, text becomes a metaphor for context. Such a rethinking of cultural events opens them up for inexhaustible interpretations and discoveries of new meanings (Geertz 1973; Hobart 1985).

At the same time, such a metaphoric view of context as text underscores the potential dangers of absolute individualization of performance situations (Scharfstein 1989, 59–66). Each single utterance, each single performance of repeated and repeatable text, could be likened to a poem, or any singular artistic creation. In fact, Robert Georges (1969, 1976) has foreseen this quandary into which contextual analysis could lead, although he regards it a virtue, not a vice. According to him, "the total message of any given storytelling event is generated and shaped by and exists because of a *specific* storyteller and *specific* story listeners whose interactions constitute a network of social interrelationships that is *unique* to that particular storytelling event" (1969, 324; my emphasis).

Theoretically, contextual description increases the specificity of each folklore performance. As no two poems are alike, so no two tellings, singings, or recitings of texts duplicate each other. The likelihood that there will be a convergence of all factors that make up a folklore performance is very slight. However, context tempers the uniqueness of any utterance and its message. The social conventions and regulations, the cultural and language rules, and the genres of speech that govern folklore performance in any context would restrain the uniqueness of any event and subject it to cultural conventions of communication, of which speakers are aware and in which they have a variable degree of competence (Bauman 1977; Bauman and Briggs 1990; Hymes 1962, 1964, 1971, 1972, 1974, 135–41; Lewis 1969; Lyons 1972, 83–84; Mailloux 1983).

Pragmatically, context is the interpretant of folklore. The term *interpretant* is taken from Charles Sanders Peirce's (1839–1914) semiotics. Though the term *context* is absent from his account, a synthesis of Peirce's semiotics with linguistic, philosophical, anthropological, and folkloristic theories points to the conclusion that context functions as the intepretant of folklore messages (Bauman 1977; Ben-Amos 1971, 1977; Givón 1989, 1–2, 69–76; Goffman 1974, 440–41; Levinson 1983, 22–23; Shapiro 1983, 14–15, 49–60; Wittgenstein 1968, pp. 142–43, sec. 525; p. 188). Context, like the interpretant, is an "agent of mediation" (Shapiro 1983, 15) between signs and their objects; applying them to concrete situations (Eco 1976, 1460), it modifies and determines the meaning of words (Langer 1976, 139), and it transforms the perception and conception of objects (Hahn 1942). John Dewey (1958, 6–9, 26) early on pointed out a fact that has become axiomatic in folklore and museums studies, that the context of the fine arts museum interprets ethnographically obtained utensils as art. Karl Bühler's (1990) formulation for language is aptly applicable to folklore: "the symbolic field of language . . . provides a second class of clues for construction and understanding, one that could be covered by name *context*; thus, in general terms, the situation and the context are the two sources that in every case contribute to the precise interpretation of utterances" (169).

Such an interpretive function is particularly valuable in comparative analysis of folklore, in which fixed texts, well-formed themes, narrative patterns, and stock figures recur in different cultures. Their meanings and significance are context-dependent. Diffused as they are, their narrators, singers, and reciters are oblivious to their broad, even global distribution; for them, they have meanings one text at a time, one character in a society. In each particular case, context functions interpretively, attributing to the utterances the meanings the speakers and listeners perceive in them. When a text is stable, on either a thematic, morphological, structural, or metaphoric level, and the context is variable, it is the latter that affects the differences in the meanings texts might produce, and therefore, it is the context that functions as the interpretant of folklore texts.

Nevertheless, the context dependency of folklore appears to be subject to gradual variation. Textual stability and contextual dependency are in direct relationship to each other. The briefer and the more stable a folklore text is, the higher is its context dependency, and conversely, the longer and consequently verbally more variable a text is, the lower appears to be its contextual dependency. The meaning of proverbs, for example, is highly context-dependent and consequently abstractly indefinite (Krikmann 1984; Kirshenblatt-Gimblett 1973; Seitel 1976), whereas tales, even epics, that have a wider range for textual variation retain stability of meaning in a variety of contexts in a single culture and thus have lower contextual dependency.

Such an observation is applicable mostly to the immediate context in which a performance occurs. But as far as the context of culture writ large is concerned, even longer and looser texts cannot extricate themselves from its constraints. Even those texts that have an apparently lower context dependency draw their specific meanings from the broad context of their specific society, the language in which they are performed, and the cultural symbolic system that interprets them. They are equally bound by the ideology, historical knowledge, modes of thought, value system, aesthetic principles, and principles of behavior that compose the context of culture. These relations

between texts and contexts have become evident in numerous studies on specific genres and their performance in different societies.

Context and Genre

In illuminating the complexities of texts in contexts, folklorists drew on a
rich tradition of research on specific genres in different societies. A theoretical emphasis on performance, rhetoric, and social interaction played a crucial
role in grasping genre-specific relations between texts and contexts.

Proverbs are quotations from entextualized tradition (Mukařovský 1971)
in which a speaker brings to bear on a situation the full authority either of
the communal past or of an individual who is called on emblematically to
channel cultural wisdom in order to resolve a particular social conflict (Abrahams 1968a, 1968b; Arewa 1971; Arewa and Dundes 1964; Briggs 1988, 101–70).
Such an application of authority occurs in situations of litigations as well as in
informal, conflict-resolving conversations that can be pedagogical in nature.
By the very use of proverbs, a speaker claims authority. Most folklorists have
obtained the relevant ethnographic information through hypothetically
reconstructed contexts of situations; however, more recent studies attempt to
observe directly the dynamics of proverb use (e.g., Briggs 1988, 101–70).

The riddle, which has often been associated with the proverb as its complement or opposite, appears to contrast with it contextually as well. Cross-
cultural surveys of the pragmatics of riddling indicate its prevalence among
children and youth rather than the elderly. Pedagogically riddles instruct, but
without morals. People pose them in situations of ritual crises rather than
social conflicts. In African societies, in addition to their purely entertaining value, riddles serve to instruct pubescent initiates, and in medieval European and Asian cultures, they were part of courting behavior and wedding
ceremonies—a past practice that tales and ballads reflect (Tale Types 851, "The
Princess Who Cannot Solve the Riddle," and 851A, "Turandot;" Child No. 1,
"Riddles Wisely Expounded"). They create a cognitively fictive world, with a
reversed relation to the phonetic or semantic verbal order a culture knows.
Riddles invoke humor rather than judgment, and play and fantasy rather
than ethical values, as proverbs do. People perform them in association with
other genres of entertainment rather than in conjunction with legal procedures (Burns 1976).

The contexts of ballad singing have similarly largely been situations of
entertainment. In eighteenth- and nineteenth-century Scotland, for example, farmhands performed them during work and in leisure and festive times
(Buchan 1972, 255–70; 1985, 62–65). In the urban centers of England, even earlier

literature and documents attest to singing on streets and in the marketplace (Würzbach 1990), and together with recitation (Goldstein 1976), ballads have been the main staple of male pub singing (Dunn 1980; Pickering 1982, 1984; Renwick 1980). The broad range of textual variations of ballads appears to be more performer- rather than context-dependent (e.g., Niles 1986; Porter 1976, 1986). Singers maintain a relative thematic stability of the ballads, adhering to their own tradition and personal style, contributing thereby to a low degree of context dependency of ballad texts. Yet in words, symbols, images, and themes, they draw on local, current, and historical events, ethical values, and cultural mores that provide the broader context for creativity, interpretation, and understanding (Pickering 1982; Renwick 1980; Toelken 1986a, 1986b). The need to examine the communicative context of singing is well recognized (Andersen 1991; Pickering 1984).

Of all the folklore forms, narratives have been subject to contextual analysis more than any other genre, albeit most studies have focused on a single aspect of storytelling rather than encompassed the entire situation. Contextual analysis of folktales has evolved through studies of the roles of narrators, either itinerant or resident in specific societies, the repertoire of individual narrators, the telling of occasions and events, and the narration of specific genres. The social interaction in narrating situations and the poetics of performed texts in context, observed or reconstructed, have been among the recent research directions (Bauman 1986; Bauman and Briggs 1990; Mills 1991).

Emerging Definitions of Context

Methodologically, there are several proposals for the contextual analysis of folklore forms. Richard Bauman proposes that the field worker in folklore organize the data around six broad foci: "(a) *context of meaning* (what does it mean?); (b) *institutional context* (where does it fit within the culture?); (c) *context of communicative system* (how does it relate to other kinds of folklore?); (d) *social base* (what kind of people does it belong to?); (e) *individual context* (how does it fit into a person's life?); (f) *context of situation* (how is it useful in social situations?)" (1983, 367). Kaivola-Bregenhøj (1992) distinguishes in the narrating process the situational context, the linguistic context (Brown and Yule 1983, 46–50), the cultural context, the cognitive context, and the generic context. And in the discussion of the context of ballads, Barre Toelken proposes to examine "(1) the immediate *human* context of performance . . . (2) the *social* context . . . (3) the *cultural-psychological* context . . . (4) the *physical* context . . . [and] (5) the *time* context, the occasion on which the performance takes place" (1986, 36).

Operationally, these and possibly other categorizations of contexts are instrumental for research purposes. However, the two key and polar terms that are fundamental to contextual analysis and are inclusive of kinds of contexts are *context of culture* and *context of situation*. Both terms are Malinowski coinages. The context of culture (Malinowski 1965, 18) comprises the reference to, and the representation of, the shared knowledge of speakers, their conventions of conduct, belief systems, language metaphors and speech genres, their historical awareness, and ethical and judicial principles. Context of culture is the broadest framework for the perception and interpretation of folklore. The concept draws on a broad spectrum of eighteenth- and nineteenth-century trends of thought, ranging from Romanticism to Marxism and from cultural evolution to psychoanalysis. Common to these intellectual movements is the principle of aesthetic dependence on national, ethnic, economic, religious, social, and ideological factors. Accordingly, any aesthetic expression is rooted in and explained by its context of culture, which in turn it reflects. Within folkloristic anthropological discourse (Bauman 1983), culture as a whole is the context on which aesthetics, and folklore as art, depends. Culture comprises the set of symbols, ideas, beliefs, and knowledge that interprets folklore utterances for speakers and listeners. In the literal interpretation of the term *context* as a frame for communication, *context of culture* serves as the broadest contextual circle that embraces all other possible contexts.

In contrast, the situation is the narrowest, most direct context for speaking folklore. The exploration of the situation as a context for the performance of folklore has been, by far, one of the most stimulating recent research directions. Malinowski considered the situation of speaking as the key for the interpretation of verbal messages. Dealing with cryptic phrases that people exchange in the course of action when they are familiar with each other and with their task at hand, Malinowski considered the concept of situation as a keystone in his ethnographic theory of language; he saw it as playing a crucial function in the formation of meaningful statements (1946, 306–9).

Malinowski himself drew on the formulations of linguists and psychologists. Among them was Philipp Wegener, who proposed a theory of situation (*Situationstheorie*) for language. In his psychologically oriented typology, Wegener distinguished three situations in which context provides ways of understanding single-word utterances: situations of perception, situations of remembrance, and situations of consciousness (Wegener in Abse 1971, 135–38). More directly, Malinowski found support for his ideas in discussions with and in reading the work of A. Gardiner. According to Gardiner's theory, speech requires the occurrence of a speaker, a listener, a word, and "the speaker and the listener must be in the same spatial and temporal situation" (1932, 49; see also 49–52). Karl Bühler formulated a model of speaking along similar lines. He drew on Plato's dialogue on language, *Cratylus* (1990, 30–39), emphasizing the instrumental, communicative nature of language. Bühler constructed a triangular model representing the speaking situation with sender (expression)/receiver (appeal) and a message that represents objects and states of affairs (1990, 35).

In linguistics, "the context theory is perhaps the most influential single factor in the growth of twentieth century semantics" (Ullmann 1959, 65). For folklore studies, Roman Jakobson (1896–1982) provided the link by which Czech structuralism, American pragmatism, and London linguistics converged in the formulation of a starting point for the emergence of contextual analysis. He considers context to have a referential function in verbal communication: "The addresser sends a message to the addressee. To be operative the message requires a context referred to ('referent' in another, somewhat ambiguous, nomenclature), sizable by the addressee and either verbalized or capable of being verbalized" (Jakobson 1960, 353). As methods have evolved and awareness of the use of the concept of context in other disciplines has grown, the context of situation has changed from a passive referent to a scene of interactive relations between speakers and their words. Trends in several fields either helped to forge such a conception of the situation or developed it in parallel directions. In psychology, contextualism was initially a theory of perception (Pepper 1938; Hahn 1942), but in recent years, psychological studies have proposed to account for context as an interactive reality (Rosnow and Georgoudi 1986). In philosophy, both American pragmatists and ordinary language philosophers considered context to be central for understanding and interpretation. John Dewey articulated this approach in regard to thought and art (1931, 1934). Among the ordinary language philosophers, Wittgenstein insisted on the importance of context for determining the significance of words (1968, secs. 525, 539, 652, 686; pp. 181, 188), while Austin (1962), followed by Searle (1969),[2] considered speech as a form of action in a situation (Goodwin and Duranti 1992, 16–19). In terms of folklore, most significant has been the dramatological model in sociological analysis that exposed the complexity of face-to-face and framed interaction (Goodwin and Duranti 1992, 22–25). A later influence has been that of Bakhtin and his circle, who conceived of literature as a theme and as an act, in dialogic terms in which context is "potentially unfinalized" (Bakhtin 1986, 147); these ideas have been further developed in American literary theory (e.g., Culler 1981). Yet of all these trends, most crucial in its influence on contextual analysis was the ethnography of speaking

(Hymes 1962, 1964, 1971, 1972; see Brown and Yule 1983, 35–58; and Goodwin and Duranti 1992, 25–27), especially in its direct impact on folklore studies (Bauman 1977, 1983; Bauman and Briggs 1990).

The context of situation is an interactive arena in which the speakers' age, status, and gender gain symbolic significance in their communication. Similarly, code, style, and measure, intonation and dramatization, genre and its conventions, and time and place of performance convey meanings. In the totality of the situation, its different components interact on each other, having the capacity to constantly redefine and renegotiate the framework for communication (Auer and di Luzio 1992; Gumperz 1982, 130–52; 1992). Within the context of situation, there is a correlation between the semantic values of its various components. For example, old age implies authority and traditionality and is appropriate for the speaking of proverbs, but not for riddling, which challenges the established cognitive system and for which youth is more suitable. In an interactive context of situation, age itself, and for that matter, other components, is negotiable.

Seemingly narrowly defined, the context of situation is still a complex analytical entity and infinite reality that we can neither observe nor comprehend with our finite human minds. On the one hand, the location of performance may include items that have little or no bearing on the communication, and their enumeration may result in the fallacy of inventory (Young 1985, 116; Silverstein 1992) or inclusiveness and false objectivity (Briggs 1988, 13). On the other hand, certain aspects, like the psychological disposition of the speakers, crucial as they are, may have only a covert presence in the context, or may relate to events that are beyond the boundaries of the situation altogether. What, then, is the scope of the context of situation? Young (1985), like Quine (1961, 60), proposes to apply the principle of relevance. Therefore, "not only is not all of the surround context but also not all of the contexts are in the surround" (Young 1985, 116). Although the principle of relevance is subjective and lacks precision, it is compatible with the interpretive nature of contextual theory.

Folklore In and Out of Context

Methodologically, the interpretation of context of situation has been further compounded by the demands of folklore research. Folklorists have a dual paradoxical goal of obtaining texts and observing their performance in society undisturbed by the folklorist's own presence. From that perspective, Goldstein proposes to view contexts as *natural, artificial,* and *induced* (Goldstein

1964, 80–90; Briggs 1986, 11–13). These concepts are relevant to inventory-focused field projects. They describe the degree of scholarly intervention in the performance, and also can be turned around to suggest the ways narrators and singers interact with the collectors (Haring 1972; Mills 1991). Yet it is misleading to describe any collecting situation as either natural or artificial, evaluating it in terms of some ideal uninterrupted performance.

Context is a value-free concept, and no one contextual situation is privileged over any other. Therefore, any investigative situation constitutes its own context, regardless of its approximation to any imagined or real researcher-free performance. The presence of a folklorist in a recording situation is meaningful for any narrator or singer and can serve to enhance his position in the community or to present to an outsider the traditions with which he and his community identify. The contexts in which people perform folklore forms in their own society are *events*. An event, "the root metaphor contextualism" (Sarbin 1977, 4), is a culturally defined context to which the speaking community allocates forms of discourse and that has known rules and conventions for folklore performance. It is possible to violate the rules of an event but not those of a context, because a performance that is in violation of one set of conventions has its own context. No utterance can be out of context, because any new situation has its own context, within or outside the cultural system of communication. Furthermore, if such a violation is deliberate and meaningful, it implies a higher degree of context dependency, because the performance acquires its significance from being counter to traditional convention and rules. The performance of folklore forms can be within their culturally defined events or outside their boundaries, but they can never be out of context.

In a technological world, people present their traditions in print, in mass media, in festivals of folklore revival, and in exhibitional displays before tourists. The performance of folklore in such contexts involves self-reference, drawing attention to its own traditionality. Its condemnation as inauthentic and the emergence of the contrast between genuine and spurious folklore that such performances inspire (Handler and Linnekin 1984; Handler 1988) involve terms of evaluation in which traditionality has a privileged positive position. However, such events, productions, and performances have their own contexts that are authentic unto themselves and in which an account of the traditionalization process is required for their interpretation (Hymes 1974; Bauman and Briggs 1990). Therefore, the concept of context has challenged folklore research not only in traditional societies, but also in modern settings. It involves the extension of the idea of folklore into new contexts

(Boyce 1990; Schwartzman 1984), and in the analysis of the display of traditionality, as in the case of folklorism, the exhibitory context imbues folklore with political and sentimental implications and meanings (Abrahams 1981; Bausinger 1990; Bendix 1988, 1989.)[3]

Notes

1. There is no discussion of context in the summative symposia that survey the accomplishments of folklore scholarship in the first half of the twentieth century (Thompson 1953). According to *The Centennial Index of the Journal of American Folklore*, the term appears first in Miller (1952), and since then, particularly in the sixties, it has become a standard term in folklore scholarship in the United States.

2. In a later essay, John Searle (1980) incorporates the context of culture into the context of situation, pointing out the importance of the background of speech.

3. An expanded version of this essay is Ben-Amos (1995). I would like to thank Roger Abrahams, Charles Briggs, Lee Haring, and Amy Shuman for their insightful and valuable comments on its earlier version.

Bibliography

Abse, D. Wilfred. 1971. *Speech and Reason: Language Disorder in Mental Disease and a Translation of the Life of Speech by Philipp Wegener.* Charlottesville: University Press of Virginia.

Abrahams, Roger D. 1968a. "Introductory Remarks to a Rhetorical Theory of Folklore." *Journal of American Folklore* 81, no. 320:143–58.

———. 1968b. "A Rhetoric of Everyday Life: Traditional Conversational Genres." *Southern Folklore Quarterly* 32:44–59.

———. 1981. "Shouting Match at the Border: The Folklore of Display Events." In *"And Other Neighborly Names": Social Process and Cultural Image in Texas Folklore*, edited by Richard Bauman and Roger D. Abrahams, 303–21. Austin: University of Texas Press.

Andersen, Flemming G. 1991. "Technique, Text, and Context: Formulaic Narrative Mode and the Question of Genre." In *The Ballad and Oral Literature*, edited by Joseph Harris, 18–39. Cambridge, MA: Harvard University Press.

Arewa, E. Ojo. 1970. "Proverb Usages in a Natural Context and Oral Literary Criticism." *Journal of American Folklore* 83, no. 330:430–37.

Arewa, E. Ojo, and Alan Dundes. 1964. "Proverbs and the Ethnography of Speaking Folklore." In *The Ethnography of Communication*, edited by J. J. Gumperz and Dell Hymes. Special issue, *American Anthropologist* 66, no. 6, pt. 2:70–85.

Auer, Peter, and Aldo di Luzio, eds. 1992. *The Contextualization of Language.* Amsterdam/Philadelphia: John Benjamins.

Austin, J. L. 1962. *How to Do Things with Words.* Oxford: Oxford University Press.

Bakhtin, M. M. 1986. *Speech Genres and Other Late Essays.* Translated by Vern W. McGee. Edited by Caryl Emerson and Michael Holquist. University of Texas Press Slavic Series, no. 8. Austin: University of Texas Press.

Bascom, William R. 1953. "Folklore and Anthropology." *Journal of American Folklore* 66, no. 262:283–90.

——. 1954. "Four Functions of *Folklore*." *Journal of American Folklore* 67, no. 266:333–49.

——. 1977. Frontiers of Folklore: An Introduction. In *Frontiers of Folklore*, edited by William Bascom, 1–16. Boulder, CO: Westview Press.

——, ed. 1977. *Frontiers of Folklore.* AAAS Selected Symposium 5. Boulder, CO: Westview Press.

Bauman, Richard. 1983. "The Field Study of Folklore in Context." In *Handbook of American Folklore*, edited by Richard M. Dorson with Iota Gale Carpenter, 362–68. Bloomington: Indiana University Press.

——, ed. 1977. *Verbal Art as Performance*. Rowley, MA: Newbury House.

Bauman, Richard, and Charles L. Briggs. 1990. "Poetics and Performance as Critical Perspectives on Language and Social Life." *Annual Review of Anthropology* 18:59–88.

Bausinger, Herman. 1990. *Folk Culture in a World of Technology*. Translated by Elke Dettmer. Folklore Studies in Translation. Bloomington: Indiana University Press.

Ben-Amos, Dan. 1971. "Toward a Definition of Folklore in Context." *Journal of American Folklore* 84, no. 331:3–15. Reprinted in *Toward New Perspectives in Folklore*, edited by America Paredes and Richard Bauman. Austin: University of Texas Press, 1972.

——. 1995. "Kontext." *Enzyklopädie des Märchens* 8:217–37.

Bendix, Regina. 1988. "Folklorismus: The Challenge of the Concept." *International Folklore Review* 6:5–15.

——. 1989. "Tourism and Cultural Display: Inventing Traditions for Whom?" *Journal of American Folklore* 102, no. 404:131–46.

Boyce, Mary E. 1990. "Story and Storytelling in Organizational Life." PhD diss. Fielding Institute.

Briggs, Charles L. 1986. *Learning How to Ask: A Sociolinguistic Appraisal of the Role of the Interview in Social Science Research*. Cambridge: Cambridge University Press.

——. 1988. *Competence in Performance: The Creativity of Tradition in Mexicano Verbal Art*. Philadelphia: University of Pennsylvania Press.

Brown, G., and G. Yule. 1983. *Discourse Analysis*. Cambridge: Cambridge University Press.

Buchan, David. 1972. *Ballad and the Folk*. London: Routledge and Kegan Paul.

——. 1985. "Performance Contexts in Historical Perspectives." *New York Folklore* 11, nos. 1/4:61–78.

Bühler, Karl. 1990. *Theory of Language: The Representational Function of Language*. Translated by Donald Fraser Goodwin. Amsterdam/Philadelphia: John Benjamins. Originally published 1934.

Burns, Thomas A. 1976. "Riddling: Occasion to Act." *Journal of American Folklore* 89, no. 352:139–65.

Culler, Jonathan. 1981. "Convention and Meaning: Derrida and Austin." *New Literary History* 13, no. 1:15–30.

Dewey, John. 1931. "Context and Thought." *University of California Publications in Philosophy* 12:203–24.

——. 1958. *Art as Experience*. New York: Capricorn Books. Originally published 1934.

Dorson, Richard M. 1972. "Introduction: Concepts of Folklore and Folklife." In *Folklore and Folklife: An Introduction*, edited by Richard M. Dorson, 1–50. Chicago: University of Chicago Press.

Dundes, Alan. 1977. "Who Are the Folk?" In *Frontiers of Folklore*, edited by William R. Bascom, 17–35. American Association for the Advancement of Science (AAAS) Selected Symposia Series, no. 5. Boulder, CO: Westview.

Dunn, Ginette. 1980. *The Fellowship of Song: Popular Singing Traditions in East Suffolk*. London: Croom Helm.

Eco, Umberto. 1976. "Peirce's Notion of Interpretant." *Modern Language Notes* 91, no. 6:1457–72.

Gardiner, Alan H. 1932. *The Theory of Speech and Language*. Oxford: Clarendon Press.

Geertz, Clifford. 1973. "Deep Play: Notes on the Balinese Cockfight." In *The Interpretation of Cultures*, 412–53. New York: Basic Books.

Georges, Robert A. 1969. "Toward an Understanding of Storytelling Events." *Journal of American Folklore* 82, no. 326:313–28.

———. 1976. "From Folktale Research to the Study of Narrating." *Studia Fennica* 20:159–68.

———. 1980. "Toward a Resolution of the Text/Context Controversy." *Western Folklore* 39, no. 1:34–40.

Givón, T. 1989. *Mind, Code and Context: Essays in Pragmatics*. Hillsdale, NJ: Lawrence Erlbaum.

Goffman, Erving. 1974. *Frame Analysis: An Essay on the Organization of Experience*. New York: Harper and Row.

Goldstein, Kenneth S. 1964. *A Guide for Field Workers in Folklore*. Hatboro, PA: Folklore Associates for the American Folklore Society.

———. 1976. "Monologue Performance in Great Britain." *Southern Folklore Quarterly* 40:7–30.

Goodwin, Charles, and Alessandro Duranti. 1992. "Rethinking Context: An Introduction." In *Rethinking Context: Language as an Interactive Phenomenon*, edited by Alessandro Duranti and Charles Goodwin, 1–42. Cambridge: Cambridge University Press.

Gumperz, John J. 1982. *Discourse Strategies*. Cambridge: Cambridge University Press.

———. 1992. "Contextualization Revisited." In *The Contextualization of Language*, edited by Peter Auer and Aldo di Luzio, 39–53. Amsterdam/Philadelphia: John Benjamins.

Hahn, Lewis Edwin. 1942. *A Contextualistic Theory of Perception*. Berkeley, CA: University of California Press.

Handler, Richard. 1988. *Nationalism and the Politics of Culture in Quebec*. Madison: University of Wisconsin Press.

Handler, Richard, and Jocelyn Linnekin. 1984. "Tradition, Genuine or Spurious." *Journal of American Folklore* 97, no. 385: 273–90.

Haring, Lee. 1972. "Performing for the Interviewer: A Study of the Structure of Context." *Southern Folklore Quarterly* 36:383–98.

Hobart, Mark. 1985. "Texte est un con." In *Contexts and Levels: Anthropological Essays on Hierarchy*, edited by R. H. Barnes, Daniel de Coppet, and J. R. Parken, 33–53. Oxford: JASO.

Honko, Lauri. 1984. "Folkloristic Studies on Meaning: An Introduction." *Arv* 40:35–56.

Hymes, Dell. 1962. "The Ethnography of Speaking." In *Anthropology and Human Behavior*, edited by T. Galdwin and W. C. Sturtevant Washington, 13–53. Washington, DC: Anthropological Society of Washington. Reprinted in *Readings in the Sociology of Language*, edited by Joshua Fishman, 99–138. The Hague: Mouton, 1968.

———. 1964. "Introduction: Toward Ethnographies of Communication." In "The Ethnography of Communication," edited by John J. Gumperz and Dell Hymes. Special issue, *American Anthropologist* 66, no. 6, pt. 2:1–34.

———. 1971. "The Contributions of Folklore to Sociolinguistics." *Journal of American Folklore* 84, no. 331:42–50.

———. 1972. "Models of the Interaction of Language and Social Life." In *Directions in Sociolinguistics: The Ethnography of Communication*, edited by John J. Gumperz and Dell Hymes, 35–71. New York: Holt, Rinehart and Winston.

———. 1974. *Foundations in Sociolinguistics: an Ethnographic Approach*. Philadelphia: University of Pennsylvania Press.

Jakobson, Roman. 1960. "Closing Statement: Linguistics and Poetics." In *Style in Language*, edited by Thomas A. Sebeok, 350–77. Cambridge, MA: MIT Press.

Jones, Steven. 1979a. "Dogmatism in the Contextual Revolution." *Western Folklore* 38, no. 1:53–55.

———. 1979b. "Slouching Towards Ethnography: The Text/Context Controversy Reconsidered." *Western Folklore* 38, no. 1:42–47

Kaivola-Bregenhøj, A. 1992. "The Context of Narrating." In *Folklore Processed in Honour of Lauri Honko on his 60th Birthday 6th March 1992*, edited by R. Kvideland et. al. 153–66. Studia Fennica Folkloristica 1. NIF Publications, no. 24. Helsinki: Suomalaisen Kirjallisuuden Seura.

Kirshenblatt-Gimblett, Barbara. 1973. "Toward a Theory of Proverb Meaning." *Proverbium* 22:821–27. Reprinted in *The Wisdom of Many: Essays on the Proverb*, edited by Wolfgang Mieder and Alan Dundes, 111–21. New York: Garland, 1981.

Krikmann, A. 1984. "On Denotative Indefiniteness of Proverbs." *Proverbium* 1:47–92.

Langer, Susanne K. 1976. *Philosophy in a New Key: A Study in the Symbolism of Reason, Rite, and Art*. Cambridge, MA: Harvard University Press. Originally published 1942.

Levinson, Stephen. 1983. *Pragmatics*. Cambridge: Cambridge University Press.

Lewis, David. 1969. *Convention: A Philosophical Study*. Cambridge, MA: Harvard University Press.

Lyons, John. 1972. *Structural Semantics: An Analysis of Part of the Vocabulary of Plato*. Oxford: Blackwell.

Mailloux, Steven. 1983. "Convention and Context." *New Literary History* 14, no. 2:399–407.

Malinowski, Bronislaw. 1946. "The Problem of Meaning in Primitive Languages." In *The Meaning of Meaning*, edited by C. K. Ogden and I. A. Richards, 296–336. New York: Harcourt, Brace and World. Originally published 1923.

———. 1965. *The Language of Magic and Gardening. Coral Gardens and Their Magic*. Vol 2. Bloomington: Indiana University Press. Originally published 1935.

Miller, Robert J. 1952. "Situation and Sequence in the Study of Folklore." *Journal of American Folklore* 65, no. 255:29–48.

Mills, Margaret A. 1991. *Rhetorics and Politics in Afghan Traditional Storytelling*. Philadelphia: University of Pennsylvania Press.

Mukařovský, Jan. 1971. "Prislovi jako soucast kontextu" [The proverb as a component of context]. In *Cestami poetiky a estetiky*. Prague: Ceskosloven sky spisovatel. Originally written 1942–43.

Niles, John D. 1986. "Context and Loss in Scottish Ballad Tradition." *Western Folklore* 45, no. 2:83–106.

Paredes, Américo, and Richard Bauman, eds. 1972. *Toward New Perspectives in Folklore*. Austin: University of Texas Press.

Pepper, Stephen C. 1938. *Aesthetic Quality: A Contextualistic Theory of Beauty*. New York: Scribner's Sons.

Pickering, Michael. 1982. *Village Song and Culture*. London: Croom Helm.

———. 1984. "Popular Song at Juniper Hill." *Folk Music Journal* 4, no. 5:481–503.

Porter, James. 1976. "Jeannie Robertson's *My Son David*: A Conceptual Performance Model." *Journal of American Folklore* 89 no. 351:7–26.

———. 1986. "Ballad Explanations, Ballad Reality, and the Singer's Epistemics." *Western Folklore* 45, no. 2: 110–24.

Quine, Willard van Orman. 1961. *From a Logical Point of View: LogicoPhilosophical Essays*. 2d ed. New York: Harper and Row.

Renwick, Roger deV. 1980. *English Folk Poetry: Structure and Meaning*. Philadelphia: University of Pennsylvania Press.

Ricœur, Paul. 1971a. "The Model of the Text: Meaningful Action Considered as a Text." *Social Research* 38:529–62.

——. 1971b. "What Is a Text? Explanation and Interpretation." In *Mythic Symbolic Language and Philosophical Anthropology: A Constructive Interpretation of the Thought of Paul Ricœur*, edited by David M. Rasmussen, 135–50. The Hague: Martinus Nijhoff.

Rosnow, Ralph L., and Marianthi Georgoudi, eds. 1986. *Contextualism and Understanding in Behavioral Science: Implications for Research and Theory*. New York: Praeger.

Sarbin, T. R. 1977. "Contextualism: A World View for Modern Psychology." In *Nebraska Symposium on Motivation*, edited by A. W. Lanfield, 1–41. Lincoln: University of Nebraska Press, 1977. Reprinted in *The Social Context of Conduct: Psychological Writings of Theodore Sarbin*, edited by V. Allen and K. E. Scheibe, 15–36. New York: Praeger, 1982.

Scharfstein, Ben-Ami. 1989. *The Dilemma of Context*. New York: New York University Press.

Schwartzman, Helen B. 1984. "Stories at Work: Play in an Organizational Context." In *Text, Play, and Story: The Construction and Reconstruction of Self and Society: 1983 Proceedings of The American Ethnological Society*, edited by Stuart Plattner and Edward M. Bruner, 80–93. Washington, DC: American Ethnological Society.

Searle, John R. 1969. *Speech Acts: An Essay in the Philosophy of Language*. Cambridge: Cambridge University Press.

——. 1980. "The Background of Meaning." In *Speech Act Theory and Pragmatics*, edited by. J. R. Searle, F. Kiefer, and M. Bierwitsch. Dordrecht: Reidel.

Seitel, Peter. 1969. "Proverbs: A Social Use of Metaphor." *Genre* 2, no. 2: 143–62. Reprinted in *Folklore Genres*, edited by Dan Ben-Amos, 125–44. Publications of the American Folklore Society Bibiliographica and Special Series, vol. 26. Austin: University of Texas Press, 1976.

Shapiro, Michael. 1983. *The Sense of Grammar: Language as Semiotic*. Bloomington: Indiana University Press.

Silverstein, Michael. 1992. "Contextualization Revisited." In *The Contextualization of Language*, edited by Peter Auer and Aldo di Luzio, 39–53. Amsterdam/Philadelphia: John Beruamins.

Thompson, Stith, ed. 1953. *Four Symposia on Folklore*. Indiana University Publications Folklore Series, no. 8. Bloomington: Indiana University Press.

Todorov, Tzvetan. 1984. *Mikhail Bakhtin: The Dialogical Principle*. Translated by Wlad Godzich. *Theory and History of Literature*, vol. 13. Minneapolis: University of Minnesota Press.

Toelken, Barre, 1986a. "Context and Meaning in the Anglo-American Ballad." In *The Ballad and the Scholars*, edited by D. K. Wilgus and Barre Toelken, 29–52. Los Angeles: William Andrews Clark Memorial Library.

——. 1986b. "Figurative Languages and Cultural Contexts in the Traditional Ballads." *Western Folklore* 45, no. 2:128–39.

Ullmann, Stephen. 1959. *The Principles of Semantics*. Glasgow University Publications, no. 84. 2d ed. London: Blackwell and Mott.

Ward, Donald. 1977. "The Satirical Song: Text versus Context." *Western Folklore* 36, no. 4:347–54.

——. 1979. "The Performance and Perception of Folklore and Literature." *Fabula* 20, no. 1/3:256–64.

Wilgus, D. K. 1973. "The Text Is the Thing.'" *Journal of American Folklore* 86, no. 341:241–52.

——. 1986. "The Comparative Approach." In *The Ballad and the Scholars*, edited by D. K. Wilgus and Barre Toelken, 1–28. Los Angeles: William Andrews Clark Memorial Library.

Wittgenstein, Ludwig. 1968. *Philosophical Investigations*. Translated by G. E. M. Anscombe. Oxford: Blackwell.

Würzbach, Natascha. 1990. *The Rise of the English Street Ballad, 1550–1650*. Cambridge: Cambridge University Press.

Young, Kathrine. 1985. "The Notion of Context." *Western Folklore* 44, no. 2:115–22.

9

TWO BENIN STORYTELLERS

LAMENTS ARE PREMATURE ABOUT THE DISAPPEARANCE OF TRADITIONAL storytelling in Africa. The forces of change, such as the emergence of modern urban life, the spread of Islam and Christianity, and the increased volume of mass communications media may affect oral literature, but they have not eradicated it. In spite of all predictions to the contrary (Crowder 1965), folklore continues to be viable in both rural and urban Africa. Its persistence in a situation of cultural change hinges not only on the number of traditionally functioning narrators and singers, but also on the ability of these artists to respond creatively to novel and foreign cultural elements. Their reaction to films, radio, and records is not imitative but innovative. They switch principles of narrative-art performance, blend genres of folklore, and form new kinds of actions of artistic communication.

The delineation of these modifications is not an easy task. The comparative analyses of traditional and modern oral texts, or even photographs of different storytelling situations, are insufficient. At most, these are documentations of the end results of gradual transformations in verbal art, the dynamic ingredients of which it is still necessary to uncover. Furthermore, as in any comparative folklore study, the establishment of equivalent categories is essential. What aspects in modern African culture could we legitimately consider to be continuations of traditional elements? What are the dynamics of change in folklore performance? The complexity of these problems becomes immediately apparent to whoever researches the folklore of modern Africa.

In 1966, my wife and I spent almost a year in Benin City, in midwestern Nigeria, during which time I studied the traditional communicative forms and techniques of the Edo people. I recorded and interviewed traditional professional storytellers, both in the urban center and the rural surroundings of Benin.[1] In Bini,[2] as in many African languages, though by no means all, there are names for folkloric events. These terms are descriptive and epitomize the attributes of storytelling, singing, and dancing situations from the speaker's point of view. The Bini of midwestern Nigeria conceive of two kinds of communicative events in which storytelling is likely to take place: *ibota* and *okpobhie*.[3] The first is a family evening entertainment, as the term *ota*, "evening," indicates:

> In the early evening hours after the daily work has been completed, the family may gather in the *ikun*, the central room in the house, and discuss household matters, tell traditional narratives (*okha*) and sing songs (*ihuan*). Once gathered in the *ikun*, the members of the family take their seats according to their age and sex. The head of the household usually sits near the ancestral altar, the children congregate in one corner on the floor, and the rest of the family sit on the mud benches along the wall. No restrictions or rites are involved with telling stories in the *ibota*. Whoever wishes may tell a story or start a song. However, two or three people often tell most of the narratives. The head of the household assumes a rather passive role as listener in the *ibota* and allows his wives and children to display their knowledge of Benin oral tradition. (Ben-Amos 1967, 54)

The head of the household may extend an invitation to a professional narrator to entertain the family during an *ibota*; however, this is rather unlikely. The presence of such an artist would involve subsequent modifications in the basic attributes of the situation that would transform it into the second folkloric event, *okpobhie*. This term consists of two elements: the first, *kpe*, means to play a musical instrument, as in *kpema*, "to drum"; the second element, *vbie*, means "to sleep." Combined, the term conveys the notion of playing or "drumming while others are asleep" (Melzian 1937, 143). *Okpobhie* usually takes place in the context of large festive occasions. These could be either rites of passage such as naming a newborn (*ihenl*), a wedding (*irhioha*), or burial ceremonies (*irorinmwin*), or the annual family sacrifice to the ancestors (*eho*). The general festivities that engulf Benin in conjunction with the celebration of *igwe*, the annual ritual in honor of the Oba's (the king of Benin's) ancestors, also serve as frame occasions for the *okpobhie*. The *okpobhie* is an open-ended and multimedia event in which a wide range of play activity is permissible. Traditionally, professional storytellers, singers, and dancers could provide entertainment for the participants. If space allows and the crowd is sufficiently large, several kinds of artists can provide amusement simultaneously until daybreak.

Thus the *ibota* and the *okpobhie* differ from each other in their initial causes, duration, composition and size of audience, narrative skill of performers, and consequently, in the span of attention the listeners devote to a performer. While they listen all night long to a single storyteller during the *okpobhie*, they diffuse their attention among several narrators during the *ibota*. Further, while the *ibota* is, by and large, an event of relaxed conversational exchanges, the *okpobhie* can include a wide range of possible entertainment, including singing, dancing, and music playing. Those occasions in which the main activity centers around a single professional storyteller share in common with the *ibota* the basic repertoire of traditional Benin narratives.

The Bini enjoy stories about their past, and for good reason. The Benin kingdom was one of the main West African empires, and its traditional history is abundant with tales of intra- and intertribal warfare, conquests, and victories. The Benin empire reached its political peak in the fifteenth and sixteenth centuries, during which time the sovereignty of the Oba was respected as far west as Lagos. The territorial nucleus of this historically mighty empire is limited by comparison to these historical boundaries. It corresponds roughly to present-day Benin Division, and consists of Benin City, its preindustrial urban center, and "several hundred compact villages ranging in size from less than 20 to (in one case only) more than 6000 souls. The great majority of the villages had populations of less than 1,000; 400 or 500 hundred may be taken as typical" (Bradbury 1967, 8). The Oba is certainly the political, religious, and social center of Benin culture. Yet, throughout its folklore, art, beliefs, and even its political system, there are undertones of tensions between the rural areas and the court. Benin is basically a village society with a superposed or inner-grown urban, royal structure. The cultural tension between the two segments of the population has never completely subsided.

Transformations that occur within the *okpobhie* can best be demonstrated comparatively by our focusing on the storytellers. For that purpose, let us examine two narrators, one traditional and the other innovative, in terms of their acquisition of narrative skill, instrumentalization, degree of dramatization, belief system, and conception of selves. These are the areas in which change was most pronounced and that most significantly altered the nature of the *okpobhie*. Neither of these professional artists is representative of the average storyteller in his generation. Both achieve a high degree of excellence in their performances, and their reputations are widespread. The effective introduction of any innovation requires the persistent efforts of a capable artist. For comparative purposes, his traditional counterpart should be equally prominent as a narrator.

Such a storyteller is Aimyekagbon. During our stay in Benin City, I became a close friend of his. In times of trouble, he often turned to me for help and confided intimate personal matters to me. Originally, Aimyekagbon was from the village of Erua, some twenty miles east of the city, but at the time we met, he lived in Benin. He had resided there for a couple of years after spending most of his artistic life in the rural parts of Benin Division. No one either in his nuclear or extended family was a professional storyteller. His father was a common villager who did not hold any significant position in the rural society. Aimyekagbon's motivation in learning the art of storytelling was purely economic, at least in his retrospective view. At first, he had made several unsuccessful attempts at other occupations: He helped his brother to farm palm trees but had an accident and could not continue in this work. He began to treat the sick with medical herbs but could not earn his livelihood doing so. At that point of frustration, Aimyekagbon happened to listen to a performance of a professional storyteller who visited his village. As he watched the artist and the audience's reaction to his narration, Aimyekagbon realized the esteem the Bini had for their traditional tales about the glorious past. "A narrator will never starve among them," he said to himself and decided to learn the art of storytelling.

Aimyekagbon's training period lasted a year, during which time he learned to play the *akpata* and acquired a substantial repertoire of tales and songs. His teacher also passed on to him some professional secrets—that is, several cautionary measures a narrator must take in order to ensure his safety.

The search for economic security also motivated Erhengbo, the younger and innovative narrator, to learn the art of professional narration. But here the similarity between the two ends. They differ completely in the next stages of their artistic development in terms of actual exposure to Bini tradition, acquisition of narrative skill, and accumulation of tale repertoire. While Aimyekagbon learned mostly the rural versions of Bini tradition, Erhengbo heard these stories at their most "authoritative source," namely the royal palace. Since the age of ten, he had lived in Benin, after his family moved to the city from the nearby village of Ofunmwegbe, where he was born. His father, who was active in the social and political life of the court, took his child along with him to the various official functions and social gatherings at the palace. These occasions provided Erhengbo with the necessary exposure to Benin traditional narratives. Particularly attractive to him were the details about the Oba's wars of conquest. While as a child Erhengbo was content with passive overhearing of tales, as be reached adolescence, he became inquisitive and began to ask deliberately for explanations of palace rituals, meanings of symbols, and functions of institutions. He no longer accepted tales at their face value. Contradictions had to be reconciled, obscure points needed clarification, and any tale required satisfactory verification by at least two sources. Thus, while Aimyekagbon formally apprenticed himself to a single master and followed the Benin pattern of acquisition of a specialized skill, Erhengbo learned the traditions of Benin in a customary accumulative process of obtaining general knowledge. It was only in the last stage of his development that he turned this information into art.

This transformation did not take place without the introduction of new symbols into the storytelling event, the most important of which is the change in instrumentation. Professional Bini storytellers accompany their narration with the *akpata*, a musical instrument widely known in Africa. It is a seven-stringed bow-lute (*pluriarch*) made out of a triangular resonant box with seven rods attached at its bottom. The seven strings, which are made from either metal wires or palm-tree fibers, are wound around the rods on the one end and tied to a bar on the resonant box on the other. The distributional center of the *akpata* seems to be the Congo, and Benin serves as the utmost northwestern limit of the area (Laurenty 1960; Sodenberg 1956, 196–76). Regardless of this ethnographic fact, the Bini consider two traditional figures as the inventors of the *akpata*: Arhuanran (fifteenth and sixteenth centuries) and Oba Ewuakpo (seventeenth century).[4] Both were folk antiheroes, tragic figures who were part of the king's family but failed to live up to their royal status. Arhuanran, a foolhardy giant, was the son of Oba Ozolua and the brother of Oba Esigie. In spite of Arhuanran's right of succession to the throne according to the primogeniture rule, his brother cleverly deceived him and ascended to the royal position himself. After his defeat, Arhuanran committed suicide by drowning. The Bini say, "You can still hear him play the *akpata* in the lake." Oba Ewuakpe, the second mythical inventor of the *akpata*, did ascend to the throne, but the Bini rebelled against him by withdrawing all social and economic support. They paid him neither visits nor taxes. In these dire hours of poverty and isolation, Ewuakpe invented the *akpata* and played to relieve his grief. These myths of origin represent the symbolic meaning of the *akpata*. The instrument stands for suffering, social rejection, and defeat. Although the Oba himself, center of all Benin knowledge, learns to pluck the *akpata* in his youth, any other narrator who plays it in the palace is bound to suffer misfortune (Egharevba 1949, 71). To avoid it, he must break the instrument he played before the king. Thus the *akpata* stands in direct contrast to the established order and further symbolizes the marginal and deprived people in Benin.

The contrary is true of Erhengbo's musical instrument, the drum, *ema*. Drums are put to multipurpose use in Benin; they accompany dances in family rites, cults, rituals, curative ceremonies, and entertainment. They are at the center of social and cultural life in Benin. Hence the substitution of an *akpata* by a drum has a symbolic and not simply musical implication. It introduces

cultural conformity to the communicative event of storytelling. In his performance style, Erhengbo carries this symbolic transformation of the event even
further. Traditional Benin narrators such as Aimyekagbon tell their stories in
a reserved manner, letting the words, not their mimicry, impress the listeners.
In contrast, Erhengbo has increased the degree of dramatization of his narration. He and his assistants enact face-to-face combat and other battle scenes
of the tales, in all of which Erhengbo personifies the winning protagonist.
A casual observer may suspect that modern movies inspired this dramatization of narratives. Indeed, it is quite possible that they triggered Erhengbo's
transformation of the storytelling situation into a folk drama. However, the
performance itself draws on the central ritual in Benin culture, *igwe*, the
annual celebration of honor to the Oba's ancestors.[5]

This ritual culminates ten days of festivities, in one of which, *iron*, there is
a dramatization of the ancient conflict between the Oba and the Uzama, the
seven hereditary chiefs in Benin. The Uzama challenge the Oba, and a battle
between them and the Oba's defenders ensues. The struggle rages back and
forth four times until the Uzama admit defeat. In that respect, Erhengbo's
innovation is twofold: First, he deritualized *iron* into drama by delocalizing
and detemporalizing the event; he moved it from its central position both in
space—the square in front of the Oba's palace—and in time—the beginning
of the new year—and moved it into the homes of the Bini, where it serves
particularly the purposes of amusement. Second, by the very same process,
he extended the range of possibilities of the *okpobhie*, a secular entertaining event, by introducing into it symbols of royalty. The court tradition also
manifests itself in Erhengbo's art in his selection of repertoire. In his tales of
the past, obas are the protagonists, not the antagonists, as is the case in many
narratives told by *akpata* players.[6]

In conjunction with these transformations in the narration situation,
there is a complete change in the belief system that the artists associate with
their performances. Aimyekagbon, perhaps more than any other traditional
narrator, is preoccupied with the mystique of *akpata* playing. He rigidly follows the temporal rules of musical-narrative entertainment; he tells stories
only at night. For him, the art of accompanied narration has absolute fasci-
nation. Once a storyteller starts, he is spellbound by his own art, completely
removed from the tribulations of daily life. Consequently, he is likely to
neglect all his other duties. According to Aimyekagbon, such an intrusion
of the nightly relaxation into the working hours of the day can cause insan-
ity. Other dangers are awaiting the narrator at dark: His melodies and voice
attract the *eniwaren ason*, the night people, and the *azen*, the witches. They

constitute an elusive audience whose response is unpredictable. Whereas the human audience constantly responds by joining the narrator in the songs interspersed in the tale, the *eniwaren ason* and the *azen* do not voice any reaction to the narration. While the artist plays, they are dancing, yet he cannot see them. If he tires out and stops playing while they are in the midst of the dance, they might hurt him, either by cutting the strings of the *akpata* or even by blinding him. In order to avoid these dangers, the *akpata* players have to devote the first melody of each performance to the night people, and later, they have to offer them cola nuts and wine. Aimyekagbon resorted to more strict protective devices: He constantly wore a white robe whenever he played the *akpata* to signal to the night people his affinity with them.

None of these beliefs and fears does Erhengbo associate with his performance. Two things could account for this elimination. The first is factual and biographical; the second is cognitive and symbolic. Traditional *akpata* players learn from their teachers about the possible dangers of their art and the protective measures that they have to take to ensure their safety. Since Erhengbo did not go through any formal apprenticeship and did not have a single instructor, he remained completely uninformed about the possible traditional hazards of his profession. Furthermore, such a belief system would no longer be functional within the new *okpobhie*. The substitution of the *akpata* and the musical narration by the drum and the dramatic representation of tales involve also the replacement of the artist's notions of suffering, tribulation, and social rejection by a sense of order, security, and social confidence. A narrator who is well entrenched within the social system need not fear the dangers that hover at its margins (Douglas 1966).

If nothing else, Erhengbo could feel confident economically. When I met him in 1966, he used to perform in *okpobhie* three times a week: on Mondays, Wednesdays, and Fridays. In fact, his busy schedule prevented us from establishing as close a friendship as I had with Aimyekagbon and, consequently, at times his reconstruction of his artistic growth is indefinite. It was his assistant who told me about the economic aspects of his work. Erhengbo's charge per performance was four to eight pounds, which he shared with his three or four assistants. The variation in price depended on the length of his performance. He also appeared before Bini associations in Lagos, Ibadan, and Port Harcourt. In 1966, the admission fees for an evening of "Erhengbo and His Group: Concert and Dance" were five shillings for a double ticket. Aimyekagbon could not envision such an economic success even when he was at the peak of popularity. Aimyekagbon said that he used to appear from two to four times a week, and also that he traveled as far as Ibadan and Lagos.

During the political campaigns in Nigeria in the 1950s and 1960s, the parties recruited him to provide entertainment for their village rallies. Nevertheless, he could not rely on storytelling as his single source of livelihood. At all times, he also was either a farmer or a native doctor. His narrative skill served as an essential, yet not exclusive, element for his social identification. Erhengbo, on the other hand, does not have any other professional involvement aside from his narrative-dramatic performance. Furthermore, he has a new conception of self. Whereas traditional storytellers regard themselves as narrators and *akpata* players, *okp'akpata*, Erhengbo considers himself to be an actor.

The role of a professional actor is hardly traditional in Benin culture. Quasi-dramatic performances take place only within ritualistic contexts in which they function in a religious-political rather than a theoretical capacity. Hence Erhengbo probably derived the notion of acting as a profession from external sources, either the Western or Indian films popular in Benin or the Yoruba dramatic performances with which he might have been familiar. In either case, the external influence at most just triggered a change. For the substantive modifications in the performance of storytelling, Erhengbo delved into traditional Benin cultural resources and his own recollections of childhood and adolescent experiences.

Thus a combination of both external and internal factors effected these transformations of the communicative event of *okpobhie* and the cultural conception of *okpobhie*. So far, the extent of these changes is relatively limited. Dramatic narration has not made musical narration outmoded. Every professional storyteller I interviewed, including Aimyekagbon, mentioned at least five pupils he had taught in the previous few years. The general appeal of the *akpata* is not fading away, though it may be more pronounced in the villages than in Benin City itself. Such a decline in its popularity may be due to the emergence of new modes of entertainment and the increase in the number of possible alternative performances within the *okpobhie*. Consequently, the share of traditional storytellers in these events dwindles somewhat. Furthermore, the invitation of a professional entertainer to an *okpobhie* generates some prestige and social appreciation toward the host. Since the hiring of a dramatic troupe costs more than the engagement of an *akpata* player, he has lost some of his prestige value. Yet, in spite of Erhengbo's success, he does not have any disciples. The youths who assist him in his performance do it mostly for the economic benefit and do not intend to become actors. In that respect, Erhengbo is, so far, a singular innovator who extended the capabilities of the *okpobhie* and modified the symbolic meaning of the performance in this event. Whether such an innovation will become stabilized in Benin culture remains to be seen.

Yet the very possibility of introducing changes into the *okpobhie*, even if they are only idiosyncratic for the time being, is indicative of the cultural conception and definition of the communicative event. The *okpobhie* lacks religious sanctions and rigid social regulations. Traditionally, variety was one of its basic attributes, as both singers and narrators could have equally been its valued entertainers. Probably this very intrinsic flexibility of the event made innovation desirable, even inevitable. Hence Erhengbo could creatively change the kind of performance and the content of the *okpobhie* without violating the cultural, artistic, and behavioral rules of this event.

Notes

1. This research was conducted in 1966, under a grant from the Midwestern Universities Consortium for International Activities, to whom I am grateful. I also would like to thank my helpful assistants in the field, Samuel Idah, Robinson Ahanon, and Solomon Amadasu, and Dr. Rebecca Agheyisi, who read and commented on this essay.

2. The terms *Benin*, *Bini*, and *Edo* are all found in the literature. The first two, possibly of Yoruba derivation, are used by Westerners. The former commonly refers to the city and the kingdom, the latter to the tribe and its language. *Edo* is the term the people themselves use for their capital city, kingdom, language, and the tribe.

3. The concept of a communicative event has been developed by Dell Hymes (1964). In this connection, see also the model for the particular event of storytelling as developed by Robert A. Georges (1969).

4. There is, of course, great uncertainty about the actual dating of the Benin kings. These dates follow Egharevba (1960), 27, 38–40. For a modern literary interpretation of this tragic figure, see Ogieriaikhi (1966).

5. A documentary color film describing this royal ritual was prepared by Robert E. Bradbury and Francis Speed ([1962] 1963).

6. See, for example, Sidahome (1964). These tales are narrated by the Ishan narrators; however, they bear similarity to the narratives of the Benin *akpata* players.

Bibliography

Ben-Amos, Daniel. 1967. "Storytelling in Benin." *African Arts / Arts d'Afrique* 1, no. 1: 54–59.

Bradbury, R. E. 1959. "Divine Kingship in Benin." *Nigeria* 62: 186–207.

———. 1967. "The Kingdom of Benin." In *West African Kingdoms in the Nineteenth Century*, edited by Daryll Forde and P. M. Kaberry, 1–35. Oxford: Oxford University Press.

Bradbury, Robert E., and Francis Speed. *Benin Kingship Rituals*. Ethnographic video online. London: Royal Anthropological Institute.

Crowder, Michael. 1965. "Tradition and Change in Nigerian Literature." *Tri-Quarterly* 5:117–28.

Douglas, Mary. 1966. *Purity and Danger: An Analysis of the Concepts of Pollution and Taboo*. London: Routledge and Kegan Paul.

Egharevba, Jacob U. 1949. *Benin Law and Custom*. Port Harcourt, Nigeria: Niger Press.

———. 1960. *A Short History of Benin*. 3rd ed. Ibadan: Ibadan University Press.

Georges, Robert A. 1969. "Toward an Understanding of Storytelling Events." *Journal of American Folklore* 82, no. 326:313–28.

Hymes, Dell. 1964. "Introduction: Toward Ethnographies of Communication." In *The Ethnography of Communication*, edited by John J. Gumperz and Dell Hymes. Special issue, *American Anthropologist* 66, no. 6, pt. 2:1–34.

Laurenty, J. S. 1960. *Les cordophones du Congo Belge et du Ruanda-Urundi*. Annales du Musée Royal du Congo Belge Tervuren. Sciences de l'Homme, n.s., vol. 2. Tervuren: Musée Royal du Congo Belge.

Melzian, Hans. 1937. *A Concise Dictionary of the Bini Language of Southern Nigeria*. London: Kegan Paul, Trench, Trubner and Co.

Ogieriaikhi, Emwinma. 1966. *Oba Ovanramwen and Oba Ewuakpe*. London: University of London Press.

Sidahome, Joseph D. 1964. *Stories from the Benin Empires*. London: Oxford University Press.

Sodenberg, Bertil. 1956. *Les instruments de musique au bas Congo et dans les regions avoisinantes: Etude ethnographique*. Publication no. 3. Stockholm: Statens Etnografiska Museum.

10

INDUCED NATURAL CONTEXT IN CONTEXT

FOLKLORE STUDENTS OF SEVERAL GENERATIONS HAVE GROWN UP on Kenneth Goldstein's *A Guide for Field Workers in Folklore* (1964). When they prepared to go into the field, they used his *Guide*, and they consulted it again when they arrived there. His cogent advice followed them, tucked conveniently in their pocket or pocketbook, reassuring them in doubt and offering solutions in uncertain situations. In the loneliness of the field, the *Guide* became a companion to which researchers turned in crisis and in joy. Goldstein's sound advice, to make "safety copies of all recordings and notes" (1965, 143), followed them wherever they went. He also advised, among other things, that if pay an informant they must, they should consider it as a gesture of "good will and friendship" rather than "a payment of incentive" (170), and counseled that for their own sake, they should stay away from "hostile factionalism" that is inevitably present in any community (73).

When the *Guide* first appeared, one reviewer welcomed it as "an attempt to bring together ideas, suggestions, and theoretical statements which reflect a needed cross-disciplinary point of view," and "highly recommended" it as "stimulated and provocative" (Black 1966, 353). Another hailed it as an "excellent field manual" that "is designed to make [the fieldwork] experience . . . much richer," noting his "praiseworthy ethnographic bias" (Dundes 1965, 547). And in the *Journal of American Folklore*, Arthur J. Rubel emphasized the significance of the book for anthropologists: "It reflects current anthropological interest in cultural cognitive systems" (1965, 369). Almost thirty years later, in a book devoted solely to research and method in oral traditions and the verbal arts, in the midst of a list consisting of the most recent books in the field, Ruth Finnegan mentions Goldstein's *Guide* and comments parenthetically that it "is still useful despite its date" (1992, 57). Later, she points out that his "categories of 'natural,' 'artificial,' and 'induced natural' contexts . . . can be criticized and extended, but are still extremely illuminating distinctions to start from" (76).

Both reviewers and casual commentators singled out the *Guide*'s contribution to the practice of fieldwork in folklore. They welcomed its interdisciplinary nature. However, in the hindsight that thirty years may provide, it appears that they failed to fully apprehend the range of Goldstein's disciplinary borrowing. In most cases, they have been misled by Goldstein's own explicit statements, focusing on his synthesis between methods in folklore and anthropology. A closer reading, however, reveals another discipline looming right behind these two academic siblings in the study of culture. Its presence becomes apparent in Goldstein's casual statements, anecdotal examples, and formal methodological concepts. Consequently, in practice and in purpose, the *Guide*'s contribution to folklore extends far beyond fieldwork, implicitly proposing a research direction that was new at the time of its publication. Since Goldstein himself hardly pursued this direction systematically, and since others have not joined him with sufficient vigor to form a scholarly trend, the novelty of this direction has not worn off, and its promise awaits fulfillment.

Goldstein alluded to the rudiments of such a research direction in his *Guide*. At the same time, he clouded them with some ambiguity and a certain degree of duality of purpose inherent in the book that has obscured his ultimate vision of folklore. Every guidebook or manual has, by definition, an ideal addressee. A tourist guide's readership is self-explanatory; a sex manual aims at the inexperienced, unimaginative, or simply bored lover. Goldstein wrote his book for the consummate folklore collector: "He is the most important element in the scholarship of folklore" because all further "evaluation, interpretation and analysis" (1964, 2) are dependent on the materials the collector harvests in the field. For Goldstein, folklore collecting was the ultimate scholarly experience, and although he realized that its enjoyment depends on temperament, he implicitly hoped that the book would make all folklorists of varying persuasions converts to collecting. Realistically yet optimistically, he states,

> This book cannot make a folklorist a collector. A methodology is only one of the requirements for successful collecting. More important is the individual who would become a collector. If he does not have the inclination, temperament, or personality for collecting, he will not become a successful field worker merely by using the methods and techniques given here. While it is true that his inclination can be changed by inspired instruction, temperament and personality go so much deeper that it is unlikely that they could sufficiently affected. Still, anyone is capable of doing a certain amount of collecting, though not in the "field." One can collect from family, friends, and neighbors, and to such collectors the basic requirements for obtaining data will apply as much as they do to qualified field workers. (Goldstein 1964, 9)

Goldstein's message filters through the conditionals, the "if," the "while," and the "still": collecting folklore itself will be an inspirational experience. Although he knew otherwise, the initial negative statement that opens the quoted paragraph transforms at the conclusion into an expectation that all folklorists will discover the joy of collecting. The "collector" is both the main protagonist and the addressee of the *Guide*. Goldstein advises him; evaluates his action; places him in real, fictive, or hypothetical situations; rescues him out of complex relationships; and weaves both story and theory around his personality.

At the same time, Goldstein cast his ideal collector in another role—that of a scientist. He prepared the *Guide* out of "a concern with the status of the discipline of folklore. It is part of a larger effort to raise the discipline to the level of a science (a social science retaining close ties with the humanities, to be sure)" (1964, 13). The *Guide* would clearly spell out the principles for adequate description of folklore processes: "Such documentation, which is essential if folklore is to achieve scientific status, can be supplied only by trained professional folklorists guided by a body of theory, or by amateurs trained by such professionals" (14). In short, Goldstein's collector has a dual mission: Not only does he have to save folk songs, folktales, proverbs, riddles, and customs from real or alleged oblivion, but he has to conduct his rescue operation along scientific principles.

According to the views that dominated folklore research up to the forties and the fifties, lagging behind other disciplines in the social sciences, there was a clear distinction between collecting, which still had to be accurate and detailed to have any value, and analysis, which ensued as the scientific research stage, involving primarily type classification and motif identification. Such a division is clearly apparent in the discussions at a midforties conference (Anon. 1946), in a set of four midcentury symposia (Thompson 1953) from which Goldstein quotes, and in several studies to which he refers (Addy 1902; Burne 1902; Crooke 1902; Dorson 1953, 1957a, 1957b; 1964, 1–20; Dundes 1962; Grainger 1908; Jones 1946; Leach 1962; Lindgren 1939; Opie 1953; Seligmann 1902; Skeat 1902).

However, for Goldstein, these two roles were inseparable. He recognized that the scientific process began in the field and before, and could not be delayed until the material reached the archive. The formulation of the research problem, the selection of informants, the questions posed to them, and the context of collecting all have direct bearing on any procedures to which a subsequent scientist would subject the collection. Goldstein thus removed the scientific work in folklore from the desk to the field. Goldstein would have agreed with his contemporary, the philosopher of science Norwood R. Hanson, who, in the course of discussing another discipline, pointed out that "by the time a law has been fixed into [a hypothetico-deductive] system, really original physical thinking is over" (1969, 70).

But where could Goldstein find the necessary models for such a conception of the collector as a scientist? They were absent from folklore scholarship. MacEdward Leach, Goldstein's mentor, wrote about the problems of collecting oral literature (1962), but he defined his issues in historical, not scientific, terms, assessing, among other things, the impact of the collector's historical assumptions concerning the origin of folklore in a specific region on the data that he recorded (quoted in Goldstein 1964, 19). Anthropology, with its emphasis on the exotic, could have been helpful, but not sufficiently so, particularly since Goldstein was emphatic that his *Guide* would serve the fieldworker in "essentially rural, agriculturally-based, non-industrial communities," and he took a guarded attitude toward "its application to non-folk, aboriginal, non- or pre-literature areas of the world" (Goldstein 1964, 10). In short, Goldstein requires his fieldworker to act in the dual roles of collector and scientist, yet at the same time, he is rather vague about the models of scientific folklore toward which he aspires.

Yet, although Goldstein did not articulate his sources of scientific inspiration, his *Guide* provides some preliminary clues, which he amplified in some of his later works. In his introductory presentation to his book, Goldstein states, "The *Guide* is based on collecting experiences and experiments conducted in 'folk' communities" (1964, 10). Now, Goldstein's prose is rarely alliterative, and the phrase "experiences and experiments" immediately stands out. Historically, folklore has not been an experimental science. Occasionally, some fieldworkers came on experimental situations serendipitously—a classic case is the Zuni rendition of the Italian version of "The Cock and the Mouse" (Tale Type 2032, "The Cock's Whiskers") that Frank Hamilton Cushing told them and a year later recorded as a native Zuni tale (Cushing 1901, 411–22; reprinted in Dundes 1965, 269–76; see Cushing 1979, 1990). The few occasions in which experimentation has been used in folklore deliberately occurred when psychologists applied their trade to tales and songs (Bartlett 1920, 1932), or when folklorists sought to confirm or refute the role of memory in oral transmission (see Dundes 1965, 246–47).

Therefore, the apparently casual use of the term *experiments* is deliberate and symptomatic, indicating some notions Goldstein had in mind but did not make sufficiently explicit and revealing his orientation toward experimental psychology. Indeed, he clearly listed books in "the fields of psychology"

(Goldstein 1964, xiii) among the works that he read in preparing his *Guide*, and he deferred to psychology as the only field in which he felt a lack of competence, yet recognized its import to his scientific fieldwork. He stated, "The present work does not include methods requiring special training and techniques, such as psychological or projective tests designed to obtain information about personality functioning. When a revised edition of this book is made, it should include one or more chapters on such techniques by persons properly qualified to instruct in them" (11).

Until Albert Lord (1960) had fully developed Parry's formulaic theory, memory had been thought to have a central role in oral transmission, and hence experiments concerning the remembrance of things past seemed to test the central process of oral transmission. But Goldstein wished to extend the role of experimentation in folklore to other areas, such as creativity, the rise and decline of tradition, aesthetic principles, and the role of the individual in the formation and continuation of tradition. For him, the field was for the folklorist what the laboratory was for the psychologist. While he glorified collecting, his *Guide* put an equal emphasis on experimentation with oral tradition. In that sense, Goldstein was a proponent of experimental folklore. In a later study that resulted directly from his fieldwork "experiences and experiments" in Scotland, Goldstein specifically cast the scientific procedures of folklore in these terms. His essay "Experimental Folklore: Laboratory vs. Field" (1967) not only set up a pair of opposites that had been crucial to his conception of folklore, but actually named as "experimental folklore" the direction that he implicitly outlined for the discipline in his *Guide*.

From such a perspective, the *Guide* is not just a handbook for fieldwork, but a proposition for the construction of folklore on the basis of experimental principles. Goldstein preferred the kind of scientific psychology methodology that develops and confirms knowledge through experiments. He tended to formulate folklore as a positivistic science, and in spite of his academic background in statistics, he did not select analytical models from sociology, in which quantitative statistical analysis has provided the positivistic scientific basis, but rather turned to psychology—and specifically, cognitive psychology—as the more appropriate and more relevant model for the science of folklore.

Some European folklorists—Wesselski (1931, 127–31), Anderson (1951), and Ortutay (see Anderson 1956, 5–6)—preceded Goldstein in conducting experiments in folklore. While he acknowledged and criticized them (1967, 73), it is necessary to point out a major difference between Goldstein's experimental folklore and the experiments that preceded him. Anderson, Wesselski, and even Ortutay conducted their experiments within the framework of the historic geographic method. The first sought to confirm, and the second to falsify, the theory of oral diffusion of narratives. Memory, forgetfulness, and narrative re-creation have been some of the core concepts of a diffusion theory that presupposes exclusive reliance on oral transmission. Therefore, when Anderson sought to validate such a theory, he considered it necessary to confirm the reliability of memory in narrative recall. In contrast, Wesselski, who considered print to be the stabilizing factor in folktale transmission, set out to demonstrate the unreliability of memory.

But Goldstein took a completely different path of research. He was not so much concerned with the diffusions of tales or songs, nor with the possibility of the dependence of this process exclusively on oral means, memory, and recall. Rather, he sought to examine experimentally the dynamics of folklore in society. For Goldstein, folklore is a science of social and verbal interaction. To be sure, memory, recall, and verbal creativity are part of his concerns, but he regards them as significant processes in and of themselves and not as instruments in the diffusion of texts. Furthermore, the folklorists and the psychologists before him experimented with folklore in situations that were analogous to the psychological laboratory, whereas Goldstein preferred the natural context of folklore performance in society. For him, this was the only context in which experiments could be valid. In spite of Goldstein's personal and emotional attitude toward field collecting and his many singer-friends, he conceived of the field as the science laboratory of folklore and his "natural context" as the ideal situation for experimental folklore.

Significantly, Goldstein illustrated his typology of contexts (1964, 80–87) with only two specific examples. The first of them, which involves an experiment, concerns the question of recall:

> For many informants the loss of situational familiarity and meaning is so great that they cannot perform effectively. One of my informants in northeastern Scotland could not recall his songs in an artificial context. Outside of his shoe repair shop he felt lost when attempting to sing his songs. I brought him his shoe-mending equipment and asked him to fix my shoes and sing his songs. The attempt was a failure. I took him at his word when he told me: "If you come tae me shop, I'll fairly fill yer tape wi' song while I mend yer sheen there." In the natural context of singing while working in his own shop, he performed some thirty ballads without pause, hesitation, or memory loss; in the artificial context I was able to garner only imperfect and fragmentary texts and tunes. Needless to say, the only meaningful observations of his performance style worth reporting would be those made in the natural context of his shop. (85)

The second example, in which Goldstein addresses the impact of natural context on the singing style of another Scottish informant, illustrates his division between the roles of scientist and collector that a fieldworker may have. "My duty," Goldstein states, "obviously, is to describe her performance styles as observed in natural context; the artificial context was valuable only for obtaining the texts and tunes of the material themselves" (86–87). The scientist, in other words, must conduct his observations and experiments in the natural state of folklore; for the collector, on the other hand, the artificial context may do.

When natural context is unobservable, the experimental scientist can resort to the manipulation of situations and induce the natural context (Goldstein 1964, 87–90; 1968). Logically, the concept of induced natural context is an oxymoron. Induced labor, as many mothers know, is no longer natural, even if it is distinct from some more radical medical interventions. But in the context of experimental folklore, the concept makes sense. It is an experimental situation in which the fieldworker, as scientist, manipulates his informant, causing harm to none, in order to simulate a situation that takes place in society without the fieldworker's presence. It is a collecting situation that is natural and in which the collector minimizes his presence so as to minimize, in turn, his influence on the data to be collected.

Ruth Finnegan, who is sensitive to the ethical issue of "covert" actions by a fieldworker, finds it a valuable concept and method. She writes,

> But there is also a variety of "natural induced" contexts in which the performers know their performances are being recorded but do not find performing in this kind of situation strange. Thus researchers sometimes exploit local conventions by inviting a praise singer to perform at a party, contributing towards the cost of putting on a memorial ceremony, or acting as host for a regular session of riddling and story-telling, whilst not concealing the presence of a tape-recorder in the background (often ignored). Since, after all, performances regularly depend on the instigation of groups and individuals it may not seem unnatural for the researcher to take and overt role. Such settings clearly have some advantages over fully "natural" contexts. Merely waiting around hopefully may mean never having access to certain genres or events. The practice of induced settings may even be a locally recognized one, as in putting on displays for a visitor or for special occasions. Compared to "artificial" settings, "induced" performances may be closer to the normal interactions, particularly if involving an audience—often important for performance. (Finnegan 1992, 80–81)

Goldstein himself offers two examples of induced natural context taken from his own "experiences and experiments":

> Having found out what the normal context for riddling was in northeastern Scotland, I invited six of my informants over for a social evening on Saturday night. When the moment seemed appropriate, I led the conversation in the directions of riddles and posed one that I had heard from an informant who was

not present. I then took the role of a participant observer and was able to study the situation in depth during the two hours that the riddling session went on. In the meantime, my wife sat in the background and made notes on each of the riddles posed. Since there was usually five or six minutes [break] between the time when a riddle was recited and the answer was given, she had sufficient time to write out each riddle and indicate the name of the poser. I made notes on my observations of the riddling context immediately after my informant friends left the house later that evening. By playing the role of the instigator, I was able to hide the real purpose of the evening from every one of the other participants, thereby assuring a more natural context.

I have also been able to avoid using accomplices from among the folk by having a member of my own family play that role on certain occasions. Wishing to observe marbles games in action as played by the children in the neighborhood, I had one of my daughters bring several of her schoolmates to our home so that I could observe them while they played on our rear lawn. Generally, such games were never played in the presence of adults because most of the home owners on the block were angered by the children digging holes in their lawns in order to play their marbles games. My daughter introduced her friends to me and asked if it was all right to play marbles. After I gave my permission, my daughter dug the hole for the game about 15 feet from where I was sitting (according to a pre-arranged plan), so that the game would be in full view to me. I busied myself pretending to be writing letters, but actually was taking notes on the situation. (Goldstein 1964, 89–90)

The natural and the induced natural contexts are methodological concepts in Goldstein's experimental folklore. Yet a method without a theory is like a play—actions without a purpose that have no consequences. What, then, are the theoretical foundations of the science of folklore that Goldstein builds in his *Guide*? Having broken with the diffusion theory of folklore that the historic-geographic school addressed, and not having embraced the literary-historical approach that his mentor, MacEdward Leach, taught, Kenneth Goldstein set in his *Guide* the foundations for a new folklore theory, a theory of cognitive folklore. Goldstein's theory of cognitive folklore seeks, in a sociological-psychological and interactional tradition, to infer from human actions how people process their traditions in their minds and how they apply these traditions in their daily lives and culturally defined specific occasions and social events. While the *Guide* reflects a certain degree of preoccupation with the adequacy of documentation as a basis for the formation of folklore as a science, the details Goldstein asks his fieldworkers to note indicate his goal of establishing folklore as a social science that deals with psychological issues of tradition. Natural and induced natural contexts are the only situations that will yield reliable scientific observations having any value toward the formulation of a theory of cognitive folklore. While such a theory may, in the final analysis, offer some universal principles, Goldstein conceives of human cognition as cultural dependent and situationally conditioned. Therefore, it is necessary to observe traditional performances and actions within their cultural and situational contexts. His *Guide* spells out the basic requirements for scientific observation, documentation, and experimentation that would establish cognitive folklore as a social science.

Bibliography

Addy, S. O. 1902. "The Collection of Folklore." *Folk-Lore* 13, no. 3:297–99.

Addy, Sidney O., Charlotte S. Burne, William Crooke, Walter Skeat, C. G. Seligman, and John Roscoe. "The Collection of Folklore." *Folklore* 13, no. 3:297–313.

Anderson, Walter. 1951. *Ein volkskundliches Experiment.* Folklore Fellows Communication, vol. 141. Helsinki: Soumalainen Tiedeakatemia.

———. 1956. *Eine neue Arbeit zur Experimentellen Volkskunde.* Folklore Fellows Communication, vol. 168. Helsinki: Soumalainen Tiedeakatemia.

Anonymous. 1946. "Conference on the Character and State of Studies in Folklore." *Journal of American Folklore* 59, no. 234:495–527.

Black, Robert A. 1966. "Review of *A Guide for Field Workers in Folklore*, by Kenneth S. Goldstein." *Ethnomusicology* 10, no. 3:352–53.

Burne, Charlotte S. 1902. "The Collection of Folklore." *Folklore* 13, no. 3:299–302.

Crooke, William. 1902. "The Collection of Folklore." *Folklore* 13, no. 3:302–7.

Cushing, Frank H. 1901. *Zuni Folk Tales.* New York: G. P. Putnam's Sons.

———. 1979. *Zuni: Selected Writings of Frank Hamilton Cushing.* Edited by Jesse Green. Lincoln: University of Nebraska Press.

———. 1990. *Cushing at Zuni: The Correspondence and Journals of Frank Hamilton Cushing, 1879–1884.* Edited by Jesse Green. Albuquerque: University of New Mexico Press.

Dorson, Richard M. 1953. "Collecting in County Kerry." *Journal of American Folklore* 66, no. 259:19–42.

———. 1957a. "Collecting Folklore in Jonesport, Maine." *Proceedings of the American Philosophical Society* 101, no. 3:270–89.

———. 1957b. "Standards for Collecting and Publishing American Folktales." *Journal of American Folklore* 70, no. 275:53–57.

———, ed. 1964. *Buying the Wind.* Chicago: University of Chicago Press.

Dundes, Alan. 1965. "Review of *A Guide for Field Workers in Folklore*." *American Anthropologist,* n.s., 67, no. 3:546–47.

Finnegan, Ruth. 1992. *Oral Traditions and the Verbal Arts: A Guide to Research Practices.* London and New York: Routledge.

Goldstein, Kenneth S. 1964. *A Guide for Field Workers in Folklore.* Memoirs of the American Folklore Society, vol. 52. Hatboro, PA: Folklore Associates.

———. 1967. "Experimental Folklore: Laboratory vs. Field." In *Folklore International: Essays in Traditional Literature, Belief, and Custom in Honor of Wayland Debs Hand*, edited by D. K. Wilgus and Carol Sommer, 71–82. Hatboro, PA: Folklore Associates.

———. 1968. "The Induced Natural Context: An Ethnographic Folklore Field Technique." In *Essays on the Verbal and Visual Arts: Proceedings of the 1966 Annual Spring Meeting of the American Ethnological Society*, edited by June Helm, 1–6. Seattle: American Ethnological Society.

Grainger, Percy. 1908. "Collecting with the Phonograph." *Journal of the Folk-song Society* 3, no. 12: 147–62.

Hanson, Norwood R. 1989. *Patterns of Discovery: An Inquiry into the Conceptual Foundations of Science.* Cambridge: Cambridge University Press.

Jones, Louis C. 1946. "A Student Guide to Collecting Folklore." *New York Folklore Quarterly* 2:148–53.

Leach, MacEdward. 1962. "Problems of Collecting Oral Literature." *PMLA* 77, no. 3:335–40.

Lindgren, Ethel J. 1939. "The Collection and Analysis of Folk-Lore." In *The Study of Society: Methods and Problems,* edited by F. Bartlett et al., 328–78. London: Routledge and Kegan Paul.

Lord, Albert B. 1960. *The Singer of Tales.* Harvard Studies in Comparative Literature 24. Cambridge: Harvard University Press.

Opie, Peter. 1953. "The Collection of Folklore in England." *Journal of the Royal Society* 101:697–714.

Rubel, Arthur J. 1965. "Review of *A Guide for Field Workers in Folklore.*" *Journal of American Folklore* 78, no. 310:359–60.

Seligmann, Charles G. 1902. "The Collection of Folklore in England." *Folk-Lore* 13, no. 3:310–12.

Skeat, W. 1902. "The Collection of Folklore." *Folk-lore* 13, no. 3:307–10.

Thompson, Stith, ed. 1953. *Four Symposia On Folklore.* Indiana University Publications Folklore Series, no. 8. Bloomington: Indiana University Press.

Wesselski, Albert. 1931. *Versuch einer Theorie des Märchens.* Prager Deutsche Studien 45. Reichenberg, Germany: i. B. F. Kraus.

11

THE NAME IS THE THING

*D*URING THE 1996 ANNUAL MEETING OF THE AMERICAN *Folklore Society (AFS), several folklorists called for the replacement of the term* folklore *with one that would better represent current activities in the field and that would be free of any negative connotations. A new term would enable folklorists to center themselves in both scholarship and public affairs. In defense of* folklore, *the present essay begins by comparing the addresses given at the celebration of the term's centennial and those delivered at its 150th anniversary. In the United States, where folklore has suffered the greatest damage, there is a correlation between the departure of folklorists from the academy and their move into the public sector and the devaluation of the meaning of folklore.[1]*

The Centennial: The Science of Folklore

Fifty years ago, as the world woke up from the nightmare of the Second World War, folklorists in England and the United States commemorated the centennial of *folklore*. In their respective presidential addresses to the British Folklore Society and the AFS, Lord Raglan and Melville Herskovits each surveyed the territories of the same discipline and found them as different as could be. For Raglan, folklore was in a state of depletion. The study of superstitions, the mainstay of Thoms's definition of folklore, was "gloomy and barren," or simply not attractive. The subject matter of folklore was "tending toward exhaustion," and comparative studies had lost their luster, since any new discovery only repeated what was already known (Raglan 1946, 98).

Raglan offered a three-pronged solution to rescue folklore from its doldrums. First, he proposed to make folklore into "a historical science" that would study the evolution of customs and costumes. Second, he suggested "dialect [as] another subject which has received little scientific study" (1946, 102) and implicitly could and should be an object of folklore research. Finally, he turned to vernacular architecture, "local house types," as a subject of folkloric scientific inquiry. In concluding his address, Raglan did not "suggest that the members of the Society should abandon their quest for superstitions and quaint survivals. These must remain one of the subjects of their study" (105). But as a way of strengthening the scientific aspect of folklore, he proposed "to collect and publish in convenient form, information on all aspects of folk life, using the term in its widest sense, in the hope of enabling us to find out how and why changes in customs and fashions come about, and thereby developing a real science of folklore" (105).

In hindsight, this was a disappointing research program. From the scholar who had offered us, ten years earlier, the classic study of *The Hero* (1936), in which he formulated an analytical model for the heroic personality in tradition, we could have expected a more innovative and rigorous agenda, but Raglan couched his argument in personal anecdotes and grounded it in the local landscape of the English countryside. His science of folklore was British through and through. The researchers were city and country gentlemen, and their objects were communities of miners and farmers. The Trobriand Islanders, the Nagas of Assam, and the Ashanti were the symbolic distant other, about whom, paradoxically, more information was available than "about our own fellow-countrymen" (1946, 100). His approach to the science he espoused was, at best, amateurish. He found research topics "interesting" (101, 102) without formulating a theory, a hypothesis, or a broader frame of knowledge that would offer a reason for his interest.

Furthermore, the directions for the rejuvenation of the science of folklore might have been new to Raglan, but hardly to anybody else. No doubt, there has been immense progress in his three targeted areas since 1946, but by that time, substantial research on these subjects had already been made. The historical study of everyday life had been fermenting in France at least since the establishment of the *Annales d'histoire economique et sociale* (1929) by Marc Bloch (1886–1944) and Lucien Febvre (1878–1956).[2] As a systematic field of study, dialectology dates to the mid-nineteenth century (Chambers and Trudgill 1980; Francis 1983). In fact, Raglan's selection of dialect as a new challenge for folklore research is somewhat baffling, since the first book that has the word *folklore* in its title also has the term *dialect* in the title (Sternberg 1851). Finally, the study of vernacular architecture flourished in continental Europe and England during the interwar years (Fox 1943; Peate 1940). However, Raglan, not an academic, did not bear the responsibility of acknowledging previous scholarship when advancing new ideas.[3]

In contrast, across the Atlantic, Melville Herskovits surveyed the fields of folklore from an academic perspective that had been shaped by his anthropological education and research experience in Africa and the Americas. Quoting Stith Thompson (1940, 866), he first noticed the worldwide acceptance of the term in European languages, then pointed out that this linguistic diffusion did not imply conceptual uniformity: "In Germany, *Volkskunde* has from the beginning been treated as a subject of far wider scope than the folklore of England. . . . In the Latin countries, both of Europe and the New World, the concept of the scope of folklore varies between the limits set by the English and the German views" (Herskovits 1946, 92). In France, he further remarked, van Gennep had not considered folklore "a simple collection of trivial unrelated facts, which are more or less curious and amusing, but a synthetic science that is concerned in particular with rural life and peasants and those of them who live in industrial and urban surroundings" (92–93).[4] Throughout his address, Herskovits juggled the American, the German, the French, and the English views in order to achieve his desired redefinition of *folklore* as the study of oral literature.

Though it was problematic, encumbered by conflicting approaches and contradictory theories and methods, for both Raglan and Herskovits, folklore was a science writ large. Raglan projected folklore as a historical science of everyday life that was concerned with behavior, speech, dress, and housing. His words rang fresh within the context of English folklore. By comparison, Herskovits's science of folklore was in the anthropological tradition that Franz Boas had initiated in the United States (Bronner 1986; Stocking 1996) and that William Wells Newell articulated in his programmatic essay (Newell 1888) and other writings (Newell 1898). Herskovits (1946) concluded that in spite of the ambiguities of the term and the dilemmas folklorists faced, "Folklorists . . . have succeeded over the century just ending, in welding our discipline firmly into the structure of scientific scholarship" (94). For him, "what we call folklore . . . which to many seems trivial, to many seems dull . . . may become the most attractive and serious of sciences" (94). While Herskovits reached out for textual support for his ideas all the way across the Atlantic, quoting Andrew Lang from A. R. Wright (1931, 11), it was clear that he had in mind the particular American configuration of folklore that Newell delineated around the same time that Andrew Lang did.

No doubt, fifty years ago, the perception that folklore was welded "firmly into the structure of scientific scholarship" was somewhat premature. With no departments to speak of, no research institutes, and no training programs, individuals rather than universities bore the burden of folklore. Their accomplishments and future plans were, then and now, a source of pride and inspiration. In their studies, they spanned the gamut of cultures from regional

Americana to German, Spanish, African, and other immigrant lores to the folklore of the American Indians in the East, the Plains, and the West (*Journal of American Folklore* [*JAF*] 1946; Gayton 1947).

The absence of nationalism as a component of folklore was unique to the American configuration of folklore. Nationalism was crucial in the transformation of the German *Volkskunde* from avocation to science (Riehl 1859), and functioned to catalyze folklore scholarship in smaller European nations (Alver 1989; Basgoz 1972; Dow 1991; Gillis 1994; Herzfeld 1982; Hutchinson 1987; Kapferer 1988; Snyder 1959; Wilson 1976), but regional diversity and multiple ethnicity have left no space for the popular nationalistic spirit. It did not figure in the American folklore paradigm that William Wells Newell constructed (Abrahams 1988; Bell 1973) and on the basis of which Herskovits formulated his redefinition of folklore.

Similarly absent from Herskovits's thesis is the "affable condescension to the 'common people'" that Wright (1931, 9) discerns in Henry Bourne's *Antiquities Vulgares* (1725) and traces of which are still apparent in Lord Raglan's commemorative address. Such a sentiment is inherent in the attitude of antiquarians who collected popular objects (Elsner and Cardinal 1994; P. Levine 1986; Pomian 1987; Stagl 1995), but, as Herskovits points out, "in the American [academic] scene, the problem posed by the antiquarian point of view in folklore was ... peripheral" (1946, 94).[5] Rather, he sets out to show that in America "the presence of Indians . . . [had a role] in shaping the conceptualization of our discipline, even for American folklorists whose primary concerns were far removed from anthropological studies" (94).

By reaching out to the formative era of folklore in America, Herskovits evokes intellectual roots that stretch even further into European intellectual history. Implicit in his redefinition of folklore as oral literature is not only a restatement of an anthropological division of labor in nonliterate societies (Bascom 1953; Zumwalt 1988) but also the adoption of a humanistic perspective that seeks to embrace literate and nonliterate peoples on equal terms. Six years after Herskovits's statement, the Italian folklorist Giuseppe Cocchiara (1981, 13–28) exposed the roots folklore had in Renaissance humanism and the role it played in shaping the human sciences in the nineteenth and twentieth centuries. In the 1940s, unbeknown to Western scholars, Mikhail Bakhtin considered the writings of Rabelais as the earliest indications of folkloristic consciousness (Bakhtin 1968, 4).[6] But none could have stated the position of folklore in the human sciences more clearly than Cocchiara's eighteenth-century countryman, Giambattista Vico (1688–1744), who wrote, employing the term *mythology*, "The first science to be learned should be mythology or the interpretation of fables; for, as we shall see, all the histories of the gentiles have their beginnings in fables, which were the first histories of the gentile nations. By such a method the beginning of sciences as well as of the nations are to be discovered, for they sprang from the nations and from no other sources" (Vico 1984, 51).

Fifty Years Later: Lamentations for Folklore

In her 1996 AFS presidential address, Jane Beck, taking a cue from a lawyer who said to Shalom Staub, "You need a new word for yourselves," makes the diagnosis that "the term *folklore* helps to marginalize the discipline." Therefore, she suggests that we "consider the possibility [of changing the name of our field] seriously. We should have," she argues, "a term for the discipline so that people will recognize it as the profound study that it is. We have much to offer other fields; why not change the name and at the same time do a little redefining?" (Beck 1997,134). Barbara Kirshenblatt-Gimblett (1996) identifies the term *folklore* as a liability, proposing to "change our name to enhance our survival" (252). Following the principle of "truth in advertising," she argues that "it is time to assess where we find ourselves, those trained as folklorists and those who identify themselves as folklorists, and ask what name best describes what we do" (252).

Kirshenblatt-Gimblett has a far more drastic agenda than just changing the name *folklore*. She well understands that a name change is not a minor verbal cosmetic operation, but that it signals the death of a discipline. She regards herself as a passive witness to that historical process and thinks that what is left for her is to give folklore a proper burial. Invoking a biological model, she says, "Disciplines are not forever. . . . We are the beneficiaries of the fragmentation of the great omnibus disciplines of the seventeenth and eighteenth centuries—cosmography, geography, statistics, and philology. During the latter half of the nineteenth century, as these fields broke up into their subspecialties, they either disappeared or became a shadow of their former selves" (1996, 249).

Similar metaphors dominate the article in which Regina Bendix advocates "a Frazerian ritual slaying of the name *folklore* to make room for the installation of one or more new names" (1998, 238; emphasis in the original). Both marketing and ideological considerations motivate her aggressive attitude toward *folklore*. She argues that "the name *folklore* impinges on the field's efficacy" (236; emphasis in the original), constraining it in "the marketplace of ideas" in which folklorists have broadened the scope of their research, "from remote villages to what Marc Augé calls the 'non-places' of supermodernity" (Augé 1995; Bendix 1998, 236). In "the *marketplace of professionals*, the name literally stands in the way of getting jobs" (Bendix 1998, 236). In the ideological arena, she considers folklore contaminated by its use by national and racial movements and hence assumes "that the ideology inscribed in the field of folklore has during the past century and a half latently or even overtly assisted in a horrifying number of deaths" (238), and therefore, guilty by association, it should be eliminated.

In the first centennial of folklore, leading scholars charted its future with new visions, directions, and challenges. How, then, in less than half a century, could folklore fall? How, then, in less than a quarter of a century, could folklore shift from the interdisciplinary highway of ideas into a dead-end alley? How did the "New Perspectives" (Paredes and Bauman 1972) dull into no prospect at all? How could folklore sink so low in the eyes of its practitioners that a retiring president, a former president, and a board member of the AFS could respectively declare *folklore* an undesirable term that should be dumped from our professional discourse, removed from the name of our society, and eliminated altogether as a symbol of our professional identity?

To be sure, the messages of Beck, Kirshenblatt-Gimblett, and Bendix are not the first signals of trouble in the house of folklore, nor have these three distinguished folklorists been the only messengers. Frustrations have encroached on folklore and folklorists from every corner. Negative connotations of the term in popular use; ambiguities of professional identity; economic instability; apparent academic disrespect on the one hand and pilferage of folklore subjects, concepts, and theories by other disciplines on the other hand: All have amounted to a real threat to folklore's scholarly integrity. When a group of folklorists met in Santa Rosa at the annual meeting of the California Folklore Society on April 27–29, 1990, they bemoaned and deliberated on these very issues, and when the meeting ended, Robert Georges concluded it, motivational style, with a call to arms: "And I want to see how many people say, 'I'm a folklorist!' Raise your hands! How many people are proud of it? Raise your hand! How many of you think we should continue the good fight? Raise your hands! Good. Thank you very much for coming and participating" (Georges 1991, 126).

Turning the culture of folklorists into the culture of organization (Gones et al. 1988) could be as ominous as spreading despair. It is the losing team that needs its cheerleaders most. Both the message of doom and the rallying shouts signal a condition of folklore that stands in sharp contrast to the views folklorists expressed just fifty years ago. At that time, Lord Raglan's criticism of folklore studies was severe but not destructive; Herskovits's redefinition of folklore as oral literature aimed at strengthening its intellectual and academic position.

Hence we must ask ourselves, what road has folklore traversed in the past half century that its own custodians call for its execution? Why does folklore seem to sink to such low depths that its own rescue mission turns into a funerary chorus? And why are the praise songs of fifty years ago lamentations? Some answers, I suspect, recalling a line from the era of *When We Were Good* (Cantwell 1996) are "blowing in the wind"; others, however, are in our deeds.

Folklore in the Academy: Entrance and Exit

First, it is necessary, as Beck (1997) proposed, to take stock of our discipline. How different is its position in the universities now than fifty or even one hundred years ago? When and where has its wheel of fortune made its downward turn, if indeed it has made such a turn, and what are the reasons for the decline in aspiration and collective self-confidence? Even without engaging in a sophisticated statistical analysis, it is clear that folklore is not thriving in an academic environment in the United States. It never was. There has never been a "golden age of folklore," McNeil (1980, 943) notwithstanding. Although the AFS was admitted into the American Council of Learned Societies in 1945, the universities virtually barred folklore from their structure. No celebratory rhetorics, or even enumeration of courses and departments (Baker 1971, 1986; Boggs 1940, 1945; Camp 1989; Clements 1988; Dorson 1950, 1961, 1965, 1972a; 1972c, 3–10; Hand 1960), can camouflage the fact that numerically folklore has but a pitiful presence in US higher education. By any quantitative measure we apply—number of departments, number of students, financial support for research, publications—only delusionary grandeur may create a fata morgana of self-importance. During the period of institutional growth in the 1950s and 1960s, and the continuous trickle up to the present, departments of folklore have been established in less than one tenth of 1 percent of US colleges and universities.[7]

This regrettable situation stands in contrast to the original intention of the founders of the AFS. They were motivated by a commitment to scholarship. Among them were distinguished members of distinguished universities, or young and visionary scholars whose later accomplishments reflected their early ideals and goals. Their first meeting took place at University Hall at Harvard University (*JAF* 1888, 3; McNeil 1980, 781), a gesture that had, no doubt, practical reasons, but also symbolic implications. Their journal was to publish only those articles that "seem to possess sufficient scientific status" (*JAF* 1888, 7) and exclude popular and philosophically speculative essays. But the scientific model they envisioned lacked bases in the scientific establishments. Many of the founders had faculty positions, but not in folklore departments, which did not exist at the time. This pattern of relations between the Society and the universities continued for over sixty years. Researchers highly regarded for their work on folklore in their respective disciplines did not find it necessary or desirable to have folklore as a distinct discipline.

The establishment of the Folklore Institute and the doctoral degree program in 1949, and the Department of Folklore in 1963 at Indiana University and the Folklore Program at the University of Pennsylvania in 1962 (Samuelson 1983), represented a new era for folklore in the United States. A formal educational program that would constitute folklore as an independent discipline required a framework, delineated boundaries, constructed an intellectual pedigree, and defined fundamental theoretical concepts. All these factors bestowed on folklore a distinct professional identity. But that change from an elusive existence to a clear presence has proven both a blessing and a curse. On the one hand, the faculty members appropriated portions out of existing fields such as anthropology, literature, history, linguistics, and ethnomusicology, and recombined them into the paradigm of folklore. On the other hand, with no sufficient number of departments in which to place graduating folklorists, there was no way to carry this newly lit torch. While folklore has achieved recognition within the academy, with only a few departments in the entire country, it has remained a discipline in isolation.

In order to overcome this paradoxical turn of events, Dorson searched for a strategy for folklore, fully aware of the dynamics of university recruitment:

> The crux of the matter lies in the departmental structure of American universities. Departments are composed of scholars holding the PhD in a common field, and they recruit new members with the same doctorate. In smaller institutions, the president may hire new members, but he places them in a department of their fellow-PhDs. The problem for the new doctor of folklore, and his sponsors, is to persuade a department composed of doctors in English, or anthropology, or history, or foreign languages, or music, to give him a home. A number of such departments have taken in their token folklorists, but each negotiation represents a struggle; many institutions possess no folklorists, and too often, especially now, if the folklorist moves to a more attractive situation his vacancy is gobbled up by hungry chairmen, former colleagues, or harassed deans to use for a Milton specialist or an urban anthropologist, or it may simply vanish. (Dorson 1972a, 107)

Under such circumstances, the placement of a newly minted folklore doctorate in a university faculty became a familiar struggle. When the postwar growth in US higher education came to a standstill, the folklore graduate pressure at the gates of the academy came to naught. The new doctorates in folklore joined the academic proletariat that rose in numbers in other fields as well, and became part of a national intellectual unemployment line consisting of thousands of personal frustration stories.[8]

The success in getting the proverbial foot in the academic door turned disastrous when this very door was quick to shut firm again. The growth that took place in the 1960s and early 1970s oversupplied the demand that theoretically it should have opened up. Yet facing such an economic dilemma, no one even contemplated scaling down the development of folklore. All the speakers in the panel entitled "The Academic Future of Folklore" (Dorson 1972a) save one endorsed Dorson's position, emphasizing different aspects of his strategy for expansion, depending on personal experience and orientation. The only uncomfortably dissenting voice was that of Robert Byington (Dorson 1972a, 113–14), who, continuing a dialogue he had initiated a year earlier (Sweterlitsch 1971), pointed the way toward the exit sign from the university and onward to applied folklore. At that time, Byington's agenda for the future of folklore was still somewhat vague, but the program for an opportunistic defection from the university clearly emerged in the conclusion of his statement:

> What I am saying is that whether [the folklorist] teaches one course, directs a program, chairs a department, or works for church or state, the trained folklorist, *qua* folklorist, is going to find more and more work; he need merely look around for it. And if this sounds like an endorsement of Applied Folklore, I mean it to. I see "pure" and "applied" on a *single* continuum, not as disparate or antithetical activities. If I appear to emphasize the latter in these concluding comments, it is only because I agree with what Dick Dorson almost but not quite said, viz., that, whether we like it or not, higher education is entering an era of unprecedented accountability to the public at large—meaning, among other things, that those disciplines with demonstrable social value are likely to fare better that those without it. Folklore has a great opportunity here. Let's not blow it. (Quoted in Dorson 1972a, 114; emphasis in the original)

In spite of the strong support for Dorson's academic strategy for folklore, the lone dissenting voice on that panel won the day. There is a direct, continuous line of action from the 1971 Middle Atlantic Conference on Folk Culture, held at Point Park College in Pittsburgh and devoted to the theme of applied folklore, to the formation of an AFS committee on applied folklore to the "Proposal for the Establishment of a Center for Applied Folklore" to the lobbying effort that culminated in the successful legislation of the 1976 American Folklife Preservation Act.[9] Burt Feintuch and the participants in the 1985 conference "Folklife and the Public Sector: Assessment and Prognosis" (Feintuch

1988) concur in this historical interpretation. I defer to another occasion a discussion of Byington's claim that "'pure' and 'applied' [folklore are] on a single continuum" (Dorson 1972a, 114) and whether the dichotomies between the two are indeed mistaken (Kirshenblatt-Gimblett 1988).

At this point, it is sufficient to note that the AFS has made a deliberate choice: Rather than rising to the challenge that folklore has encountered in the universities, establishing itself as the indispensable discipline that it is, it has sought an alternative model for development outside the academic structure. Serious scholars have assumed that since the academic route is closed, it might be possible to open up a new course of action. They found a precedent for such an action during the period of the Great Depression, when the federal government included folklore among the projects designed for the employment of writers, teachers, and local historians (Botkin 1939; Hirsch 1987, 1988, 1996; Mangione 1972, 265–85; Penkower 1977, 136–58). This massive collecting project was not initiated by the AFS, nor did it have a rigorous methodological design, but by its conclusion, the academic and nonacademic members of the Society appreciated its significance and listened without critical comments to Botkin's description of his publication plans for this material (*JAF* 1946, 520–22). With the progress of folklore in the universities stalled, the turn toward public folklore as applied folklore was later rechristened in the early 1970s (Baron and Spitzer 1992; Feintuch 1988; Gross Bressler 1995), receiving not only a passive blessing but also the active involvement of the members and officeholders of the AFS:

> In the opinion of folklorists who followed that route, being a conscious and conscientious public folklorist depends less on employment venue than the primacy of collaboration with traditional artists and communities in the representation of their cultural expression. Public folklorists do many or all of the following over the arc of a career: research and writing to describe and interpret folk cultures; teaching students to know, respect, and further research diverse cultural expression; producing media documents and curating exhibits and festivals that present traditional communities and the issues they face; addressing public policy and market conditions that affect access to tangible and intangible resources necessary for sustenance of traditional culture; and working with native scholars to assist groups in documenting their own cultures. (Baron and Spitzer 1992, 2).

While public folklore indeed has expanded the employment opportunities for the professional folklorists who have made it their choice, there has been one thing that they have encountered in the public arena for which they have not bargained: *folklore* in scholarship and *folklore* in the community have divergent meanings. As a discipline, folklore has not incurred negative evaluations. Its difficulty in making headway within the academic structure may have to do with its nonscholarly tradition, but not because it "suggests falsity, wrongness, fantasy and distortion" (Kirshenblatt-Gimblett 1996, 246). Archer Taylor (1952) has observed that "in the humanities folklore has won for itself only a small place. This is not surprising because it has not been able to free itself completely from the antiquarian and dilettante tradition of collecting curiosities. Proverbs, tales, ballads, customs, or superstitions are thought to be quaint and are recorded and studied for that reason" (59). If, then, folklore is tainted, it is necessary to distinguish between its various hues. During the "Mid-century International Folklore Conference" that was held at Blooming-ton, Indiana, in 1953, the negative connotation of the term *folklore* was not an issue (Thompson 1953, 248–65; 318–23); neither was it a concern in the flurry of folklore definitions that burst out in the 1950s and early 1960s (Bascom 1953, 1955; Bayard 1953; Halpert 1958; Utley 1961).

The first inkling of any negative connotation associated with *folklore* in a scholarly context appeared in "The Ditchley Park Conference Resolution." In their address to the nonacademic public, the participants acknowledged that "folklore is often regarded as a matter of fun and frivolity" (Dorson et al. 1970, 95). At that time, Dorson had not yet recovered, if he ever did, from the cutting of one million dollars from the National Defense Education Act that was targeted, among other fields, for folklore. While in his original letter he cited the journalistic ridicule of folklore, he associated the word mainly with folk singers and his pat archenemies, the "fakelorists." "Unhappily," he writes, "the study of folklore in the United States has become contaminated by ama-teurs, entertainers, and charlatans. Because the word 'folklore' is used so widely, all kinds of people pass judgment on folklore" (Dorson 1962, 163). He maintained this association in writing "The Ditchley Park Conference Reso-lution." Apparently, neither he nor the other conferees who made the associa-tion between folklore and entertainment appeared troubled by the negative connotation of inherent falsehood. The absence of negative semantics from *folklore* was not due simply to the scholarly context and to folklorists' posi-tive attitudes toward it. In fact, more general indicators suggest that folklore acquired its negative connotation in the English language relatively recently.

The standard meanings of *folklore* in the Oxford English Dictionary (2nd ed.) include "a. The traditional beliefs, legends, and customs, current among the common people; the study of these." What might be construed as a nega-tive semantic value is added as "b. Recently in extended use: popular fantasy and belief." The illustrating phrases date from 1954. The American stan-dard dictionaries suggest an even later date of attaching any negative mean-ings to *folklore*. Only the third edition of the authoritative *Webster's New*

International Dictionary of the English Language includes as a third definition the description of folklore as "a widely held unsupported specious notion or body of notions." This phrase is absent from the second edition of the same dictionary. The more popular versions of the dictionary, such as *Webster's New Collegiate Dictionary*, represent similar developments. The seventh edition does not include any negative connotation for folklore, and only in the ninth and tenth editions (published in 1977 and 1994 respectively) is there a listing for the third meaning: "3: a widely held unsupported notion or body of notions," and "3: an often unsupported notion, story, or saying that is widely circulated."[10]

Admittedly, by their very nature, dictionaries lag behind any semantic development of language in society, and therefore it would be erroneous to assume that *folklore* acquired its negative value in English and American uses only at the second half of the twentieth century. Earlier dates are probable. Dorson stated as matter of course in 1972 that "to the layman, and to the academic man too, folklore suggests falsity, wrongness, fantasy, and distortion" (1972b, 1). Regardless of the precise year, however, it is clear that implicating "folklore" with any negative association is a secondary and a relatively recent phenomenon. But this has been the meaning and the range of association encountered by folklorists who work in the public sector. In academic contexts, this negative connotation has been known, but there, it has been counterbalanced by all the positive analytical associations of the term.

In analytical discourse, terms have a life of their own. *Folklore* has been defined and redefined many times over. Each country and each generation has molded the concept to suit its own intellectual concerns. Scholarly dialogues provide sufficient room for disagreements, nuances, and shifts in meanings, emphases, and purposes *within* a continuous discourse. The *folklore* of "New Perspectives" (Paredes and Bauman 1972) is not identical with the *folklore* of "Theorizing Folklore" (Briggs and Shuman 1993), yet the identity of the term provides conceptual continuity that makes any difference meaningful.

In scholarship, the meaning of *folklore* is subject to negotiation, but in the community at large, politicians and the public seek a definite unambiguous answer to the question, "What is *folklore*?" Once folklorists step into the public arena, they fall into the trap of intellectual closure, and by doing so terminate their own inquiry.

The semantic shifts of *folklore* that dictionaries document represent an extension of meanings from the particular to the general. As tall tales, legends, folk tales, superstitions, and ballads represent lies, fiction, fantasy, and irrationality, so does the general category to which they belong. When *folklore* extends its social base and becomes a widely circulated term, it broadens its meaning to include connotations that might be in conflict with its learned sense. Jane Beck is a folklore scholar and a proud public folklorist; Barbara Kirshenblatt-Gimblett (1988) is academically based but has formulated the theoretical foundation for the public excursion of folklore. If Kirshenblatt-Gimblett (1996) is correct in her description of *folklore*, the meaning of the term outside scholarly discourse is in itself a survival of nineteenth-century theories of culture and folklore, a learned idea that has become a *gesunkenes Kulturgut* in the public domain. There it preserves meanings that scholars held previously but no longer hold. Yet despite her awareness that "the notion of folklore as error" is an error in itself and only part of "popular understanding" (252), she is ready to give up her hard-gained insights for an idea that she knows is wrong. She no doubt knows that folklore has not been "the science of tradition" she claims it to be (252), at least not for the last fifty years, ever since Herskovits pointed out that "the nonsense tales about psychiatrists that go the rounds of University faculty clubs are 'lore' and the intellectuals who tell them are a 'folk'" (Herskovits 1946,100), and she knows that the concepts of folk and tradition have been critically examined over and over (Ben-Amos 1984; Dundes 1977; Glassie 1995; Handler and Linnekin 1984; Hobsbawm and Ranger 1983; McDonald 1997; Shils 1981; Simpson 1921); in folkloristics (Kirshenblatt-Gimblett 1988), these concepts hardly have the same meanings she imputes to them, drawing on notions prevailing in the general public.

Even some publications for lay readership have taken notice of these conceptual changes. For example, *Merriam Webster's Encyclopedia of Literature* (1995) clearly states, "After World War II the study of folklore lost its restrictions of class and even of educational level; any group that expressed its inner cohesion by maintaining shared traditions qualified as a 'folk,' whether the linking factor was occupation, language, place of residence, age, religion, or ethnic origin. Emphasis also shifted from the past to the present, from the search of origins to the investigation of present meaning and function" (424). The entry, by the way, does not include a single negative word about folklore, neither as a discipline nor as a subject matter.[11] Nowadays, it is the professional folklorists who lag behind their own image.

The excursion into public folklore has brought on a mental fatigue that brings to the surface personal and professional doubts: "Maybe in fighting to keep the name, we'll lose our life as a field of study. Shall we uphold the name, defend what we do in terms of it, and correct misconceptions of what folklore is and what folklorists do?" (Kirshenblatt-Gimblett 1996, 252). Within the discipline, there could not have been any other reply than a resounding positive affirmation. The negative reply that Beck, Bendix, and Kirshenblatt-Gimblett so loudly voice is a direct consequence of their exchanging scholarly for popular presentations of folklore. They have adopted the perception of the field as it exists in popular culture, and they understandably do not like it, but instead of changing their orientation, they opt to shift the terminological framework of their ideas to suit their new context of operation.

Within the public arena, folklore festivals have replaced the country shows that exhibited freaks of nature. Now the festivals put on display the oddities of modern societies, the storyteller, the craftsperson, and the musician. Such festivals and public presentations do indeed marginalize folklore, making it a quaint curiosity. The association of such public displays with scholarship, now that trained scholars put them on, makes folklore appear like a freak discipline itself. From this perspective, folklore is the domain of survivals and marginal characters. But this is a distorted view of folklore as a discipline. When folklorists are engaged in such activities, they begin to accept their image as reflected in curved mirrors. They do not like what they see. Who would? But instead of getting out of the field of warped reflections, they think that a change in name would change the way they look (see Lapierre 1995).

What Is in a Name?

The semantic changes that *folklore* has experienced in general use have clearly affected folklorists who have entered the public arena, and even those who limit their discourse to analytical modes are aware of them. No doubt, there is a certain degree of mutual semantic interference emanating from the different contexts in which *folklore* occurs. Possibly, the contradictory uses of *folklore* as an aggregate of false and irrational notions, and *folklore* as a discipline governed by logic and systematic theories and methods, make the maintenance of such a distinction even more difficult. Yet the naming of a science has an important function in the history of thought, and it should not be discarded because of some external linguistic developments. The consideration of the negative meanings of *folklore* not as new philological developments but as "atavism, a return of the repressed, a deep layer in an archeology of our knowledge" (Kirshenblatt-Gimblett 1996, 246) turns *folklore* itself into a survival, ignoring the diachronic dynamics of language and equating *folklore* with its Latin root, *vulgus*, that appears in Thomas Browne's *Pseudodoxia Epidemica: Enquiries into Vulgar and Common Errors* (1646), one of the books that the canonical history of the field regards as a precursor of folklore research (Dorson 1968, 23).

The name of the discipline is like a site in the archaeology of knowledge, formulating a science into a layered progression of ideas that are interrelated in either positive or negative ways. A name frames evolutionary as well as revolutionary cycles within a discipline, providing it with an identity and a reference (Kuhn 1962). Pre-Newtonian and post-Newtonian physics differ radically from each other, but they are physics just the same. Any new theory, idea, or definition would be meaningless unless it were conceived in relation to previous thought in the same discipline. The interdisciplinary forays in which folklorists have always engaged have changed directions and fields in different historical periods and different countries, yet even these deliberate digressions from the core concerns of folklore become significant only when they stand in relation to an identified discipline. Then they can expand its scope or narrow its focus, shift courses of inquiry, and turn folklore theories upside down, but all these creative thoughts will have cognitive structure provided by the name of the discipline.

There are no free names in a language. Each word, even if it is a neologism, as *folklore* was 150 years ago, comes with its semantic load. Searching for a new term of identity, we would be like orphans scrounging to adopt new parents, only to find out that they have their own troublesome genealogies and complex family relationships that we would have no choice but to inherit. In order to appreciate Thoms's new term, it is necessary not only to relate it to the concept he tried to replace, as Dorson did (1968, 1–43), but also to examine the connotations that *folk* and *lore* had in the English of 1846.

As Schulze (1949) documents them, both terms were in use in archaic and poetic language. *Folk* as a synonym for *people* occurs quite often in Chaucer's poetry (Oizumi and Miki 1991). As a term that was available to Thoms, Schulze suggests it did not yet have, or no longer had, any association with its Latin root *vulgus* (1949, 11). *Lore* was clearly a term taken out of the Romantic vocabulary of the eighteenth century, particularly that of the Scottish poets who sought to revive their vernacular writings. Its earliest use is from the seventeenth century in Samuel Butler's (1612–1680) satiric poem "Hudibras": "Learned he was in Med'c'nal Lore" (Butler 1967, 35), but during the eighteenth and nineteenth centuries, there was a noticeable increase in its use and in its range of applications. As used by different poets, it meant "the learning of a people." James Beattie (1735–1803) writes in his poem "The Minstrel" (1771) about "the lore of Rome and Greece" (Gilfillan 1854, 24), and William Falconer (1732–69) invokes in his poem "The Shipwreck" (1762) those "unskilled in Grecian or in Roman lore" (Gilfillan 1854, 241). In the nineteenth century, Percy Bysshe Shelley (1792–1822) had the character of Mahmud in his play

Hellas (1822) say to Ahasuerus, "Thou art an adept in the difficult lore of Greek and Frank philosophy" (Ingpen and Peck 1927, 3:42, lines 741–42), and earlier, in 1817, he wished to "mould [the] growing spirit [of his son] in the flame of Grecian lore" (3:162, lines 49–51). William Wordsworth (1770–1850) wrote in 1822 about the monks in the monastery of Old Bangor (Wales) who "by their prayers-guard the store of Aboriginal and Roman lore" (Knight 1885, 7:12).

In other verses, the term pertains to specific forms of discourse. Within a theatrical context, John Cunningham (1729–73) suggests to the listeners in his poem "A Prologue, Spoken by Mr. Diggs, on opening the Edinburgh Theatre in 1763," "So the fair fields of fancy we'll explore, And search the gardens of dramatic lore" (Cunningham 1766, 148). In his poem "To My Lyre," Henry Kirke White (1785–1806) writes that "no academic lore has taught [him] the solemn strain to pour" (Roger, et al. 1853, 16), but in spite of its current resonance, the term should not be interpreted anachronistically. In still other poems, *lore* acquires meanings that anticipate its usages in the post-Thomsian era, after the coinage of the term *folklore*. In a poetic dialogue between his character Lochiel and a wizard, Thomas Campbell (1777–1844) has the wizard say that "the sunset of life give[s] [him] mystical lore" (Roger, et al. 1853, 36), and Falconer mentions in "The Shipwreck" "the tales of hapless love in ancient lore" (Gilfillan 1854, 188), while White recalls "treasur'd tales and legendary lore" in his poem "Childhood" (Roger, et al. 1853, 2). This particular phrase has enjoyed, evidently, some popularity, as Oliver Goldsmith (1728–74) also wrote it into his poem "The Hermit: A Ballad" (1765). He considers the hermit "skill'd in legendary lore" (Goldsmith 1884, 105). Poetic usage increasingly associated *lore* with concepts, forms, and roles that later became part of the conceptualization of folklore. Beattie writes in his poem "The Minstrel," "Whate'er of lore tradition could supply from Gothic tale, or song or fable old" (Gilfillan 1854, 19), and Shelley says in "Laon and Cythna" (1771),

> Yes, from the records of my youthful state,
> And from the lore of bards and sages old,
> From whatsoe'er my weakened thoughts create
> Out of the hoes of thine aspirings bold,
> Have I collected language to unfold
> Truth to my countrymen. (Ingpen and Peck 1927, 1:301, lines 100–105)

In his poem "The Lady of the Lake" (1809–10), Walter Scott (1771–1832) refers to "Tine-man forged by fairy lore" (Scott 1900, 167). Other compounds, *ancient lore*, *philosophic lore*, *poetic lore*, and *literarian lore*, occur in the writings of these and other Romantic poets (Schulze 1949, 17–39).

In 1830, sixteen years before Thoms's coinage, the June issue of the *Gentleman's Magazine* included an essay with the suggestion to use *lore* instead of the classical suffix *-ology*, for example, "earthlore" for geology, "starlore" for astrology, or "birdlore" for ornithology (Schulze 1949, 10). It is impossible to determine whether Thoms was aware of, or remembered, this suggestion, but if he did, *folklore* would have meant for him not only the subject matter of the lore of the people, but also the study of the people, representing the same duality that has troubled folklorists ever since.

William Thoms, antiquarian that he was, did not articulate a theory or a method to accompany his neologism; it was only later generations that shaped and reshaped its conceptual content (Legros 1962). To a certain extent, the lack of a precise dogmatic definition that students often bemoan served the discipline well, as it enabled folklorists to mold the discipline anew, formulating syntheses of new ideas and maneuvering its directions among the other fields of scholarship.

In the course of time, there have been communities of scholars that have used the name of *folklore* to support some of the most horrendous acts human beings have ever committed. The use of the idea of folklore as conceptualized in the German *Volkskunde* to support Nazi ideology (Bendix 1998; Dow and Lixfeld 1986, 1991, 1994; Kamenetsky 1972; Lixfeld 1994; Stein 1987) remains a blot on the history of folklore scholarship. But we cannot and should not whitewash it by changing our name. We should not revise our history nor change our name to suit our ideals. Nazi ideology is not "inscribed in the field of folklore" (Bendix 1998, 238) nor in any other nationalistic ideology. The Nazis used the idea of folklore often by distorting facts to suit their purposes as they twisted and turned other ideas that have their roots in European Enlightenment and Romanticism, putting them into the service of their ideology and actions (see Olender 1992).

Nationalism is an attribute that is projected onto, or imagined in, but not inherent to folklore (Anderson 1991; Ben-Amos 1983). While it is possible to understand the motivation of our German colleagues to distance themselves from the term *Volkskunde*, abused in the Nazi regime, it is not the name but the actions scholars committed at that time that is abhorrent. By retaining the name *folklore*, we would not be identifying with evil, but maintaining the memory of the potentially destructive power of our ideas while employing them constructively in our research.

Folklore among the Disciplines

The evaluation of folklore as a discipline depends on the quality of our scholarship, not our name. There is no need to use *folklore* as a scapegoat and assume that by doing so we shall achieve the prosperity that has eluded us so far. Realistically, the present state of higher education in the United States does not hold any promise for growth, whatever strategy we shall follow. The creative operations of professional folklorists in regional or ethnic communities do not contribute to the academic strengthening of folklore. Leaving the academy may be a personal choice for individual professional folklorists, but when the discipline as a community heads for the exit gates, it cannot expect to make any further headway within the learning environment from which it defects.

Obviously, it would be an understatement to suggest that there is room for improvement in the position of folklore in the academy. Even outside the structure of disciplinary-bound departments, in the broader domain of intellectual dialogue, we all would have liked folklore to fare better. If citations represent an index for the position of a field in the hierarchy of disciplines, even when size is factored into the calculation, folklore hardly has a respectable notch.[12] Our record of recognition is spotty. For any evidence of notice, it is possible to mount ten indicating neglect. The journal of biblical studies, *Semeia*, founded in 1974, is the only nonfolklore journal, to the best of my knowledge, that cites folklore specifically as a field on which its editors want to draw. In their advertisement, they announce, "*Semeia* is an experimental journal devoted to the exploration of new and emergent areas and methods in biblical criticism. Studies employing the methods, models, and findings of linguistics, folklore studies, contemporary literary criticism, structuralism, social anthropology, and other such disciplines and approaches, are invited" (*Semeia* 1974, 2; see Wilder 1974, 3). Some current anthropologists point out that "thanks to careful work of the Opies and numerous folklorists, we have collections of the verbal art of children—their jump rope and 'counting out' rhymes, hand-clap songs, jokes, riddles and chants—and their games" (Goodwin 1997, 4). Similarly, Susan Seizer acknowledges the leadership of folklore in some particular areas of social analysis as she notes that "in the past two decades anthropologists have joined linguists and folklorists in significantly extending the study of speech acts and their contexts under the rubric of verbal performance" (Seizer 1997, 62).

Others are not so generous. In her 1978 theoretical book, *On the Margins of Discourse: The Relation of Literature to Language*, Barbara Herrnstein Smith discusses proverbs extensively. By that time, folklorists had made some major strides in the rhetorical, literary, functional, and structural analyses of proverbs. Her own theoretical insights parallel and complement folkloristic formulations, yet her only references in folklore studies are to Archer Taylor's classic *The Proverb* (1931) and Ruth Finnegan's *Oral Literature in Africa* (1970). In the decade during which performance theory in folklore was brewing, she comments in a note, "Of all the relations a speaker may have to someone else's words, perhaps the most interesting is in his *performing* of them, as when an actor recites the lines of a play or when we read a poem, either aloud or to ourselves. Performing is quite distinct from either quoting, depicting, or referring to an utterance—or, of course, saying it. The relation is, however, a complex matter in its own right" (Smith 1978, 208). During the 1970s, there was already a substantial folkloristic literature on the subject, but Smith did not find it meaningful and left folklore on the margin of theory. So did Mary Louise Pratt. In retrospect, her book *Toward a Speech Act Theory of Literary Discourse* (1977) reads like a period piece of the 1970s. It deals with literary texts but skirts the boundaries of face-to-face communication. She draws on significant linguistic studies on narrative, but finds no use for any of the folkloristic research and theoretical formulation of that decade.

Fortunately, it is possible to notice the winds of change, and the term *folklore* does not necessarily obscure important scholarship and its appreciation. We can obviously point to some of our own members [of the America Folklore Society], such as Susan Stewart (1991), who has joined the ranks of major literary theoreticians and incorporates folklore theory and subjects in her work as a matter of course. In addition, we can also identify literary scholars with no previous folklore connections who turn to folklore scholarship without hesitation, finding it relevant to their own concerns. Casual reading that has not been motivated by the anxiety of recognition has turned up essays by Nancy Armstrong (1992) and Harriet Goldberg (1984, 1993). A deliberate search may or may not yield more essays. The issue at hand is the indication that the substance of folklore and its scholarship is not impeded by any negative meaning of the term *folklore* connotes in other contexts.

Among historians, the attitude toward folklore and the folk is more problematic. When they seek to use broad strokes to portray US society in history, some select a point of view that obscures folklore, others uphold its importance, and still others skirt their way around it. For example, Michael Kammen, a 1973 Pulitzer Prize–winning historian, constructs the US search for cultural identity in terms of competing categories: national versus folk. Scholarship receives but a dismissing note in his description: "Obviously, some interest in folklore and folk culture could be found in the United States prior to the interwar years. It emerged as an academic enthusiasm late in the 1880s, when not one but two professional associations were formed. Scholarly essays soon began to appear, journals were published, and even some state-based organizations such as the Virginia Folk-Lore Society founded in 1913" (Kammen 1991, 426).

He continues his description of the interest in folklore in the United States during the interwar years on the basis of publications in popular magazines and on the prestige government personalities accord the presentation of folk-lore. The interest of wealthy folk art collectors receives more attention than the interest of any scholars who researched folklore in that era and whose work is presented in a patchy and unsystematic way in the service of the historical picture Kammen wishes to present (1991, 426–43).

The American Historical Review forum that appeared in 1992 represents a most serious approach to the issue of folklore in industrial society. Centered around Lawrence Levine (1992), three other historians—Robin Kelley (1992), Natalie Zemon Davis (1992), and T. J. Jackson Lears (1992)—address the issues of conceptualizing *folk* and *folklore* in relation to mass media communication. Their discussion shifts from a theoretical to an empirical examination of the issues, drawing on interdisciplinary scholarship that includes folklore studies, without the slightest hesitation about the intellectual value of either term as an effective means for the conceptualization of ideas. If *folk* represents a marginal group in the lecture of one historian, another retorts that the conception of margin itself is a problematic issue. In their entire discussion, there is no trace of Jane Beck's concern that the marginality of the *folk* is contagious and affects folklore (Beck 1997, 123).[13]

Another historian finds *folklore* inadequate for his own purposes and opts for William Graham Sumner's *folkways* instead. Seeking to construct the historical changes in US culture, David Hackett Fischer (1989, 7–11) finds *folklore* an inadequate concept. Curiously, in his reasoning, he draws on hesitations and doubts that are apparent in folklore scholarship. He points out that James Deetz, Henry Glassie, and Dell Upton prefer the use of the term *vernacular* rather than *folk* in reference to architecture (Fischer 1989, 8); subsequently, he selects to modify the term *folkways*, ridding it of any biological connotations that Sumner (1906) imputed to it originally, and proceeds to use the term in a way that has a close semantic affinity with the current use of *folklore*.

Such terminological nuancing is part of any intellectual discourse. Fine-tuning of terms is necessary for the presentation of ideas. In the process, some uphold and others modify the term *folklore*. No doubt some writers confound the term, while others see through its layered meaning. In the final analysis, we cannot be responsible for how others view us, only for what we do. Our actions give meaning to our name. There are no unlucky stars or unlucky names for disciplines.

The moments of self-evaluation that punctuate the history of our discipline could serve as constructive, critical self-examination; those may become our theoretical and methodological turning points. But in these moments, let us not lose sight of the fundamentals of folklore and the intellectual traditions from which we draw and to which we attempt to contribute. Contrary to its image in popular and public culture, folklore is not a research of the eleventh hour. The urge to preserve and display the past fuels community action, not the activities of the folklorist who records in order to analyze and interpret. By the traditionalization of ideas, beliefs, and artistic forms and by the transformation of behavior into customs, communities preserve, commemorate, and even construct their past. In the course of research, speakers do not identify their songs, proverbs, tales, dresses, and buildings as traditional unless they are so conceived by their communities. Consequently, the communal process of traditionalization and the scholarly search for tradition converge, giving the false impression that folklore itself is a discipline that perches on the eleventh hour-line. But this is a case of blurred vision. Like other social and humanistic disciplines, folklore contemplates what has already been done and said, and, in most cases, has but a weak predictive capability. Casting our observations into models, hypotheses, and scenarios may be heuristically valuable but is not essential. In that respect, folklore joins a host of other disciplines that are descriptive and interpretive rather than prescriptive or predictive.[14] The map of these disciplines may be changing, and if so, the interest of historians, linguists, anthropologists, and literary theoreticians in our subject matter only strengthens the position of folklore. Folklorists, who know their own subject more profoundly than students of other disciplines, could formulate research questions that reflect their knowledge and at the same time relate their interest to broader intellectual concerns. If the genres of scholarship are somewhat blurred now, if their boundaries are crossed, and if their territories are newly appropriated, it does not mean that they all turn into a muddled thought, lacking the discipline, language, and history that their names signify.

To end, I would like to shift from folkloristics to folklore and conclude with a parable from the Hasidic tradition: "Rabbi Zusya said, 'In the coming world, they will not ask me: "Why were you not Moses?" They will ask me: "Why were you not Zusya?"'" (Buber 1947, 251).[15]

Notes

1. A previous version of this essay, entitled "How to Blame Others for Sinking Deeper in a Hole We Have Dug for Ourselves," was presented at the annual meeting of the AFS in Pittsburgh in October 1996. I would like to thank Ilana Harlow for inviting me to participate in the panel she organized in commemoration of the 150th anniversary of the coinage of *folklore* and for the meticulous editing of this essay; to Jane Beck and Regina Bendix for sharing with me prepublication versions of their articles, being fully aware that I am critical of their positions; and to Robert St. George for bibliographical help.

2. Outside the field of folklore, the historian Marc Bloch (1931) advocated the use of folklore in the study of history. Methodologically, he demonstrated the significance of folklore, among other factors, in his study of French rural history.

3. Following the war period, The Folk-Lore Society in England was headed by a series of nonacademic presidents (Dorson 1961, 17–19). Later, Dorson (1965) commented, "Folklore, the subject created and once highly honored in England, now languishes, not for the lack of interest or talents, but for want of academic recognition" (242).

4. Herskovits quotes van Gennep in French; the translation is mine.

5. The antiquarian perspective, however, was central to affluent collectors whose activities later on became a subject of scholarly research into the history of US folk art collections and exhibitions; see Rumford (1980) and Vlach (1985). I would like to thank Robert St. George for these references and clarification of some of the issues related to this movement of interest in US folk art.

6. Bakhtin wrote his book on Rabelais as a doctoral dissertation that he submitted to the Gorky Institute (Clark and Holquist 1984, 263).

7. Dorson (1972a, 107) cites the figure of 2,600 as the number of institutions of higher education. Any growth or decline that occurred since then does not change the situation significantly.

8. The declining state of higher education in the United States has become in itself a subject of research, analysis, criticism, and self-reflection. Books on this theme are published and republished as the crisis continues. In 1972, Dorson referred to Nisbet (1971); one of the later volumes on the state of the university is Readings (1996).

9. The members of the committee were Richard Bauman (chairman), Robert A. Byington, Henry Glassie, Rayna Green, and Harry Oster. The committee report and the proposal for the Center appear in (Stekert 1972, 33, 38–39).

10. I could not examine the eighth edition of the dictionary.

11. *Merriam Webster's Encyclopedia of Literature* does not credit individual articles, and it is hence impossible for me to determine whether the entry *folklore* was written by trained folklorists or an editorial staff member.

12. Uriel G. Foa suggested that a measure for the prestige of academic fields could be made by analyzing "the frequency with which scientists in one discipline quote papers from other disciplines, and relat[ing] these findings to the relative status of the disciplines involved" (Thayer 1967, 149). See also my comments on this issue and the general problem of this essay in Ben-Amos (1973, 117–19).

13. The relativity of the construction of margins and center is discussed in Davis (1992); Kelley (1992); Lears (1992); and Levin (1992).

14. There is voluminous literature on the scientific nature of the social sciences and the humanities. A starting point for reading on this subject is Nagel (1961, 447–606).

15. In the Hebrew version of his book (1957, 481), Martin Buber notes that he heard this version from Yehudah Yaari. Zusya of Annopol (d. 1800), a Hasidic preacher whose sermons and sayings were edited in the book *Menorat Zahav* (1902) (see Rabinowicz 1996, 563–64).

Bibliography

Abrahams, Roger D. 1988. "Rough Sincerities: William Wells Newell and the Discovery of Folklore in the Late-19th Century America." In *Folk Roots, New Roots: Folklore in American Life*, edited by Jane S. Becker and Barbara Franco, 61–76. Lexington, MA: Museum of Our National Heritage.

Alver, Brynjulf. 1989. "Folklore and National Identity." In *Nordic Folklore: Recent Studies*, edited by Reimund Kvideland and Henning K. Sehmsdorf, with Elizabeth Simpson, 12–20. Bloomington: Indiana University Press.

Anderson, Benedict. 1991. *Imagined Communities: Reflections on the Origin and Spread of Nationalism*. Rev. ed. London: Verso.

Armstrong, Nancy. 1992. "Emily's Ghost: The Cultural Politics of Victorian Fiction, Folklore, and Photography." *Novel* 25, no. 3:245–67.

Augé, Marc. 1995. *Non-places: Introduction to an Anthropology of Supermodernity*. London: Verso.

Baker, Ronald, L. 1971. "Folklore Courses and Programs in American Colleges and Universities." *Journal of American Folklore* 84, no. 332:221–29.

———. 1986. "Folklore and Folklife Studies in American and Canadian Colleges and Universities." *Journal of American Folklore* 99, no. 391:50–74.

Bakhtin, Mikhail. 1968. *Rabelais and His World*. Translated by Helene Iswolsky. Cambridge, MA: MIT Press.

Baron, Robert, and Nicholas R. Spitzer, eds. 1992. *Public Folklore*. Washington, DC: Smithsonian Institution Press.

Bascom, William R. 1953. Folklore and Anthropology. *Journal of American Folklore* 66, no. 262:283–90.

———. 1955. "Verbal Art." *Journal of American Folklore* 68, no. 269:245–52.

Basgoz, Ilhan. 1972. "Folklore Studies and Nationalism in Turkey." *Journal of the Folklore Institute* 9, no. 2/3:162–76.

Bayard, Samuel P. 1953. "The Materials of Folklore." *Journal of American Folklore* 66, no. 262:1–17.

Beck, Jane C. 1997. "Taking Stock: 1996 American Folklore Society Presidential Address." *Journal of American Folklore* 110, no. 436:123–39.

Bell, Michael. 1973. "William Wells Newell and the Foundation of American Folklore Scholarship." *Journal of the Folklore Institute* 10, no. 1/2:7–21.

Ben-Amos, Dan. 1973. "A History of Folklore Studies—Why Do We Need It?" *Journal of the Folklore Institute* 10:114–24.

———. 1983. "The Idea of Folklore: An Essay." In *Fields of Offerings: Studies in Honor of Raphael Patai*, edited by Victor D. Sanua, 57–64. Rutherford, NJ: Fairleigh Dickinson University Press.

———. 1984. "The Seven Strands of Tradition: Varieties in Its Meaning in American Folklore Studies." *Journal of Folklore Research* 21, no. 2/3:97–131.

Bendix, Regina. 1998. "Of Names, Professional Identities, and Disciplinary Futures." *The Journal of American Folklore* 111, no. 441:235–46.

Bloch, Marc Leopold Benjamin. 1931. *Les caracteres originaux de l'histoire nuvale francaise*. Oslo: A. Aschehoug.

Boggs, Ralph Steel. 1940. "Folklore in University Curricula in the United States." *Southern Folklore Quarterly* 4:93–109.

———. 1945. "The Development of Folklore in a University." In *Studies in Language and Literature*, edited by George R. Coffman, 106–11. Chapel Hill: University of North Carolina Press.

Botkin, Benjamin A. 1939. "WPA and Folklore Research: 'Bread and Song.'" *Southern Folklore Quarterly* 3:7–14.

Bourne, Henry. 1977. *Antiquitates Vulgares: The Antiquities of the Common People*. New York: Arno. Originally published 1725.

Briggs, Charles, and Amy Shuman, eds. 1993. "Theorizing Folklore: Toward New Perspectives on the Politics of Culture." Special issue. *Western Folklore* 52, nos. 2/4:109–400.

Bronner, Simon J. 1986. *American Folklore Studies: An Intellectual History.* Lawrence, KS: University Press of Kansas.

Browne, Thomas. 1646. *Pseudodoxia Epidemica: Enquiries into Vulgar and Common Errors.* London: Edward Dod.

Buber, Martin. 1947. *Tales of Hasidim: Early Masters.* New York: Schocken.

———. 1957. *Or ha-ganuz: sippurei hasidim* [A concealed light: Hasidic tales]. Tel Aviv: Schocken.

Butler, Samuel. 1967. *Hudibras.* Oxford: Clarendon.

Camp, Charles, ed. 1989. *Time and Temperature: A Centennial Publication of the American Folklore Society.* Washington, DC: American Folklore Society.

Cantwell, Robert. 1996. *When We Were Good: The Folk Revival.* Cambridge, MA: Harvard University Press.

Chambers, J. K., and Peter Trudgill. 1980. *Dialectology.* Cambridge: Cambridge University Press.

Clark, Katerina, and Michael Holquist. 1984. *Mikhail Bakhtin.* Cambridge, MA: Harvard University Press.

Clements, William M., ed. 1988. *100 Years of American Folklore Studies: A Conceptual History.* Washington, DC: American Folklore Society.

Cocchiara, Giuseppe. 1981. *The History of Folklore in Europe.* Translated by John N. McDaniel. Philadelphia: Institute for the Study of Human Issues. Originally published 1952.

Cunningham, John. 1766. *Poems, Chiefly Pastoral.* London: T. Slack.

Davis, Natalie Zemon. 1992. "Toward Mixtures and Margins." *The American Historical Review* 97, no. 5:1409–16.

Dorson, Richard M. 1950. "The Growth of Folklore Courses." *Journal of American Folklore* 63, no. 249:345–59.

———. 1961. "Folklore Studies in England." *Journal of American Folklore* 74:6–16.

———. 1962. "Folklore and the National Defense Education Act." *Journal of American Folklore* 75, no. 296:160–64.

———. 1965. "Folklore and Folklife Studies in Great Britain and Ireland: Introduction." *Journal of the Folklore Institute* 2, no. 3:239–43.

———. 1968. *The British Folklorists: A History.* Chicago: University of Chicago Press.

———. 1970. "The Ditchley Park Conference Resolution." *Journal of the Folklore Institute* 7:95–7.

———. 1972a. "The Academic Future of Folklore." *Journal of American Folklore Supplement,* 104–25.

———, ed. 1972b. *Folklore and Folklife: An Introduction.* Chicago: University of Chicago Press.

———. 1972c. *Folklore: Selected Essays.* Bloomington: Indiana University Press.

Dow, James R., ed. 1991. "Folklore, Politics and Nationalism." Special issue. *Asian Folklore Studies* 50.

———. 1991. "National Socialistic Folklore and Overcoming the Past in the Federal Republic in Germany." *Asian Folklore Studies* 50, no. 1:117–54.

———, ed. and trans. 1994. *The Nazification of an Academic Discipline: Folklore in the Third Reich.* Bloomington: Indiana University Press.

Dow, James R., and Hannjost Lixfeld, eds. 1986. *German Volkskunde: A Decade of Theoretical Confrontation, Debate, and Reorientation (1967-1977).* Bloomington: Indiana University Press.

Dundes, Alan. 1977. "Who Are the Folk?" In *Frontiers of Folklore,* edited by William R. Bascom, 17–35. Boulder, CO: Westview.

Elsner, John, and Roger Cardinal, eds. 1994. *The Cultures of Collecting*. Cambridge, MA: Harvard University Press.

Feintuch, Burt, ed. 1988. *The Conservation of Culture: Folklorists and the Public Sector*. Lexington: University Press of Kentucky.

Finnegan, Ruth H. 1970. *Oral Literature in Africa*. London: Clarendon.

Fischer, David Hackett. 1989. *Albion's Seed: Four British Folkways in America*. New York: Oxford University Press.

Fox, Cyril. 1943. *The Personality of Britain*. Cardiff: National Museum of Wales and the Press Board of the University of Wales. Originally published 1931.

Francis, W. Nelson. 1983. *Dialectology*. New York: Longman.

Gayton, A. H., ed. 1947. "Folklore Research in North America: Plan of Work and Summary Reports." *Journal of American Folklore* 60, no. 238:350–416.

Georges, Robert A., ed. 1991. "Taking Stock: Current Problems and Future: Prospects in American Folklore Studies." Special issue. *Western Folklore* 50, no. 1:1–126.

Gilfillan, George, ed. 1854. *The Poetical Works of Beattie, Blair, and Falconer*. Edinburgh: James Nichol.

Gillis, John R., ed. 1994. *Commemorations: The Politics of National Identity*. Princeton, NJ: Princeton University Press.

Glassie, Henry. 1995. "Tradition." *Journal of American Folklore* 108, no. 430:395–412.

Goldberg, Harriet. 1984. "Romance, Folklore, Literature, and Cultural Identity." *Romance Philology* 38, no. 1:41–53.

———. 1993. "The Judeo-Spanish Proverb and Its Narrative Context." *Publications of the Modern Language Association* 108, no. 1:106–20.

Goldsmith, Oliver. 1884. *Poems, Plays, and Essays*. New York: Thomas Y. Crowell.

Goodwin, Marjorie Harness. 1997. "Children's Linguistic and Social Worlds." *Anthropology Newsletter* 38, no. 4:1, 4–5.

Gross Bressler, Sandra. 1995. "Culture and Politics: A Legislative Chronicle of the American Folklife Preservation Act." PhD diss. University of Pennsylvania.

Halpert, Herbert. 1958. "Folklore: Breadth versus Depth." Journal *of American Folklore* 71:97–103.

Hand, Wayland D. 1960. "American Folklore after Seventy Years: Survey and Prospects." *Journal of American Folklore* 73:1–11.

Handler, Richard, and Jocelyn Linnekin. 1984. "Tradition, Genuine or Spurious." *Journal of American Folklore* 97:273–90.

Herskovits, Melville J. 1946. "Folklore after a Hundred Years: A Problem in Redefinition." *Journal of American Folklore* 59:89–100.

Herzfeld, Michael. 1982. *Ours Once More: Folklore, Ideology, and the Making of Modern Greece*. Austin: University of Texas Press.

Hirsch, Jerrold. 1987. "Folklore in the Making: B. A. Botkin." *Journal of American Folklore* 100:3–38.

———. 1988. "Cultural Pluralism and Applied Folklore: The New Deal Precedent." In *The Conservation of Culture: Folklorists and the Public Sector*, edited by Burt Feintuch, 46–67. Lexington: University Press of Kentucky.

———. 1996. "My Harvard Accent and 'Indifference': Notes toward the Biography of B. A. Botkin." *Journal of American Folklore* 109:308–19.

Hobsbawm, Eric, and Terence Ranger, eds. 1983. *The Invention of Tradition*. Cambridge: Cambridge University Press.

Hutchinson, John. 1987. *The Dynamics of Cultural Nationalism: The Gaelic Revival and the Creation of the Irish Nation State*. London: Allen and Unwin.

Ingpen, Roger, and Walter E. Peck, eds. 1926–30. *The Complete Works of Percy Bysshe Shelley.* 10 vols. New York: Scribner and Sons.

Jones, Michael Owen, Michael Dane Moore, and Richard Christopher Snyder, eds. 1988. *Inside Organizations: Understanding the Human Dimension.* Newbury Park, CA: Sage.

Journal of American Folklore [*JAF*]. 1888. On the Field and Work of a Journal of American Folklore. *Journal of American Folklore* 1:3–7.

Journal of American Folklore [*JAF*]. 1945. Folklore News: American Folklore Society Admitted to Constituency in American Council of Learned Societies. *Journal of American Folklore* 58:158.

Journal of American Folklore [*JAF*]. 1946. Conference on the Character and State of Studies in Folklore. *Journal of American Folklore* 59:495–527.

Kamenetsky, Christa. 1972. "Folklore as a Political Tool in Nazi Germany." *Journal of American Folklore* 85:221–36.

Kammen, Michael. 1991. *Mystic Chords of Memory: The Transformation of Tradition in American Culture.* New York: Knopf.

Kapferer, Bruce. 1988. *Legends of People, Myths of State.* Washington, DC: Smithsonian Institution Press.

Kelley, Robin D. G. 1992. "Notes on Deconstructing 'The Folk.'" *The American Historical Review* 97:1400–1408.

Kirshenblatt-Gimblett, Barbara. 1988. "Mistaken Dichotomies." *Journal of American Folklore* 101:140–55.

———. 1996. "Topic-Drift: Negotiating the Gap between the Field and Our Name." *Journal of Folklore Research* 33, no. 3:245–54.

Knight, William, ed. 1885. *The Poetical Works of William Wordsworth.* Edinburgh: William Patterson.

Kuhn, Thomas S. 1962. *The Structure of Scientific Revolutions.* International Encyclopedia of Unified Science, vols. 1 and 2. Vol. 2, no. 2. Chicago: University of Chicago Press.

Lapierre, Nicole. 1995. *Changer de nom.* Paris: Stock.

Lears, T. J. Jackson. 1992. "Making Fun of Popular Culture." *The American Historical Review* 97:1417–26.

Legros, Elisee. 1962. *Sur les noms et les tendances du folklore.* Collection d'etudes, 1. Liege, France: Editions du Musée Wallon.

Levine, Lawrence W. 1992. "The Folklore of Industrial Society: Popular Culture and Its Audience." *The American Historical Review* 97: 1369–99.

Levine, Philippa. 1986. *The Amateur and the Professional: Antiquarians, Historians and Archaeologists in Victorian England, 1838–1886.* Cambridge: Cambridge University Press.

Lixfeld, Hannjost. 1994. *Folklore and Fascism: The Reich Institute for German Volkskunde.* Edited and translated by James R. Dow. Bloomington: Indiana University Press.

Mangione, Jerre. 1972. *The Dream and the Deal: The Federal Writers Project, 1935–1943.* Boston: Little, Brown.

McDonald, Barry. 1997. "Tradition as Personal Relationship." *Journal of American Folklore* 110, no. 435:47–67.

McNeil, William K. 1980. "A History of American Folklore Scholarship before 1908." PhD diss. Indiana University at Bloomington.

Nagel, Ernest. 1961. *The Structure of Science: Problems in the Logic of Scientific Explanation.* New York: Harcourt, Brace and World.

Newell, William W. 1888. "On the Field and Work of a Journal of American Folk-Lore." *Journal of American Folk-Lore* 1, no. 1: 3–7.

———. 1898. "Review of *Notes of the Folk-Lore of the Fjort (French Congo)*, by R. E. Dennet." *Journal of American Folklore* 11, no. 4 3:302–4.

Nisbet, Robert. 1971. *The Degradation of the Academic Dogma: The University in America, 1945–1970.* New York: Basic Books.

Oizumi, Akio, and Kunihiro Miki. 1991. *A Complete Concordance to the Works of Geoffrey Chaucer.* 7 vols. New York: Olms-Weidmann.

Olender, Maurice. 1992. *The Languages of Paradise: Race, Religion, and Philology in the Nineteenth Century.* Translated by Arthur Goldhammer. Cambridge, MA: Harvard University Press.

Paredes, Américo, and Richard Bauman, eds. 1972. *Toward New Perspectives in Folklore.* Austin: University of Texas Press.

Peate, Iorwerth C. 1940. *The Welsh House: A Study in Folk Culture.* London: Society of the Lymmradorin.

Penkower, Monty Noam. 1977. *The Federal Writers' Project: A Study in Government Patronage of the Arts.* Urbana: University of Illinois Press.

Pomian, Krzysztof. 1987. *Collectionneurs, amateurs et curieux: Paris, Venise XVI–XVIII siecle.* Paris: Gallimard.

Pratt, Mary Louise. 1977. *Toward a Speech Act Theory of Literary Discourse.* Bloomington: Indiana University Press.

Rabinowicz, Tzvi M. 1996. *The Encyclopedia of Hasidism.* Northvale, NJ: Jason Aronson.

Raglan, Lord. 1936. *The Hero: A Study in Tradition, Myth and Drama.* London: Methuen.

———. 1946. "The Scope of Folklore." *Folk-Lore* 52, no. 3:98–105.

Readings, Bill. 1996. *The University in Ruins.* Cambridge, MA: Harvard University Press.

Riehl, Wilhelm Heinrich. 1859. "Die Volkskunde als Wissenschaft." In *Culturstudien aus drei Jahrhunderten,* 205–29. Stuttgart: J. G. Cotta. Reprinted in Gerhard Lutz, ed. *Volkskunde: Ein Handbuch zur Geschichte ihrer Probleme.* Berlin: Erich Schmidt: 1958.

Roger, Samuel, et al. 1856. *The Poetical Works of Rogers, Campbell, J. Montgomery, Lamb, and Kirke White: Complete in One Volume.* Philadelphia: Lippincott, Grambo and Co., 1853.

Rumford, Beatrix T. 1980. "Uncommon Art of the Common People: A Review of Trends in the Collecting and Exhibiting of American Folk Art." In *Perspectives on American Folk Art,* edited by Ian M. G. Quimby and Scott T. Swank, 13–53. New York: Norton.

Samuelson, Sue. 1983. *Twenty Years of the Department of Folklore and Folklife at the University of Pennsylvania: A Dissertation Profile, 1962–1982.* Occasional Publications in Folklore and Folklife, no. 1. Philadelphia: Department of Folklore and Folklife, University of Pennsylvania.

Schulze, Fritz Willy. 1949. *Folklore: Zur Ableitung der Vorgeschichte einer Wissenschaftsbezeichnung.* Hallische Monographien, no. 10. Halle, Germany: Max Niemeyer.

Scott, Walter. 1900. *The Complete Poetical Works of Scott.* Boston: Houghton and Mifflin.

Seizer, Susan. 1997. "Jokes, Gender, and Discursive Distance on the Tamil Popular Stage." *American Ethnologist* 24:62–90.

Shils, Edward. 1981. *Tradition.* London: Faber and Faber.

Simpson, Georgiana R. 1921. *Herder's Conception of "Das Volk."* Chicago: University of Chicago Press.

Smith, Barbara Herrnstein. 1978. *On the Margins of Discourse: The Relation of Literature to Language.* Chicago: University of Chicago Press.

Snyder, Louis L. 1959. "Nationalistic Aspects of the Grimm Brothers' Fairy Tales." *Journal of Social Psychology* 23:209–23.

Stagl, Justin. 1995. *A History of Curiosity: The Theory of Travel, 1550–1800*. Studies in Anthropology and History, vol. 13. New York: Hardwood.

Stein, Mary Beth. 1987. "Coming to Terms with the Past: The Depiction of *Volkskunde* in the Third Reich since 1945." *Journal of Folklore Research* 24:157–86.

Stekert, Ellen J., ed. 1972. "Annual Report of the American Folklore Society." *Journal of American Folklore Supplement*.

Sternberg, Thomas. 1851. *The Dialect and Folk-Lore of North Hamptonshire*. London: John Russell Smith.

Stewart, Susan. 1991. *Crimes of Writing: Problems in the Containment of Representation*. New York: Oxford University Press.

Stocking, George W. 1996. *Volksgeist as Method and Ethic: Essays in Boasiam Ethnography and the German Anthropological Tradition*. History of Anthropology 8. Madison: University of Wisconsin Press.

Sumner, William Graham. 1906. *Folkways: A Study of Sociological Importance of Usages, Manners, Customs, Mores, and Morals*. Boston: Ginn and Company.

Sweterlitsch, Dick, ed. 1971. *Papers on Applied Folklore*. Bibliographic and Special Series, no. 8. Bloomington, IN: Folklore Forum.

Taylor, Archer. 1931. *The Proverb*. Cambridge, MA: Harvard University Press.

———. 1952. "The Place of Folklore." *Publications of the Modern Language Association of America* 67:59–66.

Thayer, Lee. 1967. *Communication: Concepts and Perspectives*. Washington, DC: Spartan Books.

Thompson, Stith. 1940. "Folklore and Literature." *Publications of the Modern Language Association of America* 55:866–74.

Thompson, Stith, ed. 1953. *Four Symposia on Folklore*. Indiana University Publications Folklore Series, no. 8. Bloomington: Indiana University Press.

Utley, Francis Lee. 1961. "Folk Literature: An Operational Definition." *Journal of American Folklore* 74:193–206.

Vico, Giambattista. 1984. *The New Science of Giambattista Vico*. Translated by Max Harold Fisch and Thomas Goddard Bergin. Ithaca, NY: Cornell University Press. Originally published 1948.

Vlach, John Michael. 1985. "Holger Cahill as Folklorist." *Journal of American Folklore* 98:131–47.

Wilder, Amos N. 1974. "An Experimental Journal for Biblical Criticism: An Introduction." *Semeia* 1:1–16.

Wilson, William A. 1976. *Folklore and Nationalism in Modem Finland*. Bloomington: Indiana University Press.

Wright, A. R. 1931. *English Folklore*. New York: Jonathan Cape and Harrison Smith.

Zisel, Meshulam. 1902. *Menorat Zahav*. Warsaw: n.p.

Zumwalt, Rosemary Levy. 1988. *American Folklore Scholarship: A Dialogue of Dissent*. Bloomington: Indiana University Press.

12

A DEFINITION OF FOLKLORE

A Personal Narrative

WHEN PROFESSOR CARME ORIOL INVITED ME TO THE conference honoring the memory of the late Professor Josep M. Pujol (1947–2012), I first politely declined. "I have not read his work, except for his masterful folktale index of Catalan folktales that both of you edited," I told her.[1] "I really am not familiar with his scholarship."

"You could not have been," she replied, "unless you knew Catalan, because he wrote exclusively in Catalan.[2] But," she added, "he knew your work." And later, she sent me a copy of her then forthcoming obituary for Professor Pujol (Oriol 2012) in which she pointed out that he was influenced by the works of my teacher, Professor Richard M. Dorson (1916–81), and by my own definition of folklore. At that moment, I felt embarrassed and sad. Embarrassed, because of the lack of mutuality in our relation. He knew my work, but I did not know his. Sad, because we could not meet and I could not tell him the story of my definition of folklore, nor discuss it with him, refine my own conception of folklore, and benefit from his erudite comments and analytical insights. This was not to be. I can only tell the story of my definition of folklore to you, his students and colleagues, as a personal narrative, from a perspective that a period of forty-six years allows.

The number of years that I have just mentioned holds its own narrative episode.

My essay "Toward a Definition of Folklore in Context" was published in the *Journal of American Folklore* in 1971, but it had been written four years earlier in 1967. What prompted me to write a new definition of *folklore* was an invitation from a publisher to write an introductory textbook for folklore, and when I started to do so, I thought I would begin—where else?—at the beginning and define the book's subject. Someone on one of the various committees and editorial boards of the publishing house had a brilliant idea.

More often than not, introductory textbooks were written by senior scholars in their respective academic disciplines: senior professors, experienced teachers, and accomplished researchers. However, as Thomas Kuhn has acutely observed, these "textbooks were pedagogical vehicles for the perpetuation of normal science" (1962, 137–38). They presented linear histories of their respective disciplines, beginning at the formative stages of the currently dominant scientific paradigm. These introductory textbooks inherently suffered from three basic shortcomings: they ignored "the historical integrity of that science in its own time" (Kuhn 1962, 3); their historical narratives were, to use a term proposed by George W. Stocking (1965), "presentist"; and they validated and reaffirmed "the normal science" of their respective disciplines, rather than the agitation that permeated among younger scholars and that was likely to be symptomatic of future trends in scholarship. Reversing the process, somebody apparently proposed to commission young professionals, fresh out of graduate schools, who, by their very position and learning trajectory, would address the current and future theories and methods of their respective disciplines. The publisher set out to scout for potential writers in different disciplines, across the academic spectrum, and in spite of its limited presence in American universities, decided to include the discipline of folklore in this projected series of future-oriented introductions.

I did not know then, and do not know until this very day, who suggested to the publisher's author scout to contact me. At that time, I had but a few publications: three short articles that appeared, one each, in Switzerland (Ben-Amos 1963a), India (Ben-Amos 1963b), and Nigeria (Ben-Amos 1967a); and two in the United States (Ben-Amos 1963c, 1967c). And I had been credited for assisting my teacher at the Hebrew University, Professor Dov Noy, to edit the volume of *Folktales of Israel* (Noy 1963). None of these publications could have indicated to any publisher that I was the potential author of a future-oriented textbook on folklore. In retrospect, I would credit my friends and teachers for directing that agent to me; either they did not want to write such a textbook themselves or they thought that I could. At any rate, I had the audacity to accept the offer nonchalantly, taking for granted that I could and would accomplish the task.

The year was 1967. I started teaching at a university during the academic year of 1966–67, having a one-year renewable appointment at the Anthropology Department of the University of California, Los Angeles (UCLA). At that time, I had just returned to the United States after an eight-month period of field work among the Edo people of midwestern Nigeria (Bendel State). I arrived in Nigeria on January 15, 1966, the day of the first military coup d'etat,[3] and returned to the United States in late August 1966.

On my return, I assumed a teaching position at UCLA's Anthropology Department and maintained close personal and academic association with both the newly established African Studies Center and the by then internationally renowned Folklore and Mythology Center, which was headed by Professor Wayland Hand (1907–86) and counted among its members such distinguished scholars as D. K. Wilgus (1918–89), Donald Ward (1927–90), Sam Armistead (1927–2013), Jaan Puhvel, and Robert Georges.

That was also the first year that the American Folklore Society had its own independent annual meeting. Until then, it had alternated its annual meetings between the Modern Language Association and the American Anthropological Association.[4] When the call for paper proposals for the meeting was issued, I was in Nigeria, meeting storytellers and singers and attending rituals at the local shrines of the Edo gods. Annual scholarly meetings could not have been farther from my mind. Therefore, without a lecture scheduled on the program, I had to sit out that historical annual meeting of the American Folklore Society convened in Boston.

But when the call for paper proposals for the 1967 meeting was issued, I was eager to participate. By that time, I had already had my meeting with the publisher's literary agent and might even have signed a book contract. I thought that the first chapter of that projected book would be an appropriate subject for a conference lecture, and I sent in my proposal, which I titled "Folklore: The Definition Game Once Again."

I did not mean to undermine the significance of my own definition of *folklore*, then only vaguely verbalized, nor was the usage of such a title a rhetorical ploy that the psychoanalyst Martin Grotjahn (1904–90) diagnosed as a distinctive feature of Jewish humor: namely, self-criticism that would deflect anticipated critical comments by others (Grotjahn 1966). Neither was the title a strategy intended to disarm any objections by responding, "This is only a game."

Rather, by the midsixties of the twentieth century, the discipline of folklore was inundated with definitions and redefinitions that hampered research and obscured, rather than clarified, its boundaries, identity, subject matter, and research goals. Twenty years earlier, as folklorists around the world celebrated the centennial of William Thoms' (1803–85) coinage of the term *folklore*,[5] its reassessment and re-evaluation was in full force. The respective presidential addresses of Melville Herskovits (1895–1963; see Herskovits 1946),[6] then president of the American Folklore Society, and Lord Raglan (1885–1964; see Raglan 1946), then president of the Folklore Society in England, were concerned with the indefiniteness of *folklore*, or the inertness of the discipline that the term had initiated.

As the title of his lecture indicated, Herskovits proposed a "redefinition" of *folklore*, which was necessary because of the initial and subsequent inconsistencies that he perceived in its conceptualization. Herskovits pointed out that the *lore* in William Thoms's newly coined compound was synonymous with *literature*, yet he proposed the new term as a substitution for *popular culture*, not *literature* nor *popular literature*. For him, *popular antiquities* consisted of "manners customs, observances, and superstitions," but he also included "ballads and proverbs, etc." in the mix. Thirty-two years later, Herskovits noticed that in a recapitulation of the original coinage, Thoms repeated the same inconsistency in the first "rule" of the newly founded Folk-Lore Society, of which he was the director: "The Folk-Lore Society has for its object the preservation and publication of Popular Traditions, Legendary Ballads, Local Proverbial Sayings, Superstitions and Old Customs (British and foreign), and all subjects relating to them" (Herskovits 1946, 90). As the term became ubiquitous and gained worldwide acceptance, folklore became the object of explanatory theories that amplified its inherent discrepancies. Evolutionary theories rationalized folklore as vestiges of human primitiveness, and national sentiments upheld it as the bond that binds a nation. The quaintness of the "folk" collided with the expansion of the concept to embrace societies, regardless of their economic position. The American scene further complicated matters by having to cope with migrant and native traditions. As a solution to these multiplying dilemmas, Herskovits opted to consider folklore as *folkliterature* only (100).

Raglan took a distinctly different approach. He evaluated the state of folklore as a subject of intellectual inquiry negatively for three reasons. The first is that to confine one's studies to moribund superstitions is a somewhat gloomy and barren proceeding, little calculated to attract those who are interested in both the present and the past. Second, the class of matter that has filled our journal for so many years is obviously tending toward exhaustion. Third, many of the customs and beliefs that were new to the earlier students of folklore are now known to be, or to have been, universal in Britain, if not throughout the world (Raglan 1946, 98).

His solution itself was inconsistent with his observation. Instead of abandoning the subject and its name, as some American folklorists proposed fifty years later (see Beck 1997; Bendix 1998; Kirshenblatt-Gimblett 1998; objectors are Ben-Amos 1998 and Oring 1998), he proposed, as a few students of folklore had done before him, to reconfigure folklore as a science (see Riehl 1859; von Hahn 1864; Cox 1881; Hartland 1891; Gomme 1908; Krappe 1930; and more recently, Edmonson 1971; and Brückner and Beitl 1983), a historical science, to be exact, but its subject matter would not reflect global or even national, political, social, or economic changes, but rather, the regional historical changes in everyday life.[7]

The reconceptualization of folklore was not limited to anniversaries. Six years later, Archer Taylor (1946, 1952), then president of the American Modern Language Association, considered folklore as a representation of "associative thinking." For him, folklore deals with materials that have been shaped and handed on by associative rather than logical thinking. A ballad or a superstition is a bit of folklore in which associative thinking has been chiefly operative in its preservation. Its form, its use, and the characteristic variations of its several versions are determined by unconscious, not conscious, processes.

In his characterization of folklore, Archer Taylor invoked the concept of association of ideas that Edward B. Tylor (1832–1917; see Tylor 1958, 115–16) perceived to be at the basis of "occult science. Or he could have had in mind the principle of "pre-logical thinking" that Lucien Lévy-Bruhl (1857–1939; see Lévy-Bruhl 1919) proposed as the distinctive feature of primitive societies, and to whose writings he specifically referred in a previous essay (Taylor 1946, 104). In any case, such a concept only added coal to the fire of confusion that smoldered among folklorists at the time.

Midcentury was an ambivalent milestone for folklore. On the one hand, leading scholars could look back with pride at the major strides the discipline had taken and the tangible scholarly accomplishments of the twentieth century (Thompson 1953). But on the other hand, the attempts to frame these very achievements conceptually as the subjects of a single scholarly discipline entangled themselves by the multiple strands and lines of thought, and interdisciplinary theories and methods that were brought to bear on the themes, objects, and forms of folklore. The twenty-one short definitions that Maria Leach assembled in her valuable folklore dictionary (Leach and Fried 1949–50) exposed the pitfalls scattered on the road that led to an answer to the question of "What is folklore?" In a retrospective essay, Francis Lee Utley (1961) identified orality and tradition as the two features that recurred most often in those definitions of folklore and that could therefore be considered its common denominators. However, his proposal disregarded the many non-common denominators that plagued the discipline and prevented folklorists from articulating a comprehensive analytical conception.

The list of scholars who defined folklore in Leach's *Dictionary* reads like an examination question in a course on the history of folklore. True, some prominent names are missing. For example, Roman Jakobson (1896–1982), who contributed an excellent essay to the *Dictionary* on Slavic mythology

(Jakobson 1949) and who had by then published the influential, yet at the time little-known article that he wrote together with Peter Bogatyrëv (1893–1971) on the uniqueness of folklore (Bogatyrëv and Jakobson 1929), and Ralph Steel Boggs (1901–94),[8] the internationally known scholar of Hispanic folklore, were not included. Yet the list represented the breadth and depth of folklore scholarship in the United States in the 1940s, and the differences among the scholars stretched the idea of interdisciplinary studies to its bewildering limits.

A flurry of definition articles followed, attempting to put our house in order. Senior scholars sought to establish the disciplinary boundaries, particularly between anthropology and literature, or to merge them into a folkloristic perspective (Bascom 1953, 1955; M. A. Smith 1959; Utley 1958, 1961). In doing so, they followed the American scholarly tradition in folklore that Rosemary Zumwalt described as "a dialog of dissent" (Zumwalt 1988), while younger scholars sought to resolve the contradictions in previous theories, and forge ahead with their own answers to the puzzle of folklore (Abrahams 1963; Kongas 1963; Dundes 1965, 1966).

Scholarly history and the public space compounded the definitional frustration of folklore. In 1950, my teacher Richard M. Dorson published his article "Folklore and Fake Lore," in which he lambasted the commercial and popular use of folklore. At the core, his criticism is the distinction between folklore in society and its display in popular culture for either commercial, nationalistic, or exhibitionist purposes. In the same period, side by side with the rise of folklore in popular publications, the increased visibility of the folk song revival movement challenged the concept of folklore as a research subject (Cohen 2002; Russell and Atkinson 2004). Should the theatricality of folklore be considered to be on the same level as the performance of folklore in its indigenous society, either urban or rural, literate or nonliterate? Was it not this very phase of folklore that generated the question of authenticity (Adorono 1973; Benedix 1997; Golomb 1995; Pincus 1996)?

These issues contributed to the frustrations of my friends in folklore and my own frustrations. Slowly, the definition of *folklore* became a personal need rather than a task. It became necessary for me to distance myself from the sources of our confusion and ask myself, as simply as I could, three interrelated questions: Is folklore real? That is to say, is folklore a figment of our ideational or ideological history, or is it a social and cultural reality? And by any other name, does it still exist, and is it cognitively distinct? If so, is it universal or socially and historically ephemeral, a passing phenomenon that disappears from the socio-cultural scape as societies change? Third, how do people, behaviorally, linguistically, and cognitively, distinguish their folklore acts within their own social life? If the reality and universality of folklore are theoretical premises, its behavioral aspect is observable and subject to description, analysis, and interpretation, which are the tasks of the discipline of folklore. In my limited previous studies and research, I encountered folklore only as it was mediated in literature and available in print,[9] but in order to define it as a pragmatic social reality, I needed to encounter it in social life.

For that purpose, I drew on my still fresh experience of living among the Edo people in Nigeria in 1966 and researching their oral tradition. Listening to them telling their stories, singing their songs, citing their proverbs, and playing their music, and watching them dancing, decorating their shrines, worshiping their gods, and performing their rituals, brought me into direct contact with the reality of folklore. But at that point, it was necessary for me to translate this experience into conceptual terms of a definition that would not only describe but also frame folklore as a subject of analytical research. Such a reflexive transformation of experience required the phenomenon to be explored not only by folklore as a discipline but also by science in general to be identified. Obviously, the amount of scholarship on the philosophy of science is considerable, and I would not be able to pursue all the possible answers to this fundamental problem. The portal through which I entered into this area of knowledge was Alfred North Whitehead's essay "Process and Reality," first published in 1929 and presented at the University of Edinburgh in 1927 and 1928 (Lowe 1966; Whitehead 1961, 565–746; 1927). My definition is not an application of Whitehead's philosophy to folklore, yet his essay, or what I understood of it, helped me reorient myself from what was considered an item-oriented exploration of reality, part of the intellectual heritage of antiquarianism and curiosity collecting that was inherent in the formative stages of folklore (Dorson 1968, 1–90), to a process orientation. Folklore, I reasoned, had a reality of its own before it was put into file cabinets, before it was classified into motifs and types, and before it was the subject of romantic idealization (Abrahams 1993). What was that reality?

Other disciplines had to record and examine facts as well, but the recording was part of the observation rather than the events themselves. And at that stage, Whitehead was helpful. He proposed that we observe and study processes in nature and in society. We study reality in flow as interactions, relations and movement. Disciplines examine processes rather than static conditions. Students may freeze them for observations and scrutiny purposes, or may abstract them into ideal types as Max Weber proposed,[10] but these technical means of documentation are necessary only because of our own limited abilities of observation. All the archival research into which historians delve purports to uncover not isolated documents, but causal relations between events along a temporal axis that have an explanatory value and reveal processes in time. The concept of process is applicable to all other disciplines in the social sciences, the humanities, and, of course, the natural sciences, yet as far as folklore is concerned, it would be necessary to identify the particular process that universally exists in human societies that folklore as a discipline explores.

There is an inherent incongruity between processes in society and academic disciplines. Society and nature do not come packaged ready-made for university departments to study and, if anything, the relation between the organization of the academy and the order of society and nature is inverted. Disciplines attempt to adapt to study reality, but even then, the correspondence between the two is far from perfect. By the mid-1960s, folklore as a concept and as a discipline had a history that was long enough to extend in different directions, which complicated the demarcation of folklore in the social context. At the time, my own department at the University of Pennsylvania was named Folklore and Folklife, partially reflecting the twists and turns of its academic history rather than social changes in the United States (Miller 2004). I therefore first attempted to identify the process in society that could best be described as *folklore* before going on to deal with its academic representation.

For this purpose, following my experience in my field study, I isolated communication as the process of folklore. It could be verbal, visual, musical, or kinetic, but it had to involve the process of communication. It was not the first time that the concept had occurred in folklore scholarship (see Bascom 1955, 247), but my direct inspiration was the special issue of the *American Anthropologist* edited by John Gumperz and Dell Hymes, which they titled "The Ethnography of Communication" (1964), and in particular, Hymes' introductory essay "Introduction: Toward Ethnographies of Communication" (Hymes 1964). Hymes envisioned the ethnography of communication as a "second descriptive science comprising language" that centers holistically on communicative events and of which language is just one of the components.[11]

Such an idea of communication could provide a solid foundation for the study of folklore but, as proposed, it was both too broad and too narrow, since it excluded such nonlinguistic forms of communication as visual arts, music, and dance that were part of the paradigm of the discipline of folklore. Indeed, the history of the discipline was not a major concern for me at the time. I deliberately considered the concept of tradition[12] in folklore to be an optional, not a defining, criterion (Ben-Amos 1971). But not only past scholarship was at stake. There was a need to establish a correspondence between the socio-cultural and the scholarly-analytical conceptions of folklore. For that purpose, I proposed that folklore was a unique kind of communication that is distinct in words, in sight, in sound, in motion, and in performance.

Artistic was not an evaluative but a descriptive term, indicating the aesthetic dimension of its performance. It is artistic by the very nature of its distinction from the quotidian forms of communication that we encounter in society. Using verbal folklore as an example, speakers discern the forms of speaking folklore by employing such verbal markers as opening and closing formulas, style and register, narrative patterns, and thematic domains. These markers distinguish them from other forms of verbal communication and subject them to culturally cognizant performance rules. Folklore scholarship engages in the analysis and interpretation of these verbal genres that are conceived as artistic by the community of speakers.

At that time, I had not read the article by Peter Bogatyrëv and Roman Jakobson, "Die Folklore als eine besondere Form des Schaffens," which was published in 1929. However, by selecting the concept of art as the modifier of communication, I was probably influenced by the writings of the school of Russian formalism—to which I had been exposed through the writings of Vladimir Propp (1895–1970) that had begun to be available in English—and some students at the Folklore Institute of Indiana University to whom I referred in my dissertation.[13]

But the modification of communication as artistic, though necessary, was not sufficient. Forty-six years ago, before the exponential leap in communication technology that we are currently experiencing, it was possible to broadcast or telecast a song for millions of listeners and refer to it as a folk song. Was such communication still a folkloric event? My conclusion was that it transcended its folkloric boundaries. Society at large considered such performances as mass communication. Maybe it was folklore being displayed in another medium, but it was not a folkloric performance. Therefore, in addition to aesthetic modification, there was a need to add the social modification of folklore. Therefore, I proposed that folklore was "artistic communication in small groups," involving face-to- face communication in an event in which performers and their audiences share the same symbolic universe.

I first delivered my paper "Folklore: The Definition Game Once Again" at the 1967 Annual Meeting of the American Folklore Society in Toronto, Canada. I was scheduled to talk at a panel on "Oral and Written Literatures" chaired by Professor D. K. Wilgus (University of California, Los Angeles), in which the other speakers were Alan Lomax (New York, NY); Robert J. Adams

(Indiana University), a specialist on Japanese folklore and a classmate of mine; and Barre J. Toelken (University of Oregon), a scholar of ballads and Navajo folklore whom I barely knew at the time but who later became a good friend. I was the last. Alan Lomax (1915–2002) was the most senior scholar in the group and, appropriately enough, dominated the panel (see Cohen 2003; Szwed 2010). He spoke freely beyond his allotted twenty minutes and put the rest of us under time pressure. By the time I had my turn, lunchtime was approaching. I started setting up my argument, developing the ideas and leading up to the definition of folklore that I was about to propose, but the chairman, D. K. Wilgus, asked me impatiently to hurry up and finish my presentation. As I learned later, it was not just his hunger that prompted him to cut me short.

On my return from Toronto, I took some time to prepare my paper for publication and, on the advice of colleagues, changed its title to the more respectable and, to my taste, somewhat pretentious "Toward New Perspectives in Folklore," and mailed it to the *Journal of American Folklore*. The editor, Professor John Greenway (1919–91) rejected my manuscript. However, he made a concession and told me that he had forwarded it to Professor Américo Paredes (1915–99) of the University of Texas, who by that time was the editor-elect of the *Journal of American Folklore*. Américo Paredes later told me personally that while he did not know whether my manuscript was the last that John Greenway rejected, he remembered quite well that it was the first he approved for publication in the *Journal of American Folklore*.

Instead of my paper, John Greenway published in the *Journal* "A Note on Definitions" by Roger Welsch (1968), who was my classmate at Indiana University. By that time, he was teaching at the German Department of the University of Nebraska. He was an excellent young scholar and in 1967–68 was probably working on the translation of Kaarle Krohn's (1863–1933) *Methodology of Folklore* (1971), introducing American students to a folklore classic. He subsequently became a distinguished folklorist of the Prairie Plains, publishing eleven books and counting.[14] Welsch pointed out the futility of definitions in general and criticized my own definition in particular. He admonished folklorists for their recurrent attempts to define *folklore*, pointing out that it is in the nature of words to constantly change meanings and that the term *folklore* was not unique in that regard. Definitions, he argued, are linguistic, not folkloric, problems. His note was eloquent and sophisticated, making me realize the apparent vagueness of my own lecture. My argument was not concerned with the word *folklore* but with the social and verbal conduct that societies designate as distinct from other forms of behavior and to which scholars applied the term *folklore*.

The person who came to my defense was Richard Bauman, a friend and a classmate who, after obtaining an MA degree in folklore from Indiana University, continued his studies at the University of Pennsylvania, specializing in American civilization and anthropology. He was later to become the editor of the *Journal of American Folklore* himself and an internationally known scholar who authored many books on performance theory in folklore (Bauman 1983, 1986, 1975, 2004). He wrote,

> If ever a writer has hobbled a truly significant contribution with an infelicitous title, it is Dan Ben-Amos, with his "Folklore: The Definition Game Once Again," delivered at the Toronto meetings of the American Folklore Society in 1967. For it is abundantly obvious that folklorists have grown weary of the old game, and Roger Welsch has undoubtedly struck a responsive chord in many of his colleagues by coming forward to say so even before Ben-Amos's paper has appeared in print. The truth of the matter is, however, that Ben-Amos is not really playing games, or at least he has so rewritten the rules that the game is a brand new one, and agree or disagree with his ideas, we do ourselves little disservice to dismiss them as another tired whack at the same tattered ball. His paper will speak for itself when it appears in print, but certain points raised by Welsch need to be answered now, if only to make it possible for Ben-Amos's contribution to receive the full attention it deserves. Fortunately, this has nothing to do with the essential points of Ben-Amos's work. Insofar as the kind of exercise described above represents the definition game, Ben-Amos has explicitly dissociated himself from it. Instead—and would that he had stressed this in his subtitle—Ben-Amos has entered into a major reconceptualization of the entire field of folklore. His work must be considered in that light. For it is plain that Ben-Amos is not talking about the materials of folklore—the folklore things of the world—and he certainly does not intend to include himself among the legions of item-oriented folklorists. The significance of his contribution, rather, lies in his suggestion that folk-lore be considered in terms of communicative process, communicative action; he is doing no more and no less than advancing the concept of a behavioral study of folklore, thereby opening the way for a behavioral science of folklore. Now—while Welsch and other humanists recoil in horror and indignation—let us consider some of the implications of this reorientation for those who, like myself, find the prospect of such a science highly promising and not uncongenial. The idea of folklore as a social science is a relatively familiar one by now, recognized, if not put into practice, by most folklorists. Even the literarians seem generally inclined to grant it some legitimacy, if only on a live-and-let-live basis. But folklore as a behavioral science is something new. (1969, 167)

Later, Richard Bauman was instrumental in according attention to my definition of *folklore*. He came to the University of Texas in 1967 as a postdoctoral scholar, and when Professor Américo Paredes assumed the editorship of the *Journal of American Folklore* in 1968, starting with vol. 82 (1969), Richard Bauman became his colleague. Together they began to plan an issue devoted to folklore theory, for which Richard Bauman became a special editor.

In the summer of 1970, I was teaching summer courses at Indiana University and asked Professor Richard Dorson, by then my former teacher, to read and comment on my manuscript. He had previously been the editor of the *Journal of American Folklore* (1959–63) and was a teacher whose judgment I trusted. After reading the manuscript, he said, "The paper is fine, but you have to state in the title what is unique about your definition. How does your definition differ from all other definitions of *folklore*?"

"Well," I answered, "I am defining *folklore* in context."

"So, say so."

I immediately wrote to Américo Paredes asking him to change the title of my essay from "Toward New Perspectives in Folklore" to "Toward a Definition of Folklore in Context." And by the time he and Richard Bauman were ready to publish the theoretical issue of the *Journal of American Folklore*, he asked me for permission to use the discarded title of my paper as the title of the issue.

The concept of context that I spontaneously selected to highlight in the title, preferring it over any of the terms within the definition, was not new in folklore scholarship. In his *Guide for Field Workers in Folklore*, Kenneth Goldstein (1964, 190) distinguished between artificial, formal, informal, natural, physical, semiformal, and social contexts. Alan Dundes and Roger Abrahams considered the methodological significance of context in the analysis of folklore texts, and in a retrospective essay that I wrote twenty years after the publication of "Toward a Definition of Folklore in Context" (1971), I discussed previous uses of the concept in folklore studies and related disciplines (see Ben-Amos 1993). But in their use and in their theoretical discourse of folklore, context is a concept relating to interpretive information regarding the meanings of texts. I assumed that much, taking the integral relations of texts and their contexts for granted. By inserting the preposition *in* into the title of my essay, I intended to indicate that the definition I proposed is tenable to folklore as it exists, occurs, and is performed in context, considering all the attributes that have often figured in the definitions of folklore, secondary, optional, and, in fact, unnecessary features for definitional purposes (Ben-Amos 1983). Folklore is, therefore, "artistic communication in small groups" as it happens pragmatically in culture and society.

When it finally appeared in print, the essay and the definition received a mixed reaction. The most visible, or rather vocal, was D. K. Wilgus's "Presidential Address" (1973) delivered at the 1972 Annual Meeting of the American Folklore Society in Austin, Texas. Quoting the venerable scholar George Lyman Kittredge (1860–1941), Wilgus's address was a frontal attack on the theory, the method, and the terminology of these upstarts in folklore who collected their works between the two covers of the *New Perspectives*. Richard

Bauman's and my own essays were well represented as targets of criticism. While listening to his speech, both of us glanced at each other, with admitted satisfaction. We realized that if we, mere youngsters in the field of folklore, had roused the ire of the president of the American Folklore Society, we had done something right.

Other leading scholars at the time had a more ambivalent response. Richard Dorson, for example, who himself began his scholarship in folklore by ruffling some feathers with his neologism *fakelore*, empathized with his former students, considering them "young Turks among folklorists" (1972, 45). At the same time, in commenting about the *New Perspectives* in his own book *Folklore and Fakelore*, he expressed his own reservations, concluding that there was nothing new in this new trend (1976, 86–87), epitomizing William James' observation that a new theory is first rejected, next admitted as true but insignificant, and finally, considered not new at all (James 1907, 198).

The folklorists who were younger forty-six years ago were more receptive (e.g., Glassie 1983, 129). In my own work, I made some digressions into more traditional folklore methodologies, but even while pursuing them, this definition of *folklore* and the concept of folklore that is at its core sustained me and continued to be the fundamental premise of my studies.

Notes

1. I referred to Oriol-Pujol (2008).

2. Subsequent to our conversation, three essays of the late Josep M. Pujol appeared in English (Pujol 2013), including "Folkloric Bibliography of Josep M. Pujol" (Pujol 2013, 65–69) and a compilation of his essays in Catalan (Oriol and Samper 2013).

3. This was an obvious milestone in Nigerian history, but on arrival at the Lagos airport, I experienced it as a colossal nuisance. For historical studies and analyses of the January 15 Nigerian coup d'etat, see Akinnola (1998, 1–7); Ademoyega (1981); Luckham (1971, 17–50); Nwachuku and Uzoigwe (2004, 32–38); Nwankwo (1987, 97–124); Oyinbo (1971, 36–80); Arthur (1987, 97–124); and Panter-Brick (1970).

4. The first nine annual meetings (1889–97) of the American Folklore Society were held independently. The next four meetings (1898–1901) were held together with those of the American Society of Naturalists. The fifteenth meeting (1903) was independent again, but from 1916 to 1941, the annual meetings were held together with those of the American Anthropological Association. No meetings were held from 1942–43, and after four more independent meetings (1944–46), the American Folklore Society alternated its annual meetings between the American Anthropological Society and the Modern Language Association until 1966, when it began and continued to meet independently (Dwyer-Shick, 1979). At the time, such a schedule represented the history of academic folklore in the United States (Zumwalt 1988).

5. The term *folklore* appeared first in a letter to the editors of *The Athenaeum* signed with the pseudonym Ambrose Merton and written on August 12, 1846; see Thoms (1846); Emrich (1946); Dorson (1955; 1968, 75–90); M. A. Smith (1947).

6. See Gersehnhorn (2004) and L. M. Smith (2009).

7. By the time Lord Raglan made his proposal, the history of everyday life was already an established research trend in historical studies across the English Channel in France, where, in 1929, Marc Léopold Benjamin Bloch (1886–1944) and Lucien Paul Victor Febvre (1878–1956) had launched the *Annales d'histoire economique et sociale*, thereby initiating an influential school in historical research that incorporated everyday life into the academic scrutiny of history. For a selection of studies of historiographical research about the Annales school, see Birnbaum (1978); Bloch and Febvre (1994–2003); Burguière (2006); Burke (1990); Clark (1999); Fink (1989); Forster (1978); Harsgor (1978); Hunt (1986); and Tendler (2013).

8. He was a folklorist of international reputation who taught in the Department of Romance Languages at the University of North Carolina, where he founded the Curriculum in Folklore in 1939. For a bibliography of his publications up to midcentury, see Boggs (1951).

9. My MA thesis was entitled "In Praise of the Besht: Commentary and Motif-Index" (1964) and was later incorporated into the translation that Jerome Mintz and I published *In Praise of the Baal Shem Tov* (1970), and my doctoral dissertation was on "Narrative Forms in the Haggadah: Structural Analysis" (1967b).

10. For a selection of studies about the concept of "ideal type" in Max Weber's sociological theory, see Becker (1933–34, 1940); Burger (1976); Cahnman (1964, 1965); Rogers (1969); and Weber (1947, 1949); for the application of this concept to folklore, see Ben-Amos (1992) and Honko (1968, 1976, 1980, 1989a, 1989b).

11. The essay became one of the series of Hymes' influential contributions. Dell Hymes (1927–2009) continued to produce illustrious scholarship. He was the president of three scholarly organizations: the American Folklore Society (1973–74), the Linguistic Society of America (1982), and the American Anthropological Association (1983). Some of his major studies in folklore were collected in his books (Hymes 1974, 1981).

12. The deletion of the concept of tradition from the definition of folklore became one of its most controversial aspects. In folklore studies and in related fields, tradition was and continued to be a major idea that was explored and analyzed in scholarship and in society, regardless of its elimination by me from the defining criteria of folklore. For a selection of studies about tradition, see Anttonen (2005); Becker (1998); Blank and Howard (2013); Bronner (1998, 2011); Cashman, Mould, and Shukla (2011); Gailey (1989); Glassie (1995); Hobsbawm and Ranger (1983); Honko (1988); McDonald (1997); Shils (1981); Utley (1961); and Watson (1997). Tongue in cheek, when Linda Dégh guest edited an issue of the *Journal of Folklore Research* on "Culture, Tradition, Identity," she invited me to write an essay about tradition; see Ben-Amos (1984).

13. Today, Vladimir Yakovlevich Propp is recognized as a major folktale and literary scholar. The first translation of his groundbreaking morphological analysis of the folktale was published at Indiana University in 1958 and had an immediate influence on the students at the Folklore Institute. A second edition appeared ten years later as part of the American Folklore Society Bibliographical and Special Series. For bibliographical details of books in English by and about him and his method, see Propp (1968, 1984, 2012); Dundes (1964a); Gilet (1998); Milne (1988); and Levin (1967).

14. The latest is Welsch (2012).

Bibliography

Abrahams, Roger D. 1963. "Folklore in Culture: Notes toward an Analytic Method." *Texas Studies in Literature and Language*, no. 5:98–110.
———. 1968. "Introductory Remarks to a Rhetorical Theory of Folklore." *Journal of American Folklore* 81, no. 320:143–58.

———. 1993. "Phantoms of Romantic Nationalism in Folkloristics." *Journal of American Folklore* 106, no. 419:3–37.

Ademoyega, Adewale. 1981. *Why We Struck: The Story of the First Nigerian Coup.* Ibadan, Nigeria: Evans Brothers.

Adorono, Theodor W. 1973. *The Jargon of Authenticity.* Translated by Knut Tarnowski and Frederic Will. Evanston, IL: Northwestern University Press.

Akinnola, Richard. 1998. *History of Coup d'Etats in Nigeria.* Lagos: Media Research and Resource Bureau.

Anttonen, Pertti J. 2005. *Tradition through Modernity: Postmodernism and Nation-State in Folklore Scholarship.* Helsinki: Finnish Literature Society.

Bascom, William R. 1953. "Folklore and Anthropology." *Journal of American Folklore* 66, no. 262:283–90.

———. 1955. "Verbal Art." *Journal of American Folklore* 68, no. 269:245–52.

Bauman, Richard. 1969. "Towards a Behavioral Theory of Folklore: A Reply to Roger Welsch." *Journal of American Folklore* 82, no. 324:167–70.

———. 1975. "Verbal Art as Performance." *American Anthropologist*, n.s., 77, no. 2: 290–311.

———. 1983. *Let Your Words Be Few: Symbolism of Speaking and Silence among Seventeenth-century Quakers.* New York: Cambridge University Press.

———. 1986. *Story, Performance, and Event: Contextual Studies of Oral Narrative.* New York: Cambridge University Press.

———. 2004. *A World of Others' Words: Cross-Cultural Perspectives on Intertextuality.* Malden: Blackwell.

Bayard, Samuel P. 1953. "The Materials of Folklore." *Journal of American Folklore* 66, no. 253:1–17.

Beck, Jane C. 1997. "Taking Stock: 1996 American Folklore Society Presidential Address." *Journal of American Folklore* 110, no. 436:123–39.

Becker, Howard. 1933–34. "Culture Case Study and Ideal-Typical Method: With Special Reference to Max Weber." *Social Forces*, no. 12:399–405.

———. 1940. "Constructive Typology in the Social Sciences." In *Contemporary Social Theory*, edited by Henry E. Barnes, Howard Becker, and Frances Becker, 17–47. New York: Appleton-Century.

Becker, Jane S. 1998. *Selling Tradition: Appalachia and the Construction of an American Folk, 1930–1940.* Chapel Hill: University of North Carolina.

Ben-Amos, Dan. 1963a. "Folklore in Israel." *Schweizerisches Archiv für Volkskunde* 59:14–24.

———. 1963b. "Hebrew Parallels to Indian Folktales." *Journal of the Assam Research Society* 15:37–45.

———. 1963c. "The Situation Structure of the Non-Humorous English Ballad." *Midwest Folklore* 13, no. 3:163–76.

———. 1964. "In Praise of the Besht: Commentary and Motif-Index." Unpublished MA thesis. Bloomington: Indiana University.

———. 1967a. "Ikpomwosa Osemwegie: A Young Bini Poet." *Nigeria Magazine* 94:250–52.

———. 1967b. "Narrative Forms in the Haggadah: Structural Analysis." PhD diss. Indiana University.

———. 1967c. "Story Telling in Benin." *African Arts/Arts d'Afrique* 1, no. 1:54–59.

———. 1971. "Toward a Definition of Folklore in Context." *Journal of American Folklore* 84, no. 331:3–15.

———. 1983. "The Idea of Folklore: An Essay." In *Studies in Aggadah and Jewish Folklore*, edited by Issachar Ben-Ami and Joseph Dan, 11–17. Folklore Research Center Studies 8. Jerusalem: Magnes.

———. 1984. "The Seven Strands of Tradition: Varieties in Its Meaning in American Folklore." *Journal of Folklore Research* 21, no. 2/3:97–131.

———. 1992. *Do We Need Ideal Types (in Folklore)? An Address to Lauri Honko*. NIF Papers, no. 2. Turku: Nordic Institute of Folklore.

———. 1993. "Context in Context." *Western Folklore* 52, no. 2/4:209–26.

———. 1998. "The Name Is the Thing." *Journal of American Folklore* 111, no. 441.:257–80.

Ben-Amos, Dan, and Jerome R. Mintz, eds. and trans. 1970. *In Praise of the Baal Shem Tov*. Bloomington: Indiana University Press.

Bendix, Regina. 1997. *In Search of Authenticity: The Formation of Folklore Studies*. Madison: University of Wisconsin Press.

———. 1998. "Of Names, Professional Identities, and Disciplinary Futures." *Journal of American Folklore* 111, no. 441:235–46.

Birnbaum, Norman. 1978. "The Annales School and Social Theory [with Discussion.]" *Review (Fernand Braudel Center)*, no. 1:225–42.

Blank, Trevor J., and Robert Glenn Howard, eds. 2013. *Tradition in the Twenty-First Century: Locating the Role of the Past in the Present*. Logan: Utah State University Press.

Bloch, Marc, and Lucien Febvre. 1994–2003. *Marc Bloch, Lucien Febvre et les Annales d'histoire économique et sociale: Correspondance*. Edited by Bertand Müller. 3 vols. Paris: Fayard.

Bogatyrëv, Peter, and Roman Jakobson. 1929. "Die Folklore als eine besondere Form des Schaffens." In *Donum natalicum Schrijnen, verzameling van opstellen opgedragen aan . . . Jos. Schrijnen bij gelegenheid van zijn zestigsten verjaardag, 3 Mei 1929*, 900–913. Utrecht: Dekkera and Van der Vegt. Rev. version: *Roman Jakobson: Selected Writings*, 4, 1–15. The Hague: Mouton, 1966. Published in English as "Folklore as a Special Form of Creativity." In *The Prague School: Selected Writings, 1919–1946*, edited by Peter Steiner, 32–46. Austin: University of Texas Press, 1982.

Boggs, Ralph Steele. 1951. "Bibliography of R. S. Boggs through 1950." *Folklore Americas* 11, no. 2:1–13.

Bronner, Simon J. 1998. *Following Tradition: Folklore in the Discourse of American Culture*. Logan: Utah State University Press.

———. 2011. *Explaining Traditions: Folk Behavior in Modern Culture*. Lexington, KY.: University Press of Kentucky.

Brückner, Wolfgang, and Klaus Beitl, eds. 1983. *Volkskunde als akademische Disziplin. Studien zur Institutionelausbildung. Referat eines wissenschaftsgeschichtlichen Symposions vom 8.–10. Oktober 1982 in Würzburg*. Österreichische Akademie der Wissenschaften, Philosophisch-Historische Klasse 414. Vienna: Der Österreichische Akademie der Wissenschaften.

Brunvand, Jan Harold. 1968. *The Study of American Folklore: An Introduction*. New York: W. W. Norton.

Burger, Thomas. 1976. *Max Weber's Theory of Concept Formation: History, Laws, and Ideal Types*. Durham, NC: Duke University Press.

Burguière, André. 2006. *The Annales School: An Intellectual History*. Translated by Jane Marie Todd. Ithaca: Cornell University Press.

Burke, Peter. 1990. *French Historical Revolution: The Annales School, 1929–89*. Stanford, CA: Stanford University Press.

Cahnman, Werner J. 1964. "Max Weber and the Methodological Controversy in the Social Sciences." In *Sociology and History: Theory and Research*, edited by Werner J. Cahnman and Alvin Boskoff, 103–27. New York: Free Press.

———. 1965. "Ideal Type Theory: Max Weber's Concept and Some of Its Derivations." *The Sociological Quarterly* 6, no. 3:268–80.

Cashman, Ray, Tom Mould, and Pravina Shukla, eds. 2011. *The Individual and Tradition: Folkloristic Perspectives.* Special Publications of the Folklore Institute, 8. Indiana University. Bloomington: Indiana University Press.

Clark, Stuart, ed. 1999. *The Annales School: Critical Assessments.* 4 vols. London: Routledge.

Cohen, Ronald D. 2002. *Rainbow Quest: The Folk Music Revival and American Society, 1940–1970.* Amherst and Boston: University of Massachusetts Press.

———, ed. 2003. *Alan Lomax: Selected Writings, 1934–1997.* New York: Routledge.

Cox, George W. 1881. *An Introduction to the Science of Comparative Mythology and Folklore.* New York: H. Holt and Co.

Dorson, Richard M. 1955. "The First Group of British Folklorists." *Journal of American Folklore* 68, no. 269:333–40.

———. 1963. "Current Folklore Theories." *Current Anthropology* 4, no. 1:93–112.

———. 1968. *The British Folklorists: A History.* Chicago: University of Chicago Press.

———. 1976. *Folklore and Fakelore: Essays toward a Discipline of Folk Studies.* Cambridge, MA: Harvard University Press.

———, ed. 1972. *Folklore and Folklife: An Introduction.* Chicago: University of Chicago Press.

Dundes, Alan. 1964a. *The Morphology of North American Indian Folktales.* Folklore Fellows Communications 195. Helsinki: Suomalainen Tiedeakatemia.

———. 1964b. "Texture, Text, and Context." *Southern Folklore Quarterly* 28:251–65. Reprinted in Alan Dundes, *Interpreting Folklore*, 20–32. Bloomington: Indiana University Press, 1980.

———. 1965. "What Is Folklore?" In *The Study of Folklore*, edited by Alan Dundes, 1–3. Englewood Cliffs, NJ: Prentice-Hall.

———. 1966. "The American Concept of Folklore." *Journal of the Folklore Institute*, no. 3:226–49.

Dwyer-Shick, Susan A. 1979. "The American Folklore Society and Folklore Research in America, 1888–1940." PhD diss. University of Pennsylvania.

Edmonson, Munro S. 1971. *Lore: An Introduction to the Science of Folklore and Literature.* New York: Holt Rinehart and Winston.

Emrich, Duncan. 1946. "Folklore: William John Thoms." *California Folklore Quarterly* 5, no. 4:355–74.

Fink, Carole. 1989. *Marc Bloch: A Life in History.* Cambridge: Cambridge University Press.

Forster, Robert. 1978. "Achievements of the Annales School." *The Journal of Economic History* 38, no. 1:58–76.

Gailey, Alan. 1989. "The Nature of Tradition." *Folklore* 100, no. 2:143–61.

Gershenhorn, Jerry. 2004. *Melville J. Herskovits and the Racial Politics of Knowledge.* Lincoln: University of Nebraska Press.

Gilet, Peter. 1998. *Vladimir Propp and the Universal Folktale: Recommissioning an Old Paradigm Story as Initiation.* Middlebury Studies in Russian Language and Literature, vol. 17. New York: Peter Lang.

Glassie, Henry. 1983. "The Moral Lore of Folklore." *Folklore Forum* 16, no. 2:123–51.

———. 1995. "Tradition." *Journal of American Folklore* 108, no. 430:395–412.

Goldstein, Kenneth S. 1964. *A Guide for Field Workers in Folklore.* Hatboro, PA: Folklore Associates for the American Folklore Society.

Golomb, Jacob. 1995. *In Search of Authenticity: From Kierkegaard to Camus.* London: Routledge.

Gomme, George Laurence. 1908. *Folklore as an Historical Science.* London: Methuen.

Grojahn, Martin. 1966. *Beyond Laughter: Humor and the Subconscious.* New York: McGraw-Hill.

Gumperz, John J., and Dell Hymes, eds. 1964. "The Ethnography of Communication." Special issue, *American Anthropologist* 66, no. 6, pt. 2.

Hahn, Johann Georg von. 1864. *Griechische und albanesische Märchen.* 2 vols. Leipzig: W. Engelmann.

Harsgor, Michael. 1978. "Total History: The Annales School." *Journal of Contemporary History* 13, no. 1:1–13.

Hartland, Edwin Sidney. 1891. *The Science of Fairy Tales: An Inquiry into Fairy Mythology.* London: W. Scott.

Hasan-Rokem, Galit. 1998. "The Birth of Scholarship Out of the Spirit of Oral Tradition: Folk Narrative Publications and National Identity in Modern Israel." *Fabula*, no. 39, nos. 3–4:277–90.

Herskovits, Melville J. 1946. "Folklore after a Hundred Years: A Problem in Redefinition." *Journal of American Folklore* 59, no. 232:89–100.

Hobsbawm, Eric, and Terence Ranger, eds. 1983. *The Invention of Tradition.* Cambridge: Cambridge University Press.

Honko, Lauri. 1968. "Genre Analysis in Folkloristics and Comparative Religion." *Temeno*, no. 3:48–66.

———. 1976. "Genre Theory Revisited." Folk Narrative Research: Some Papers Presented at the VI Congress of the International Society for Folk Narrative Research. *Studia Fennica* 20:20–26.

———. 1980. "Genre Theory." *Arv: Scandinavian Yearbook of Folklore*, no. 36:42–45.

———, ed. 1988. *Tradition and Cultural Identity.* Turku: Nordic Institute of Folklore.

———. 1989a. "Folkloristics Theories of Genre." *Studies in Oral Narrative.* Edited by Anna-Leena Siikala. *Studia Fennica*, no. 33:13–28.

———. 1989b. "Methods in Folk Narrative Research." In *Nordic Folklore: Recent Studies*, edited by Reimund Kvideland and Henning K. Sehmsdorf, 23–39. Folklore Studies in Translation. Bloomington: Indiana University Press.

Hunt, Lynn. 1986. "French History in the Last Twenty Years: The Rise and Fall of the Annales Paradigm." *Journal of Contemporary History* 21, no. 2:209–24.

Hymes, Dell. 1964. "Introduction: Toward Ethnographies of Communication." In "The Ethnography of Communication," edited by John J. Gumperz and Dell Hymes. Special issue, *American Anthropologist* 66, no. 6, pt. 2:1–34.

———. 1974. *Foundations in Sociolinguistics: An Ethnographic Approach.* Philadelphia: University of Pennsylvania Press.

———. 1981. *"In Vain I Tried to Tell You": Essays in Native American Ethnopoetics.* Philadelphia: University of Pennsylvania Press.

Jakobson, Roman. 1950. "Slavic Mythology." In The *Funk and Wagnalls Standard Dictionary of Folklore Mythology and Legends*, edited by Maria Leach and Jerome Fried, 2:1025–28. New York: Funk and Wagnalls.

James, William. 1907. *Pragmatism: A New Name for Some Old Ways of Thinking.* New York: Longmans, Green and Co.

Jason, Heda. 1991. "Marginalia to P. Bogatyrev and R. Jakobson's Essay 'Die Folklore als Eine Besondere Form des Schaffens.'" *Folklore* 102, no. 1:31–38.

Kirshenblatt-Gimblett, Barbara. 1998. "Folklore's Crisis." *Journal of American Folklore* 111, no. 441:281–327.

Kongas, Elli-Kaija. 1963. "The Concept of Folklore." *Midwest Folklore* 13, no. 2:69–88.

Krappe, Alexander H. 1930. *The Science of Folk-Lore*. London: Methuen.

Krohn, Kaarle. 1971. *Folklore Methodology*. Formulated by Julius Krohn and expanded by Nordic Researchers. Translated by Roger L. Welsch. Publications of the American Folklore Society Bibliographical and Special Series, vol. 21. Austin: University of Texas Press. Originally published as *Die folkloristische Arbeitsmethode*. Oslo, Norway: Institute for Comparative Research in Human Culture, 1926.

Kuhn, Thomas S. 1962. *The Structure of Scientific Revolutions*. International Encyclopedia of Unified Science, vols. 1 and 2. Vol. 2, no. 2. Chicago: University of Chicago Press.

Leach, Maria and Jerome Fried, eds. 1949. "Folklore." In The *Funk and Wagnalls Standard Dictionary of Folklore Mythology and Legends* 1, 398–403. New York: Funk and Wagnalls Company. Reprinted as "Definitions of Folklore." *Journal of Folklore Research* 33, no. 3 (1996): 255–64.

Levin, Isidor. 1967. "Vladimir Propp: An Evaluation on His Seventieth Birthday." *Journal of the Folklore Institute* 4, no. 1:32–49.

Lévy-Bruhl, Lucien. 1910. *Les fonctions mentales dans les sociétés inférieurs*. Paris: F. Alcan. Published in English as *How Natives Think*. Translated by L. A. Clare. New York: A. A. Knopf, 1925.

Lowe, Victor. 1966. *Understanding Whitehead*. Baltimore: Johns Hopkins Press.

Luckham, Robin. 1971. *The Nigerian Military: A Sociological Analysis of Authority and Revolt, 1960–1967*. Cambridge: Cambridge University Press.

McDonald, Barry. 1997. "Tradition as Personal Relationship." *Journal of American Folklore* 110, no. 435:47–67.

Miller, Rosina S. 2004. "Of Politics, Disciplines, and Scholars: MacEdward Leach and the Founding of the Folklore Program at the University of Pennsylvania." *The Folklore Historian* 21:17–34.

Mine, Pamela J. 1988. *Vladimir Propp and the Study of Structure in Hebrew Biblical Narrative*. Sheffield: Almond.

Noy, Dov. ed. 1963. *Folktales of Israel*. With the assistance of Dan Ben-Amos. Folktales of the World. Chicago: Chicago University Press.

Nwachuku, Levi A., and G. N. Uzoigwe. 2004. *Troubled Journey: Nigeria Since the Civil War*. Dallas: University Press of America.

Nwankwo, Arthur A. 1987. *The Military Option to Democracy: Class, Power and Violence in Nigerian Politics*. Issues in Nigerian Development 7. Enugu, Nigeria: Fourth Dimension.

Oyinbo, John. 1971. *Nigeria: Crisis and Beyond*. London: Charles Knight.

Oring, Elliott. 1998. "Anti Anti-'Folklore.'" *Journal of American Folklore* 111, no. 441:328–38.

Oriol, Carme. 2012. "Josep M. Pujol (1947–2012)." *Fabula* 53, nos. 3–4:295–98.

Oriol, Carme, and Josep M. Pujol. 2008. *Index of Catalan Folktales*. Folklore Fellows Communications 294. Helsinki: Suomalainen Tiedeakatemia.

Oriol, Carme, and Emili Samper, eds. 2013. *Això era i no era: Obra folklòrica de Josep M. Pujol*. Tarragona: Publicacions Universitat Rovira i Virgili.

Panter-Brick, S. K. 1970. "From Military Coup to Civil War, January 1966 to May 1967." In *Nigerian Politics and Military Rule: Prelude to the Civil War*, edited by S. K. Panter-Brick, 14–57. Commonwealth Papers 13. London: University of London and Athlone.

Paredes, Américo, and Richard Bauman, eds. 1972. *Toward New Perspectives in Folklore*. Publications of the American Folklore Society Bibliographical and Special Series, vol. 23. Austin: University of Texas Press. 2nd ed., Bloomington, IN: Trickster, 2000.

Pincus, Leslie. 1996. *Authenticating Culture in Imperial Japan: Kuki Shuzo and the Rise of National Aesthetics*. Berkeley: University of California Press.

222 | *Folklore Concepts*

Propp, Vladimir. 1958. *Morphology of the Folktale.* Translated by Laurence Scott. Edited by
Svatava Pirkova-Jakobson. *International Journal of American Linguistics* 24, no. 4, part 3.
Publication ten of the Indiana University Research Center in Anthropology, Folklore and
Linguistics. Bloomington: Indiana University.

——. 1968. *Morphology of the Folktale.* 2nd rev. ed. Edited by Louis A. Wagner. Introduction
by Alan Dundes. Publications of the American Folklore Society Bibliographical and
Special Series, vol. 9. Indiana University Research Center in Anthropology, Folklore and
Linguistics, publication 10. Austin: University of Texas Press.

——. 1984. *Theory and History of Folklore.* Translated by Ariadna Y. Martin and Richard
P. Martin. Edited by Anatoly Lieberman. Theory and History of Literature, vol. 5.
Minneapolis: University of Minnesota Press.

——. 2012. *The Russian Folktale.* Translated and edited by Sibelan Forrester. Series in Fairy
Tale Studies. Detroit: Wayne State University.

Pujol, Josep M. 2013. *Three Selected Papers on Catalan Folklore: Traditional Literature and
Ethnopoetics; Introduction to a History of Folklores; Extraordinary Stories, Urban
Legends.* Edited by Carme Oriol and Emili Samper. Tarragona: Publicacions URV.
http://publicacionsurv.cat/llibres-digitals/biblioteca-digital/item/419-three-selected
-papers-on-catalan-folklore.

Raglan, Lord. 1946. "The Scope of Folklore." *Folklore* 57, no. 3:98–105.

Riehl, Wilhelm Heinrich. 1859. "Die Volkskunde als Wissenschaft." In *Culturstudien aus drei
Jahrhunderten,* 205–29. Stuttgart: J. G. Cotta. Reprinted in Gerhard Lutz, ed. *Volkskunde:
Ein Handbuch zur Geschichte ihrer Probleme.* Berlin: Erich Schmidt, 1958.

Rope, Jonathan. 2007. "Thoms and the Unachieved 'Folk-Lore of England.'" *Folklore* 118, no.
2:203–16.

Russell, Ian, and David Atkinson, eds. 2004. *Folk Song: Tradition, Revival, and Re-Creation.* The
Elphinstone Institute Occasional Publications 3. Aberdeen: University of Aberdeen.

Shils, Edward. 1981. *Tradition.* Chicago: University of Chicago Press.

Simpson, George Eaton. 1973. *Melville J. Herskovits.* Leaders of Modern Anthropology Series.
New York: Columbia University Press.

Smith, Llewellyn M., director and producer. 2009. *Herskovits at the Heart of Blackness* [video
recording]. Berkeley, CA: California Newsreel.

Smith, Marian A. 1947. "Thoms, *Folk-Lore* and the Folklore Centenary." *Journal of American
Folklore* 60, no. 238:417–20.

——. 1959. "The Importance of Folklore Studies to Anthropology." *Folklore* 70, no. 1:300–312.

Stocking, George W., Jr. 1965. "On the Limits of 'Presentism' and 'Historicism' in the
Historiography of the Behavioral Sciences." *Journal of the History of the Behavioral
Sciences* 1 no. 3:211–18.

Szwed, John F. 2010. *Alan Lomax: The Man Who Recorded the World.* New York: Viking
Penguin.

Taylor, Archer. 1946. "The Problems of Folklore." *Journal of American Folklore* 59 no. 232:101–7.

——. 1952. "The Place of Folklore." *PMLA* 67, no. 1:59–66.

Tendler, Joseph. 2013. *Opponents of the Annales School.* New York: Palgrave Macmillan.

Thompson, Stith, ed. 1953. *Four Symposia on Folklore.* Indiana University Publications Folklore
Series, no. 8. Bloomington: Indiana University Press.

Thoms, William [Ambrose Merton]. 1846. "Folklore." *Athenaeum,* no. 982 (August 22, 1846):
862–63. Reprinted in *The Study of Folklore,* edited by Alan Dundes, 4–6. Englewood
Cliffs, NJ: Prentice-Hall.

——. 1996. "'Folk-Lore' from 'The Athenæum,' August 22, 1846." *Journal of Folklore Research*
33, no. 3:187–89.

Tylor, Edward Burnett. 1958. *The Origins of Culture.* New York: Harper and Brothers. Originally published in 1871.

Utley, Francis Lee. 1958. "The Study of Folk Literature: Its Scope and Use." *The Journal of American Folklore* 71, no. 280:139–48.

———. 1961. "Folk Literature: An Operational Definition." *Journal of American Folklore* 74, no. 293:193–206.

Watson, Stephen H. 1997. *Tradition(s): Refiguring Community and Virtue in Classical German Thought.* Bloomington: Indiana University Press.

Weber, Max. 1947. *The Theory of Social and Economic Organization.* Translated by A. M. Henderson and Talcott Parsons. New York: Free Press.

———. 1949. *Max Weber on The Methodology of the Social Sciences.* Translated by Edward A. Shils and Henry A. Finch. Glencoe, IL: Free Press.

Welsch, Roger. 1968. "A Note on Definitions." *Journal of American Folklore* 81, no. 321:262–64.

———. 2012. *Embracing Fry Bread: Confessions of a Wannabe.* Lincoln: University of Nebraska Press.

Whitehead, Alfred North. 1927. *Symbolism.* New York: Macmillan.

———. 1961. *Alfred North Whitehead: An Anthology.* Selected by F. S. C. Northrop and Mason W. Gross. New York: Macmillan.

Wilgus, D. K. 1973. "The Text is the Thing." *Journal of American Folklore* 86, no. 341:241–52.

Zumwalt, Rosemary Lévy. 1988. *American Folklore Scholarship: A Dialogue of Dissent.* Bloomington: Indiana University Press.

INDEX

The letter t *following a page number denotes a table.*

Aarne, Antti, 42

Abrahams, Roger, ix, x–xi, 79, 89–90, 214;
    Deep Down in the Jungle, x; *The
    Man-of-Words in the West Indies*, x

academic prestige of disciplines, 196n12

Acosta, Jose de, 17

Adams, Robert J, 211–12

Adorno, Theodor, 78

Aimyekagbon, 157–59, 160–62

akpata (stringed bow-lute) and *akpata*
    players, 159, 160–61

alliteration, 49

Alvey, Gerald, 107

American Council of Learned Societies,
    xxi, 181

American Folklife Preservation Act (1976), 183

American Folklore Society: and applied
    folklore, 183, 184; Beck's address to, 179;
    and direction of research, 105–6; first
    independent meeting of, 205; Herskovits's
    address to, 175, 176–77; meetings of, 215n4;
    panel on "Oral and Written Literatures" at,
    211–12; publication dedicated to Redfield, 76;
    scholarly intentions of founders of, 181–82;
    survey by, 64; Wilgus's address to, 214–15

American folklore studies, tradition in:
    anthropological approach in, 177–78;
    as canon, 72–84; as culture, 87–88; as
    lore, 70–72; as organic mass, 85–87;
    overview of, 64, 69–70, 91–92; as
    performance, 90–91; as process, 71,
    84–85; as system of rules, 88–90. *See also*
    diffusion; oral traditions and
    transmission; translation

American Historical Review, 194

American Indians. *See* Native Americans

America's discovery and interest in folklore, 8

Anderson, Walter, 169–70

Andrzejewski, B. W., 51

d'Anghiera, Pietro Martire, 17

anonymity, 1–2, 5, 7

anthropologists: and definitions of folklore,
    87, 92n1; and Goldstein's *Guide*, 165; and
    leadership of folklorists, 192; views on
    culture, 87–88

anthropology: development of, 8, 20n2;
    folklore as part of, 68; and folkloric
    research, 105–6, 177

antiquarian approach to folklore: and
    collecting, 178, 185, 196n4; and development
    of folklore, 14; Gustavus Adolphus's
    Instructions, 14–15, 19; impact of discovery
    of America on, xv, 12–13; seventeenth
    century expectations for, 18

applied folklore, 103, 183, 184

archetypal approach to folklore, 46–47

Armistead, Sam, 205

Armstrong, Nancy, 193

artifacts, 24

artistic forms, origins of, 4

artistic works: motifs and themes in, 132;
    Ruskin's aesthetics, 117–18; transformation
    of life experiences in, 123

Ashanti storytellers, 30–31

associative thinking, 207

audiences: functional analysis and, 140; impact
    on genres, 24–25; and natural contexts, 171;
    as necessary to folkloric acts, 33–34, 211;
    part of communicative events, 30; passive
    creativity of, 27; use of metric forms and, 52

Augé, Marc, 179

authenticity, 5, 149, 208

Bakhtin, Mikhail, 10, 103, 147, 178, 196n6

ballads: affinities with other genres, 42,
    43; in antiquarian tradition, 185, 206; as
    communal creations, 27; contexts of, 144–
    45; creativity of ballad singers, 80–81; and
    irrationality, 186; truth in, 52–53. *See also*
    Child, Francis James

theoretical underpinnings, 101–2, 103, 107; and tradition, 34–35, 68–69; use of scientific principles in, 167–68. *See also* comparative studies; fieldwork

folklorists: academic inferiority complex of, 102; distinctiveness of, 100–101; outside the academy, 175, 192; placement in higher education, 182–83; work of, 184

folk song movement, 208

folkways, use of term, 194

formalism, 141, 211

Foster, George, 87

Frankfurt Institute of Social Research, 78–79

Frazer, James, 26

free motifs, 128, 132

functional approach to folklore, 47–48

Funk and Wagnalls Standard Dictionary of Folklore, Mythology and Legend, 65, 87

Gardiner, A., 146–47

Gbaya narratives, 53

genealogy of forms, 42, 45, 46

Gennep, Arnold van, 177

genres: characteristics of, xix–xx; contextual analysis of, 144–45; ethnic systems of, 49–50; folk humor, 10, 49; and motifs, 131; native genres, 48, 49; structural unity in, 44–45; superorganic and organic duality of forms, 24; as thematic categories, 41–44; as verbal formulations of mental concerns, 46–47. *See also* classification of folklore; ethnic genres; specific genres

Gentleman's Magazine (1830) on *lore*, 191

Georges, Robert, 90, 142, 180, 205

German Romanticism and folklore studies, 9, 115–17

German *Volkskunde*, 9, 177, 178, 191

Glassie, Henry, 80, 194

Goethe, Johann Wolfgang von, 115–16, 117, 127

Goldberg, Harriet, 193

Goldsmith, Oliver, "The Hermit: A Ballad," 190

Goldstein, Kenneth, 81, 86, 148–49, 168–71; *Guide for Field Workers in Folklore*, x, 165–72, 214

Gozzi, Carlo, 115–16

Great Depression, folklore projects in, 184

Green, Archie, 79–80

Greenway, John, 48, 212

Greverus, Ina-Maria, 129

Grimm, Jacob, 119

Grimm brothers, 42, 104

Grotjahn, Martin, 205

Gummere, Francis, 27

Gumperz, John, 210

Gunkel, Hermann, *Das Märchen in Alten Testament*, 42

Gustavus Adolphus (1594–1632), 14, 15, 17, 18

Hahn, J. G. von, 45, 133n3, 133n5; *Griechische und albanesisclze Märchen*, 114

Hand, Wayland, 205

Handler, Richard, 83–84

Hanson, Norwood R., 168

Harman, M., 87

Harris, Marvin, 20n2

Hartland, Edwin Sidney, 26, 66–68, 70, 72

Harvard University, 106

Hausa people, and proverbs, 58

Hebbel, Friedrich, 134n14

Henderson, M. Carole, 105

Herder, Johann Gottfried von, 9, 10, 68, 103, 104–5

The Hero, study of, 176

Herodotus, 16

Herskovits, Frances, 50–51

Herskovits, Melville: address to American Folklore Society, 175, 176–77; on antiquarian approach, 178; commentary on *lore* and *folk*, 187; on Dahomean narratives, 50–51; definition of *folklore*, 74, 87; redefinition of *folklore*, 181, 205–6

high culture, 92n7

higher education: declining state of, 196n8; folklore studies in, 106, 181–83, 184–85, 192, 196n3

historians' attitude toward folklore, 193–94, 196n2

historical processes' effect on folklore, 2–3, 4

historical scholarship, 12

historic-geographic method: criticism of, 131–32; and diffusion theory, 172; experimenters using, 169–70; and minimal narrative units, 111–13; and motifs, 124, 128, 130–31, 132. *See also* diffusion theory

DAN BEN-AMOS is Professor of Folklore and Comparative Literature in the Department of Near Eastern Languages and Civilizations at the University of Pennsylvania. He is author of *Sweet Words*; *Folklore in Context*; *Jewish Folk Literature* (in Hebrew and Russian); *Concepts and Methods in Folkloristics* (in Chinese, edited by Juwen Zhang); *Communication and Folklore* (in Estonian); and editor of *Folklore Genres*; *Folktales of the Jews* (vols. 1–3; in English and Russian); *Folklore: Performance and Communication* (with Kenneth S. Goldstein); *Cultural Memory and the Construction of Identity* (with Liliane Weissberg); and *The Diary: The Epic of Everyday Life* (with Batsheva Ben-Amos). He is editor and translator of *In Praise of the Baal Shem Tov* (with Jerome R. Mintz) and has prepared an annotated edition of *Mimekor Yisrael: Classical Jewish Folktales* (by Micha Joseph Bin Gorion, edited by Emanuel Bin Gorion, translated by I. M. Lask). He is also editor of the Raphael Patai Series in Jewish Folklore and Anthropology at Wayne State University Press. In 2006, he received the National Jewish Book Award; in 2013, he was recognized as Honorary Member of the International Society for Folk Narrative Research; and in 2014, he was given the American Folklore Society Lifetime Scholarly Achievement Award.

HENRY GLASSIE is College Professor Emeritus at Indiana University. He has received many awards for his work, including the Chicago Folklore Prize, the Haney Prize in the Social Sciences, the Cummings Award of the Vernacular Architecture Forum, the Kniffen Award and Douglas Award of the Pioneer America Society, and the Nigerian Studies Association Book Prize. He has also received formal recognition for his contributions from the ministries of culture of Turkey and Bangladesh. Three of his works have been named among the notable books of the year by the *New York Times*.

He is author of numerous books including *Passing the Time in Ballymenone: Culture and History of an Ulster Community*; *Irish Folktales*; *The Spirit of Folk Art*; *Turkish Traditional Art Today*; *Art and Life in Bangladesh*; *Prince Twins Seven-Seven: His Art, His Life in Nigeria, His Exile in America*; and *Daniel Johnston: A Portrait of the Artist as a Potter in North Carolina*.

In 2010, he received the American Folklore Society "Lifetime of Scholarly Achievement Award." In 2011, he received the Charles Homer Haskins Prize of the American Council of Learned Societies for a distinguished career of humanistic scholarship. A documentary film (by Pat Collins) on Glassie's work and thought, *Henry Glassie: Field Work*, premiered at the Toronto International Film Festival in 2019.

ELLIOTT ORING is Professor Emeritus of Anthropology at California State University, Los Angeles, and Visiting Research Scholar in the Department of Folklore and Ethnomusicology at Indiana University. He is author of *Israeli Humor: The Content and Structure of the Chizbat of the Palmah*; *The Jokes of Sigmund Freud: A Study in Humor and Jewish Identity*; *Engaging Humor*; *Jokes and Their Relations*; *Just Folklore: Analysis, Interpretation, Critique*; *Joking Asides: The Theory, Analysis, and Aesthetics of Humor*; and *The First Book of Jewish Jokes: The Collection of L. M. Buschenthal*. He is editor of *Folk Groups and Folklore Genres: An Introduction*.

www.ingramcontent.com/pod-product-compliance
Lightning Source LLC
Chambersburg PA
CBHW031125270326
41929CB00011B/1496